The International Enterprise

The International Enterprise

JAMES M. LIVINGSTONE

A HALSTED PRESS BOOK

JOHN WILEY & SONS
New York—Toronto

English language edition, except USA and Canada,
published by
Associated Business Programmes Ltd
17 Buckingham Gate, London SW 1

Published in the USA and Canada by
Halsted Press, a Division of
John Wiley & Sons Inc
New York

First published 1975

Library of Congress Cataloging in Publication Data

Livingstone, J   M   1925-
   The international enterprise.

   'A Halsted Press book.'
   Bibliography: p.
   Includes index.
   1.   International business enterprises—Management.
I. Title.
HD69.17L58   338.8'8   75-23283

ISBN 0 470-54215-2

This book has been filmset, printed and bound in Great Britain
by R. J. Acford Ltd, Industrial Estate,   76-6501
Chichester, Sussex

Contents

Preface

This book is intended for two types of reader. Firstly there is the executive whose company operates internationally or is likely to do so: secondly the student at MBA level or equivalent who needs a text covering a rapidly growing field of business.

This double market has decided the size and layout of the book, principally by keeping it reasonably short. The busy executive is not likely to be interested in a 600–700 page textbook complete with case studies and test questions. Some rather abstract issues have been omitted entirely, e.g. economic theories on comparative advantage or factor endowment as an explanation of foreign trade. Other rather marginal areas like GATT, Eurocurrencies, and so on are dealt with only in passing or are relegated to footnotes. Finally, no attempt has been made to trace through all the ramifications of the main issues.

So far as student use of the book is concerned, any teacher who wishes to base a course on it will readily identify these areas he would wish to fill out by formal teaching or discussion. There is no shortage of suitable case study material available through the major case study clearing centres, the Harvard Business School, IMEDE in Switzerland, or Cranfield in England.

This book has been written from a mid-Atlantic viewpoint, that is to say while recognizing that the U.S. Multinational Corporations are at present the major source of international business activity, it does not concentrate exclusively on them, but discusses issues as they affect smaller companies also, whether they originate in the U.S.A., Europe or elsewhere.

At a time when the multinational corporation is increasingly cast as the villain on the world scene, this book is written from a pro-business stance. The author believes that the internationalization of business does far more good on the world scene than harm. At the same time, anyone concerned with international business has to be aware of the case which can be made against some current practices. If this book helps to highlight some of the dangers and suggest how some of the criticisms can be met, it will serve a useful purpose.

1. *International Business and the International Enterprise*

DEFINING INTERNATIONAL BUSINESS

This book deals with two subjects, one general, one specific. These are international business and the international enterprise. The purpose of this section is to define the first of these.

International business comprises any type of commercial activity which involves the crossing of national frontiers: firstly, physically, by the movement of exports or the building of production plant in one country which is owned and controlled from outside that country's frontiers: secondly, by less tangible movements across frontiers, through financial transactions by way of payments for goods, capital investment abroad, or payment of royalties, licence fees, etc for the use of patents, trade marks or general knowhow.

International business is not a new phenomenon. Several of the activities outlined in the previous paragraph have been around for well over two thousand years, at least since Roman times, and indeed well before then. All of the activities described above have been practised for at least a century.

Nevertheless, it is only in the past twenty years or thereabouts that the activities have grown to vast proportions and in the process brought about very profound economic and political changes on a world-wide scale. It would scarcely be an exaggeration to describe this twenty years process as being quite as significant on the world scene as the Russian and Chinese Revolutions.

How and why has this dramatic change taken place?

Up until the 1950's the general pattern in what has been described as international business was straightforward exporting plus some traditional overseas investment. The dominant trend was of a relatively small number of industrial countries who accounted for most of the world's production of industrial and consumer goods; and a much larger number of raw material producing economies, many of them colonial territories of the manufacturing nations, who traded their produce for manufactures. In many instances the production facilities of the raw material producers were controlled by interests in the manufacturing nations, and their production was geared very specifically to the needs of the manufacturing industries of the industrial countries.

Generally the raw material, whether oil, ore, or a crop would be extracted from the source country by an enterprise manned by expatriate managerial and technical staff, shipped to the home territory of the enterprise, processed and used to meet the demands of the home market. The key processing facilities were located in, and served that home market. The overseas activities of the enterprise were largely confined to extracting and transporting homewards whatever materials were needed for the home market.

There were exceptions of course, where an enterprise might set up a manufacturing subsidiary abroad to serve a foreign market, generally another wealthy industrial market. An early example of this is to be found in some European investment in the U.S.A. The latter country began to industrialize two or three decades after the major European nations. To protect its infant industries from competition of the established industries of Europe, the U.S. government imposed high tariff barriers against imports. Some European companies, in textiles for example, met the threat to their established U.S. sales by manufacturing within the tariff walls. These companies were among the first modern multinational corporations, operating a century before the phrase was invented. They were, incidentally, to repeat the same process again and again throughout the world, in the twentieth century.

The interreaction of American and European industry in the nineteenth and early twentieth century was not a one way traffic. A chronic shortage of cheap labour in the U.S.A. accelerated the development there of labour saving devices which could in turn be exploited in the European context. In some instances these developments were introduced by their American inventors to Europe. The Singer Sewing Machine Company, for example, produced and marketed in Europe eighty years before this pattern became general for most U.S. corporations. And early in the twentieth century, the mass production techniques of the U.S. automobile manufacturers carried them into European production for individual European markets. But multinational production for multinational markets remained the exception rather than the rule until the middle of the twentieth century.

THE MULTINATIONAL EXPLOSION

Since the middle 1950's there have been at least four new developments which have transformed international business and brought about more and more direct investment by enterprises in other economies than their own.

a) The first of these was the abrupt transformation in the attitude of many of the larger U.S. corporations during the middle 1950's and the 1960's. Hitherto, for many companies, exporting had been at most a marginal activity, production outside North America a pipe dream. They had perhaps restocked a war devastated Europe but scarcely contemplated permanent markets in such a politically and financially unstable area. But in the early 1950's, surplus capacity and a post-Korean recession in the U.S. home market made Europe, now more stable if still presenting financial problems, an attractive temporary solution to excess production.

In fact, the financial difficulties were, in the long run, to prove to be the key to the next step. Once tempted into European markets, the corporations found opportunities there denied to them in the U.S., but to exploit these they had to circumvent currency blocking and import licences imposed by European governments acutely short of dollars and other hard currencies. The answer was to manufacture in Europe and remit home only the profits, not the total cost of exports. The move towards direct U.S. investment received discreet encouragement from the U.S. government anxious to reduce its dollar aid commitments: it received more overt encouragement from most European governments who saw such investment bringing in new technology and employment opportunities and an injection of dollar investment, instead of a dollar drain to pay for imports.

One of the most fascinating aspects of the U.S. postwar investment in Europe, and ultimately elsewhere, was the way that motives and restraints which loomed large at one stage became irrelevant within a few years, to be replaced by new but perhaps equally transient factors, without the whole process of investment faltering. Europe was seen first as a market for surplus U.S. production: when it proved difficult to get dollar payments for these exports, the corporations went into local manufacture, hoping to recoup by remitting home profits or selling European manufactured products back into dollar markets: and when, almost overnight, dollar remittance problems began to disappear, the new incentive of an economically unified Europe comparable in size to the U.S. domestic market appeared, investment and U.S. controlled productive capacity in Europe grew at such a pace that it was the U.S. and European governments who now endeavoured to slow down the process they had been encouraging a few years previously.

It will be necessary later in the book to look in more detail at the reasons for U.S. multinational corporation manufacturing in Europe and elsewhere appearing when it did and in the form it did, and why such investment slowed down almost as abruptly as it started. But the fact that the process did happen has had almost incalculable consequences for the U.S.A. and the world economy.

b) Compared with the impact of the American corporation going multinational the second factor, the internationalization of British industry, was small. Nevertheless the process illustrates that 'going international' was not merely an American phenomenon.

In the case of Britain, traditionally the major source of European international investment, the causes of the postwar wave were rather different. Traditional British overseas markets had often been found in the old Empire, now the new Commonwealth. With the exception of Canada, firmly in the U.S. economic sphere, British industry had largely supplied the Empire and Commonwealth with much of their manufactures and had in return imported food and raw materials from there. During the two world wars, however, these traditional markets could not be supplied and in many instances the dominions and colonies had to develop their own industries. Even when, after both wars, it was possible for these markets to buy British again, their governments were anxious to foster local industry, rather than remain merely suppliers of food and materials. The infant industries created by war conditions were now protected even against the traditional British suppliers. And country after country made it clear that if a new industry could be set up locally it would be protected against the traditional supplier.

In this situation many British companies accepted the inevitable and set up assembly or manufacturing subsidiaries overseas to retain their old customers. Direct investment from Britain, previously heavily concentrated on developing raw material supplies for the British market, began to emphasize local production as well—the U.S. pattern in Europe in miniature.

But as well as the Commonwealth declining as a source of exports, there was now Europe, assuming more and more importance to the British economy. Here the dilemma of the far-sighted British manufacturer was acute, especially after 1958 when the European Economic Community, a Common Market, came into existence. Britain was now on the wrong side of the evolving common external tariff which was to be so important a characteristic of the EEC.

Within a short time of the Market coming into existence, the British government was attempting to secure membership, in the face of French opposition, headed by President de Gaulle. For the next thirteen years it was by no means clear whether Britain would, in time, become a member. That fact affected the policy of British companies towards setting up Common Market subsidiaries. If membership was assured, then manufacturing subsidiaries on the continent might be unnecessary. If Britain did not join, then manufacturing and market subsidiaries could be vital in the light of a double handicap, namely the common tariff, and the fact that traditional export methods by sea to the most convenient continental ports had to compete with door to door delivery by continental rivals.

Britain, as it happened, did secure Common Market membership along with Ireland and Denmark in 1971. But in the years of uncertainty many British companies had set up subsidiaries, or simply bought over European companies, at best as a means of exploiting the rapid growth of European opportunities, at worst as a means of minimizing the ill effects of non-membership.

c) The third wave of international investment was that which occurred among European companies within the EEC, in part to exploit a continental-sized market, in part as a reaction to U.S. successes within Europe.

In the early years of the EEC it was the American corporations, rather than the Europeans who seized the new opportunities opening up in Europe. Disposing not only of the most up to date technology, with apparently limitless resources, the U.S. corporations appeared to be on the point of taking over entire European industries. A French critic of American multinationals was able to claim that by the middle 1960's the U.S. stake in European industry represented the third industrial power concentration in the world after the U.S.A. and the U.S.S.R.[1]

In time, of course, European companies learned that, to compete with the Americans, they too had to operate on a continental scale by investment, takeover or international amalgamation. By the early 1970's the concept of a European form of company incorporation, as an alternative to national incorporation in one of the EEC member states was being considered. And with several European currencies stronger than the dollar, European direct investment was once again moving into the U.S.A.

d) The fourth international wave of investment was just beginning when the others were reaching or had passed their peaks. This was the internationalization of Japanese industry.

The peculiar conditions of the postwar Japanese economy will be discussed later. Basically, however, the fantastic growth of the Japanese economy in little over twenty five years had reached the point where there was little manpower available for further expansion. Japan was also increasingly being criticized for its protectionist policies. Other countries had suffered from manpower shortages: indeed the EEC growth had been fuelled by mass immigration of 'guest workers' from the poorer European countries outside the affluent Common Market, as well as Turks and North Africans. In the case of Japan there was no attempt to bring in non-Japanese labour. Assembly work was diverted to lower wage economies of South East Asia. Japanese-owned factories sprang up in Taiwan, Hong Kong, South Korea and elsewhere. By the early 1970's Japanese investment was beginning discreetly to appear in Europe and North America, as Japanese living standards, and costs, began to match and surpass many Western economies.

Japanese investment depended initially on their massive balance of payments surplus. At one stage these virtually forced the Japanese to invest abroad to reduce their embarrassingly high reserves. As it happened the surpluses of the 1960's were rapidly eroded in the 1970's by two factors. The first of these was the pressure from the U.S.A. and other industrial countries in the West to compel the Japanese to revalue their currency upwards to a more realistic level and so encourage a better balance of exports and imports. The second, more traumatic, was the effect of multiplying oil prices on the Japanese economy, a country almost entirely dependent on imported oil.

The rapid erosion of the Japanese balance of payments slowed but did not stop Japanese investment overseas. Instead of using national reserves, the industrialists borrowed on the international market.

If, after the traumas of the middle 1970's, Japan resumes anything approaching its previous staggering growth performance, there seems no reason to doubt that by the 1980's the Japanese-owned multinational corporation will be almost as common a feature on the world scene as the American or European multinational.

THE TERMINOLOGY OF INTERNATIONAL BUSINESS

The study of international business is comparatively new, and evolving rapidly. The terms used by businessmen and writers on the subject, therefore, have not yet been standardized. They may vary not only from country to country, but even from individual to individual. This section and the one which follows attempt to define some common terms, particularly those which may cause some uncertainty through varying usage.

First, however, to note some terms where the meaning is widely or universally accepted. In dealing with an international corporation or company, it is usual to refer to the parent company and the subsidiary company: the former being the founder organization which has subsequently set up subsidiaries in foreign countries. The terms 'parent' or 'home country' refers to the nation state where the corporation originates and the parent company is sited: the nation states in which the subsidiaries are located are normally referred to as host countries.

Rather more confusion arises in the term applied to the whole international corporation. The term *corporation* is normally used in the U.S.A. while the term *company* might refer either to subsidiaries of the corporation at home or abroad, or small independent enterprises for whom corporation would sound grandiose. In Britain however and most countries deriving their commercial forms from Britain, *company* is the normally accepted term whether the enterprise is large or small. 'Corporation', in the British sense, normally refers to a non-commercial organization, probably owned and controlled by the state or a public body: in recent years there has been some tendency to adopt the American usage but examples are still rare.

So far as most of Europe, and those areas outside Europe which adopted their commercial practices from Europe, are concerned, the equivalent to the U.S. corporation or British company, translates as 'Society'. The variants are discussed in a later section.

It would be confusing and unnecessary to use all the variants or to switch from one term to another, perhaps even in the same sentence, depending on the national origin of whatever business unit was being discussed. Equally, it would be inaccurate to use the American or British term to cover other national forms. Some writers in the field have pioneered the use of the term 'Enterprise' and this is the term which will be used in this book, unless a more specifically national term is more appropriate.

A rather similar difficulty arises from the somewhat indiscriminate use of the term 'international' and 'multinational'. To make the confusion worse, two more terms are now being added, namely, 'transnational' and 'supranational'.

One authority has defined the four terms. At one extreme an *international* enterprise is one which engages in foreign trade but without substantial investment abroad. *Multinational* implies a degree of foreign investment of the enterprise's resources, but with a clearly defined ownership in national terms. *Transnational* would then represent a stage when ownership and control was no longer limited to one nationality and where national bias no longer existed. *Supranational* would represent the stage when the enterprise's legal incorporation was not within a nation state or states, but with a supranational authority.

Two difficulties of definition arise, basically because the definitions are not mutually exclusive. Firstly, an international enterprise might have sales companies registered and incorporated in other nation states: but whether this makes it a multinational is arguable. Secondly, most enterprises of any size, operating in more than one nation state, are likely to find that some of their equity shares are owned by foreigners and that they employ foreign executives: this, in theory, would take them into the transnational class. Finally, of course, supranational authorities with the power to offer legal incorporation do not exist, and so the supranational enterprise cannot exist.

An Alternative Approach

A simpler but less elegant definition might involve three conditions: a) when an enterprise begins to operate on an international scale, by some activity other than merely exporting though still retaining the distinction between domestic and foreign markets, this might be regarded as an international condition; b) when the distinction between the domestic and foreign markets begins to disappear, this might be regarded as a multinational condition; c) when the earlier stages have reached the point where the original nationality of the enterprise is no longer material, this might be regarded as a transnational condition.

However, no enterprise has got near the third stage. The world's largest enterprise is General Motors, but no matter how much business it transacts outside the U.S.A. and no matter how important these non-U.S. markets become, neither the shareholders nor the executives have any doubt that in the last analysis, General Motors is an American corporation subject to the control of the American government.

A Rough and Ready Approach to Definitions

At the moment, whatever distinctions are drawn by academics and writers on the subject, most business men regard international and multinational as meaning much the same thing. They rarely use the other two terms at all. This book will therefore simply use the term 'international', unless there is a very obvious and definable reason for using the other terms. Where, therefore, the very common term 'multinational corporation' is quoted, no more should be read into the term than is covered by the term 'international enterprise'—which will now be defined more closely.[2]

DEFINING AN INTERNATIONAL ENTERPRISE

This chapter began by defining international business, but delayed a definition of the individual international enterprise. In many instances international enterprise is taken as synonymous with the widely used American term 'multinational corporation'. Unfortunately there is no universally accepted definition of the latter phrase.

The most widely accepted definition of multinational corporation is of an organization whose annual turnover exceeds $100 millions and which has manufacturing facilities in six countries or more. Such a definition would classify somewhere between a third and a half of the 'Fortune 500' largest U.S. corporations in this category. This definition by Professor Vernon of the Harvard Center for International Affairs has the advantage of precision and emphasizes the significance of size in international business. It is important in considering the role of the multinational corporation in the world economy to realize that many such corporations have a global turnover which exceeds the national income of many independent nation states.

There are perhaps two qualifications which have to be made of this, the most authoritative, definition. Firstly, international enterprises exist which operate on a smaller scale than that given. Even collectively they are not of such consequence as the 200 or 300 enterprises throughout the world which would qualify under the Vernon definition. Nevertheless, smaller enterprises are multiplying in international business and cannot safely be ignored. Secondly, the element of arbitrariness involved in this precise definition can mean that, for example, two smaller enterprises with some foreign subsidiaries suddenly become a multinational corporation if one takes over the other, without there being any obvious change in the outlook of the new enterprise.

An alternative definition which has been suggested is that an international enterprise might be considered to conduct say twenty five per cent of its business in foreign markets.[3] Other definitions turn on the concept of income generating assets abroad.

The definition which will be used in the following chapters is as follows:

'An international enterprise is one which, by choice, has a permanent personality in more than one country: the personality being of such a nature that the enterprise is no longer under the complete control of a single national government on a day to day basis. In most instances this personality will have a legal status with the appropriate form of incorporation.'

By this definition, even a small enterprise with no more than a single sales company registered in another country would be, potentially at least, in the field of international business as an international enterprise.

Before discussing the case for including even very small enterprises, it would be as well to dispose of the qualifying phrases in the definition namely 'by choice' and 'control . . . on a day to day basis.' Firstly, some enterprises, shipping or airlines, for example, are virtually compelled to have overseas or foreign based offices, but are not normally regarded as being international enterprises on that account alone. They would, however, come into the category if they chose to transfer those operations to foreign subsidiaries, which they could perform in the home country. Similarly, there may be an element of choice about how an enterprise exports. If it could sell via an agent or distributor in a foreign market, but instead chooses to set up a separate marketing company in that market, by our definition it changes from being a domestic to an international enterprise. Secondly, the definition emphasizes exemption from day to day control by a one nation state. The point here is that, although in the last analysis the enterprise is subject to control (i.e. it can be put out of business by any state in whose territory it operates), no one nation state can oversee all its routine decisions.

NATIONAL CONTROL OF THE INTERNATIONAL ENTERPRISE

The definition has emphasized the importance of freedom from control by a single nation state in day to day operations. Ultimately, the enterprise is under national control in that it can be put out of·business by the decision of the national government. In the case of the parent country government, the authorities can decree that the whole enterprise including all subsidiaries elsewhere should be wound up: and only the intervention of the host country government can stop that happening even in respect of the subsidiaries. Equally any host government can decide to close down or take over any subsidiary operating within its jurisdiction no matter how large and powerful the latter may be. The fact of ultimate control does not alter the situation that day to day control cannot be imposed on the whole international by any one national government.

Day to day control depends on a complete flow of information. If, for example, a national government suspects that the enterprise is reducing its tax revenues by diverting profits abroad, through transfer pricing, etc., it needs accurate information from the enterprise before it can substantiate or dismiss the suspicion. Control is information. Can national governments secure this information?

The *de jure* situation is quite clear but the *de facto* situation is not.

The parent country government may wish information on pricing and costing from the subsidiary company which is outside its jurisdiction. Conversely the host government may want information from the parent company, again outside its own jurisdiction. Legally neither government can obtain this information directly.

Any instruction issued directly by a government to a company incorporated in another nation state will be ignored by that company if it wishes to avoid trouble with its own government. The latter will rightfully regard such an attempt to instruct a domestically incorporated company by a foreign government as an infringement of its national sovereignty and will almost certainly instruct the company not to reply. The issue has come most frequently into the open in the American context, when U.S. Federal Authorities seek information on the activities of foreign registered companies, generally to consider whether American anti-trust legislation is being breached. Occasionally, American courts will issue judgments which instruct foreign registered companies on how they may operate even outside the U.S.A. Depending on the state of relations between the U.S.A. and the foreign government, the latter will publicly or confidentially order the company to refuse to comply.

Other national governments with, perhaps, a tradition of administrative discretion appear better able to avoid direct clashes. But their powers to obtain information from companies registered elsewhere are no greater.

There is, however, for the parent country government an obvious way round the difficulty. It may require the parent company to supply the information. The subsidiary cannot readily refuse this information to its own parent organization, and it is not in a position to question the parent company on its motives for seeking the information. The only possible difficulty arises when the subsidiary is not a wholly owned one, or one where the parent has the majority stockholding. Even here, friction is not likely to arise unless the other stockholder happened to be a national government or one of its agencies.

Difficulties however arise in the other direction when the host government seeks information. It can demand and obtain information from the subsidiary. If the subsidiary does not have the relevant information on the matter, the host government has no lever to use extraterritorially. The subsidiary may ask for, but cannot compel, disclosure of headquarters information.

This can be a difficulty particularly where the host country is relatively underdeveloped and has a relatively unsophisticated administrative machine with which to check upon the activity of an international enterprise: it tends to reinforce the fears and doubts about the role of such enterprises in national development, and makes the foreign owned subsidiary a scapegoat when things go wrong in the economy.

National Control—Theoretical and Real

The relative inadequacy of the administrative machinery of an under-developed country, coupled with the inability as a host government to force disclosure by the extraterritorial parent company of an international enterprise, might seem to be a painful contrast to the powers of a highly developed parent country with a sophis-ticated administrative machine and effective means of extracting information on a global scale from the enterprise. The reality however may be rather different. Its superior information gathering and assessing abilities may be neutralized by the sheer amount of information which has to be reviewed. The enterprise cannot refuse to give information to its government, but for the latter investigating its world wide activities thoroughly can be so time consuming that a good deal of potential control may go by default. Inevitably, parent governments have to deal in a fairly rough and ready way with large scale international enterprises originating within their own territories. Setting up effective regulation may be no more a practical proposition in a developed than an under-developed country, or in a parent than in a host government.

The definition used in this book turns on the principle of person-ality, normally legal personality, in more than one country. This generally means incorporation according to the commercial legal system prevailing in different countries. This principle is potentially a very profound issue. A subsidiary company operating in another country from the parent, whether it be a shoe-string sales operation or a vast manufacturing complex, will conduct its operations in accordance with the law of the host country, with an independent legal existence. Once there are two or more legally incorporated companies in different nation states, a whole new dimension has been added to the situation. Unlike an enterprise limited to one nation state and therefore subject only to one national government, the international enterprise becomes subject to pressure from more than one national government: one aspect of this has been touched upon in the previous section. But by the same token the enterprise is not completely subject to the control of any one nation state.

That, in a nutshell, is the major issue in international business —the existence of a commercial or industrial enterprise no longer wholly subordinate to a single national government.

Potentially at least, there are problems for the enterprise, because it may be subject to mutually incompatible demands or rules of behaviour by two national governments, in the sort of situation already discussed. But there are at the same time considerable advantages and room to manoeuvre. These include, for example, causing taxable profits to occur in the country with the lowest tax rates; moving financial assets out of one national economy into another where this is in the interests of the enterprise but perhaps not in the interests of one of the nation states, either parent or host country to that enterprise. Such manoeuvres could be attempted most commonly by using the so-called 'transfer price' system already referred to, i.e. setting prices for transactions between parent company and subsidiary significantly higher or lower than would be set for transactions involving mutually independent enterprises.

In practice, thus far, few enterprises with sales companies but not production facilities incorporated abroad, find conflicting pressures from different nation states to be very much of a problem. Fewer still try to exploit the room for manoeuvre available to them in tax and currency issues. Such enterprises make no pricing distinction between selling abroad via an agent acting on commission, and their own selling subsidiary. But all enterprises could do so: and certainly many of the giants, the archetypal multinational corporations have done so on a large enough scale to threaten the economic viability of whole nation states. A major part of this book will be concerned with exploring the implications of this room for manoeuvre outside the total control of any nation state. In the meantime, however, this issue is the justification for using such a wide definition of an international enterprise. The major criticisms which are made of the activities of multinational corporations place the emphasis on their size and power relative to individual nation states. This book will argue that what makes multinational corporations unique is not essentially their size but their ability to escape from national control, by manoeuvring. Indeed, this manoeuvring ability could be exploited by much smaller international enterprises than the multinational corporations.

THE MAJOR FORMS OF LEGAL PERSONALITY

What are the mechanics of acquiring a legal personality in different nation states? International enterprises setting up in host countries normally register their subsidiaries under the appropriate form of legal incorporation. In the Western world this is probably in joint stock form; other forms of liability may be available but may not be particularly appropriate for a commercial venture.

In some instances there may be a choice between a public and private company. The choice may be very important since there may be significant differences in control, disclosure of information, employees' representation on boards, the nationality of directors, rates of taxation, etc.

Where the enterprise wishes to facilitate widespread holding of equity capital, either in the host country or internationally, a subsidiary company with share quotations in one or more stock exchanges may be appropriate, provided that control can still be effectively maintained by the parent enterprise. On the other hand, where local equity holding might be undesirable or against corporate policy, i.e. where this brought about constraints which were unacceptable to the parent enterprise, a private company form of incorporation might be more appropriate. Unfortunately, it is difficult to generalize any further than this since legislation varies enormously from country to country, albeit with discernible patterns.

The British pattern, modified, but still recognizable, is followed in most countries which were formerly dominions or colonies, and this includes the U.S.A. In the latter country there are variations between the States but overall a similar pattern. Similarly, a French pattern is found in French speaking Europe, and the former overseas territories, as well as in Spain, Portugal and so through to Latin America. A German pattern is also recognizable in Northern Europe with recent German legislation having considerable influence, particularly in respect of employees' representation.

Legal Forms of Incorporation

U.S.A.   The limited liability corporation with the suffix 'Inc' is by far the most common, with some variation according to the State of incorporation. The terms Domestic, Foreign and Alien are sometimes used in a manner confusing to the non-American. Briefly, Domestic can be applied to a corporation in the Federal State in which it is incorporated, Foreign if it is incorporated in another State, and Alien if it is incorporated outside the U.S.A.

The Major Nations of Western Europe.   The United Kingdom of Great Britain and Northern Ireland has two forms of company which can be adopted by foreign enterprise subsidiaries. These are the Public and Private Limited Liability Company. In both instances the title of the company is followed by 'Limited' normally abbreviated to 'Ltd'. The Republic of Ireland follows the same pattern as the United Kingdom though company law differs in some respects.

France. The appropriate form is the Societé Anonyme, which corresponds roughly to the British public limited liability company. The private company form is the Societé à Responsibilité Limitée (SARL) and is not normally appropriate for a foreign subsidiary.

West Germany.   Both public and private company forms are possible for the foreign subsidiary as the Aktiengesellschaft (AG) and the Gesellschaft mit beschrankter Haftung (GmbH).

Italy.   The corresponding forms are the Societa per Azione (SpA) and the Societa a Responsibilita Limitada (SRL). The former is the the more common. So far as the small European countries are concerned, as has been suggested, a rough and ready rule is that Spain and Portugal follow the French pattern with the Sociedad Anonima and the Sociedad de Responsibilidad Limitada in the former case and the Sociedade Anonima and the Sociedade por Quotas in the latter. Teutonic and Nordic countries have their equivalent of the Aktiengesellschaft. Belgium, as a bilingual country has French and Flemish forms, and Switzerland French and German.

In all instances the amount of financial information which has to be published is likely to be greater in the case of the public company, i.e. the SA or AG than for the private company. In some countries however, like Switzerland, the amount of information which has to be published is very limited indeed.

The Harmonization of Company Law and the European Company

Within the European Economic Community attempts are being made to harmonize company law, but even if this is achieved, enterprises will remain essentially national, with the suffixes Ltd, SA, AG, etc. remaining, and subject to the laws of the country in which they are incorporated.

An alternative form of incorporation which is under active consideration within the EEC is the Societas Europea (SE), an optional form of incorporation available to enterprises operating in two or more member countries of the Community. The SE form of incorporation, if it evolves, would be an alternative to, not a replacement of, the present existing national forms. Presumably, too, if harmonization of individual national company law were successful the need for an SE form of incorporation would be less obvious.

Incorporation Elsewhere in the World

Incorporation elsewhere in the world outside the Communist and Socialist States, as has been suggested, follows the pattern of the European nation whose legal code has had the most influence.

The major non-Western industrial centre is Japan. The equivalent forms of limited incorporation are the Kabushiki Kaisha (KK) and the Yugen Kaisha (YK), which, broadly speaking, follow the Western legal pattern.

THE STRUCTURE OF THE ENTERPRISE AND DISCLOSURE OF INFORMATION

The point made earlier about disclosure of information being greater in the case of a public company applies more generally than merely to joint stock companies. The situation is complicated because of the variations in the way equity capital is raised. There are a few nation states in Europe which have very active stock exchanges and some which do not. But outside Europe, North America and Japan, stock exchanges are a good deal less important, and the need to disclose information less pressing. In countries without important stock exchanges industrial financing of all types may be carried out by banks or holding companies (often with a close link with the state bureaucratic machine) and the amount of financial information which has to be disclosed may be minimal.

CLASSIFYING INTERNATIONAL ENTERPRISES

Every international enterprise is different in structure and operation. It is convenient nevertheless to be able to group according to common characteristics. This section will look at three of the best known, namely, those associated with Perlmutter, Dunning and Vernon, representing attempts to group respectively by attitude, by function, and by technological characteristic.

Perlmutter's classification is a threefold one, into what he refers to as ethnocentric, polycentric and geocentric organizations.[4]

The ethnocentric enterprise is essentially a national enterprise with foreign subsidiaries, highly centralized, with key decisions taken and key personnel centred at the parent headquarters. The enterprise operates in the interest of the parent company and all decisions are judged by this yardstick.

The polycentric enterprise, on the other hand, is a good deal more decentralized with considerably more discretion accruing to the individual foreign subsidiary, and possibly less overall control exercised by the parent company.

The ethnocentric enterprise has the weakness of unadaptability. If the culture of the parent company is American it will attempt to impose U.S. standards, rewards and penalties, in nations and cultures where these may be, at best, irrelevant, at worst, positively harmful to the development of the enterprse. The weakness of the polycentric approach is that decentralization may reach the point when the corporate existence of the enterprise is in doubt. There may be no effective control, no ability to react to events in a coherent way, no real sense of unity.

Perlmutter's synthesis is therefore the geocentric enterprise, which is a totally integrated enterprise operating on a world wide basis—a genuinely supranational enterprise.

The problems of using the Perlmutter classification are twofold. Firstly, there is the problem of assessing objectively into which of the first two categories an existing enterprise fits. Even an enterprise which is overtly ethnocentric to the point of chauvinism will scarcely admit that it regards its own nationals and methods as superior to lesser breeds without the law. In the touchy nationalistic world of today it would scarcely be tolerated outside its own frontiers. So far as possible polycentric enterprises are concerned it would be difficult to find a parent company which would admit that decentralization of decision-making ever got to the point where the enterprise was out of control. A real life enterprise is likely to contain large elements of both characteristics with neither necessarily dominating in every subsidiary.

Secondly, a geocentric attitude is essentially an ideal rather than a reflection of present conditions; and an ideal requiring slow and painful progress towards its achievement. Even the largest of the present day enterprises in the last analysis obeys the fiat of its own parent government, is aware of its own national origin and is likely to be most profoundly influenced by its own national culture. It may be a long time before many of the very large international enterprises have moved decisively to a genuinely geocentric attitude.

The second type of classification by Dunning, is rather more precise. He divides the enterprises into four groups which are classified as multinational producing enterprises (MPE), multinational trading enterprises (MTE), multinational owned enterprises (MOE) and multinational controlled enterprises (MCE).[5]

This is a very useful division in clarifying by function: the problem is that the groups are obviously not mutually exclusive, and that this therefore limits the applications to which the concept can be put.

Of the four groups the MPE is the most important. Dunning subdivides this group into three, the first two of which he defines as cost oriented and market oriented vertical organizations, i.e. he describes those organizations which move across national frontiers, in one instance to secure raw materials and in the other to secure the ultimate market. The third subdivision is on a horizontal basis, that is to say a particular process or product is replicated in various countries. Ford, Chrysler, General Motors, in so far as these corporations refer to automobile products: IBM in computers: or, in industrial gas production Union Carbide, Air Products, British Oxygen, Aire Liquide of France. All essentially are performing the same production function in different markets, on an international basis.

In some instances the third subdivision relates to what might be called high technology industry: the more complex the technology, the more difficulty it has in crossing frontiers. In other instances the technology is not so important as the production or marketing expertise, i.e. there is no great mystery about how to produce potato crisps or cornflakes: the main problem in many parts of the world may be to persuade people actually to buy and eat the products.

The second division, the MTE, represents the enterprise with one production centre relying heavily on direct exporting. In the definition suggested earlier in the chapter and to be used throughout this book, the MTE would not be regarded as an international enterprise at all, unless the exporting involved the use of subsidiary sales companies in the foreign market—a criticism perhaps of the definition rather than Dunning's classification.

Multiple ownership (MOE) appears to cover two situations. Either there would be a wide ownership of equity on an international basis, with perhaps quotations in various stock exchanges, or the enterprise might have grown out of an international merger, e.g. the British Italian Dunlop Pirelli, or the German Belgian Agfa-Gevaert. The second type of international ownership could not readily involve a very large American partner because of possible implications from U.S. anti-trust legislation.

Finally, the multiple controlled enterprise (MCE) such as Royal Dutch Shell and Unilever (both Anglo Dutch) or various oil consortia, in embryo at least, may be nearing Perlmutter's geocentric concept.

As in many other definitions such a grouping cannot be mutually exclusive if they are not to be qualified out of a realistic classification.

Vernon's classification is at once the simplest and most realistic. In his studies of the U.S. multinational he has analysed them in terms of Extractive and Industrial Enterprises.[6]

The extractive category is analysed in historical terms to establish the characteristics of different technological inputs, and the vulnerability of various industries to nationalization or simple decline. Several of his illustrations are in fact used in the next section which attempts to extend his classification.

The development of U.S. industrial subsidiaries abroad is considered in terms of a historical model, whose particular interest lies in the emphasis of the continuity of the process since the end of the nineteenth century. The most spectacular growth, and the period which has attracted most comment, has been in the last two decades, but the process is not a new one. Vernon has also attempted to suggest reasons for the different emphasis on innovation between the U.S.A and Europe. European companies have possibly been less ready both to innovate and also to move more and more into direct investment in the U.S.A. It is perhaps characteristic of the dynamism of the present situation that some of Vernon's propositions in this subject have within a year or two been overtaken by events.

The summary in the paragraphs above might appear to anyone acquainted with Vernon's work to be simplification to the point of caricature. Vernon's comments on the field of international business are so seminal that they are likely to influence comments in the field of international business, far beyond his particular studies of the American case.

A THREEFOLD CLASSIFICATION

The categories used from now on will be an adaptation of the Vernon classification and some of the examples quoted as illustrations will be developed from those used by him. Three major categories will be discussed. Two of these are traditional types of variants, i.e. variants on vertical and horizontal integration: the third is a relatively new development and less easily definable.

CATEGORY I

The international vertical pattern has already been mentioned as typical of the pre World War 2 pattern. It is therefore the most traditional, but in modern conditions the most vulnerable. The enterprise whose headquarters is in one of the developed countries supplies that developed market from raw materials grown, mined or extracted in underdeveloped areas. In some cases the vertical pattern may be virtually complete from production to retail consumption in the developed market. The U.S. and European oil corporations have operated from oil well to garage pump. In other instances the vertical operation stops at supplying other industries, e.g. copper or other metals for the industries of North America or Western Europe. All have this in common. The market which matters is in the developed country, not in the country which produces the raw materials.

The technology involved in these international enterprises helps to explain both their structure and present vulnerability. The original sources of raw materials were probably in developed regions and the technology as well as the markets developed there. But the original sources were quickly exhausted and the industries or markets which had been developed had to find alternative sources of raw materials.

In many instances it was in the economic or political dependencies of the industrial nations that alternative supplies could be easily tapped. Initially the U.S. corporations moved into Central and South America where U.S. power was effectively dominant. In the case of the European powers the colonial territories were the obvious source.

The possible conflicts of interest between the developed consumer economy and the underdeveloped host economy were in the long run obvious. They became more acute as the latter obtained political, if not economic, independence. In many instances newly independent states with highly nationalist leanings have nationalized or simply expropriated the subsidiary companies on their territories, claiming previous exploitation of their limited national wealth. Almost every underdeveloped country with foreign owned enterprises operating extractive processes has demanded at least a degree of national ownership of these assets at some time or another since the end of World War 2.

Ability to press the issue successfully has depended on a number of factors which can be used virtually as an index to the vulnerability of the international enterprise.

The most obvious factor is the complexity of the technology and the extent to which trained personnel can be replaced if expatriates are withdrawn. The level of sophistication of the host countries is constantly rising and so therefore is the vulnerability of more technologically advanced industries. Thus for example, oil, copper or most other conventional mining industries can be taken over and run after a fashion. Aluminium, uranium or more exotic minerals are at present less vulnerable to nationalization because the technology of extraction or refining is more complex.[7] The vulnerability of the Western oil companies to widespread nationalization in the middle 1970's was a graphic illustration of the fact that the technology of oil extraction and refining no longer constituted a serious barrier to host countries if they deemed it expedient to take over. The international oil companies are rapidly becoming marketing organizations, not producers.

A second factor is the control of the market and the extent to which the former owners can inhibit sales, either by organizing a boycott or by taking legal action to prevent or at least discourage outside purchasers buying from the nationalizers. The precursor of the massive oil nationalization of the 1970's was the nationalization by Iran twenty years before of the Anglo Iranian concessions and oil refinery at Abadan in the Persian Gulf. The oil company fought a series of legal battles throughout the world to discourage buying of the nationalized oil, and in time won a compromise settlement with Iran. In the 1970's after nationalization of their copper mines by the Allende Government in Chile, the U.S. Kennecott Corporation used the same methods, and in time got a settlement from the new Chilean government after the overthrow of the Marxist President Allende. But the fact that it was necessary to fight the distribution of the copper was a clear indication that production technology was no longer a safeguard. By the 1970's, too, the oil corporations could not even stop distribution.

Other factors play their part in the potential trial of strength. The ease of identification of a product, e.g. whether the oil or ore can be proved to come from a particular source or the perishability or otherwise of products. So too does the fact that the Communist countries will offer technical assistance: and increasingly nationalization attracts overt sympathy from the Third World bloc of countries in the United Nations, who have achieved virtual universal acceptance of the proposition that any nation state has the right to take over the assets of any foreign enterprise operating within its territory, particularly if the enterprise is engaged in an extractive operation.

By and large, therefore, the balance of power is moving towards the host governments and against the extractive enterprises. The future of this type of enterprise is increasingly bleak. New concessions to enterprises are for a very limited period of time with provision for concessions to revert to the host governments. Even these limited concessions are liable to be repudiated by a successor government. By the end of the century it seems reasonable to suppose that most international enterprises controlling extractive industries in the underdeveloped world and marketing the processed output in the developed world will have ceased to exist, save possibly in a marketing capacity.

CATEGORY II

The second traditional type of international enterprise follows the pattern of horizontal integration. The enterprise is supplying the same product or range of products to many different markets. The variety of these products is almost infinite—from IBM producing the most sophisticated electronic equipment to Coca Cola.

The examples quoted above manufacture throughout the world, but on the definition of an international enterprise in terms of multiple legal personality the products could in theory be manufactured by the parent enterprise factory and exported through overseas subsidiaries who might merely be order takers. The main characteristic of this enterprise is that their reputation is in their knowledge, technical or marketing, and their ability to deploy these internationally.

In general, this type of enterprise is more acceptable to the host country than the first. Indeed, if it does not produce but merely sells in the host country it will probably be under pressure to extend its activities into local manufacture, not pull out entirely. Of course, as it moves towards local manufacture it becomes more vulnerable and potentially at least has more to lose from nationalization or expropriation. Even so, hostility is likely to be less than in the case of an extractive industry because it can be claimed to bring in new technology, possibly creating more employment, probably saving scarce foreign exchange by import savings, perhaps even earning foreign exchange, by exporting in turn.

There are, naturally, possible sources of conflict, either with local industry which feels threatened or is forced to pay higher wages. More important, there can be conflict with a host government whose attitude may be ambivalent.

One useful way of looking at the situation is in terms of technological content, and even perhaps, social usefulness.

A. High technology industries. Although the initial impulse of host governments is to welcome inward investment in high technology industry, the longer term attitude, once the foreign subsidiary has begun to operate, may change to one of reserve. The issues will be discussed in greater detail in a later chapter but they can be summed up for the moment in two propositions.

i) That there is a very high probability that the new technology which is introduced remains indefinitely under foreign control, and so therefore do key sections of local industry.

ii) That the international enterprise by choice or by necessity may use in its plant an inappropriate level of technology. It may use very advanced automated processes which in practice create little employment in a less developed economy, sometimes destroying more traditional occupations than it creates through the new technology. More probably however, it will follow the opposite policy, i.e. use in its subsidiary a level of technology which is significantly less advanced than it uses in a developed country, i.e. in its own home plant. In this situation the enterprise can be made, by local critics to appear, not as the source of new technology and opportunity, but as the instrument whereby the host economy is held back by a deliberately maintained technology gap. There may be very sound reasons for a technological gap persisting without it being deliberately imposed: these will be the subject of a subsequent section. But if there is a general grievance on the part of the host economy on this score, horizontal integration becomes in a sense, vertical integration in the dimension of time, with the same enterprise operating different generations of technology in different parts of the world.

B. Industries with less sensitive technology. There are a group of industries, basically consumer oriented, soap and detergents, cosmetics, processed foods and drinks and the like which are also subject to foreign investment in many countries. Here the technology is less important than the marketing skills: what has tended to happen in these industries is that the rise in consumer expectation has occurred in the developed countries initially, generally the U.S.A. and the corporations which satisfied the need were better able to cope with the new markets as they appeared elsewhere. Although such enterprises are markedly vulnerable they are not in such hazard as the first group precisely because they do not present a threat to national development. No nation feels threatened by the presence of the Coca Cola Corporation, General Foods, or Proctor and Gamble in the way they worry about the computer industry being dominated by foreign control. They may however complain about wasted resources, and this takes us into the third group.

C. Luxury enterprises. The question of what type of industry is acceptable for purposes of investment is a difficult one particularly in the underdeveloped world. In so far as national governments wish for foreign investment they want to see it in primary industries —defining primary in its widest sense. They prefer basic or prestigious industries. Unfortunately these are not necessarily the most profitable: in a curious way luxuries may come before necessities particularly where the distribution of national income is very uneven. In many underdeveloped countries, the poor are very poor, and the rich are very rich. The obvious market may therefore be for what on any rational assessment would seem to be trivialities, e.g. imported Scotch Whisky, Swiss watches, American motor cars, etc. So far as local production is concerned it is not unknown for foreign subsidiaries to produce, for example, canned pet food while sections of the local population are on the starvation level. The criticism which this sort of situation engenders is typical of the ambivalence of attitudes to foreign invest-ment, namely, concern at the possible domination of key sectors of the economy by foreign enterprises, combined with indignation that the unpopular foreigner is not dominating the key areas, but is concentrating on what might be termed the candy floss sector. The enterprise in this situation is merely reflecting the wrong priori-ties present in the economy as a whole; it is the symbol rather than the cause of the country's faults. Nevertheless as a symbol, it is still liable to be the prime target of critics of the prevailing regime.

Thus far, issues raised in the *Category II* international enterprise have related mainly to investment in the less developed world. Most of such investment however takes place in the developed world because the skills and markets required to transplant the industries are more readily available.

The conflicts with host country national interests do not appear to be so newsworthy in the developed countries. It would however be naive to assume that xenophobia is confined to the less developed world. Most countries are ambivalent about the control of sectors of their economy by foreign enterprises, particularly where these industries are likely to be the most dynamic. The degree of anti-Americanism overt in Gaullist France and the more discreet else-where, does not arise exclusively from the Marxist left. It is to be found in the right of centre and middle of the road politician and man in the street who may, in a muddled sort of way, welcome more U.S. knowhow but not more U.S. industrial influence. In that sense everyone wants all the benefits without any of the responsibilities.

CATEGORY III

The third type of international enterprise is less easily designated but may be defined as one which, by transfer of technology from the developed to the less developed areas of the world, creates an export/import situation which is the reverse of the traditional, i.e. it creates the opportunity to export manufactured goods and products from the underdeveloped to the developed economies.

In a later chapter the phenomenon will be examined in terms of a product life cycle concept, but at the moment all that will be attempted is the defining of situations where an international enterprise will attempt to set up 'premature' production facilities in a small market, and export from there. By 'premature' production facilities in this context is meant those of a size and advanced nature which could not be justified in terms of the existing domestic market.

There are three possible types of production.

a) In the first place there has to be a relatively cheap source of labour, with, ideally, the prospect of market developing locally as standards of living rise. The motor-car industry originated in North America and industrial Europe. A characteristic of these areas now is that the market has reached saturation point. One cannot get much further than one car for every adult in the community — and in the developed areas this figure is being reached: moreover labour costs there are very high. By contrast Southern Europe is relatively sparsely developed in terms of the numbers of cars: and labour costs in Spain, Southern Italy, Greece, Yugoslavia and parts of Eastern Europe are still relatively low. It may make sense therefore for the international enterprises in this field to build plant in these regions (if political factors permit) and increasingly to supply the developed markets with products: the bonus being that the domestic markets for the new plants are likely to grow faster than the older established markets. Cars and trucks for North Europe may come from the South. Chrysler trucks manufactured in Spain are already being designed for the British markets. Even more widely spread the Ford and Volkswagen plants in Brazil are reported to be supplying components into their companies' European operations.

The examples so far given are discussed in their most striking aspect, i.e. developing nations supplying the developed. The process may be encouraged by the success of underdeveloped nations, working through UN agencies, in obtaining unilateral tariff concessions for industrial products which are being exported to developed countries.[8] But in a less marked way, the same phenomenon is observed between developed nations where labour costs vary widely. Burroughs Machine Corporation manufactures at its European factories to meet demands in the U.S. domestic market. On a smaller scale, Swedish owned textile factories in Finland and Scotland manufacture virtually exclusively for their own Swedish retail orders simply because wage costs are less than one half those of Sweden. Puerto Rican subsidiaries of U.S. corporations effectively represent the same process. These are what their Trade Union opponents would call 'runaway' industries, moving in many instances to an area where wage costs are low; or where unionization is weak or non-existent; or where the authorities will take a tough line with strikers.

b) A second type of industry also relies on cheap labour. It is however not an industry which has gone into a mature phase of technology. On the contrary it is an industry which is at the beginning of a product life cycle and whose technology is developing at an explosive rate. It would seem common sense to suggest that a high technology industry must be a capital intensive and therefore a natural industry for developed countries. This however is not always so. Heavy expenditure on Research and Development will be spent in the developed countries but heavy capital expenditure on production lines is a very different proposition. Industries based on transistors or microcircuitry, for example, are going through a phase when obsolescence in a product may occur within two years: this is in marked contrast to the automobile industry where genuine obsolescence following a genuine technical breakthrough might take two decades. It would therefore be a high risk in microcircuitry to tool up for a production run requiring several years to reach a break-even point when the particular component could become superseded between the time the production line was planned, and production actually began. Capital equipment is unadaptable but labour is highly adaptable and dispensible. Microcircuitry and transistors may therefore be an area where labour intensive production facilities can make sense, and that means transistor assembly in Taiwan, South Korea, Hong Kong and Singapore for the U.S., European and Japanese industries. Presumably if the technology ever slows down at a stage of maturity and it becomes possible to automate before obsolescence, then these assembly plants may decline, because they do not have control of the computer and data processing industries they supply in the developed world. But until then, very new technology may make employment in relatively underdeveloped areas.

c) The third type of production is arguably rather different in kind. This is manufacture under contract. An enterprise with extensive international contracts may find it useful to have some of its products made, probably to its own design and specification, in some part of the world where labour costs are cheap, then market under its own trade name in its established markets. The suppliers remain effectively barred from these domestic markets of the enterprise, since they lack the distribution channels.

This situation may develop out of the assembly operations described in the preceding subsection. Initially, the American or European enterprise may have had to create its own assembly operations in low labour cost areas like South East Asia or parts of Latin America. Within a short time however, local entrepreneurs may be offering a service, so that there may be wholly owned assembly subsidiaries whose capacity can be supplemented by contracting out to some of the independents. In time the wholly owned subsidiaries may decline in the face of local production— a situation which may suit both the buying enterprise and the host government which may prefer the industry locally owned. The limitation remains, however; access to the end market for the product remains the preserve of the foreign buyer.

The concept of 'sourcing', i.e. supplying developed markets from less developed economies is an important one, but is an area where detailed information is not readily available, because it is not in the interest of the enterprise either to reveal the source of products or components to its rivals, or to stir up trouble with domestic interests, whether suppliers or trade unions. If the entire product, e.g. a radio or casette recorder is manufactured in a low cost area some designation, e.g. 'imported' 'foreign' or 'made in . . .' will probably be a legal requirement and its non-domestic origin, at least, will be obvious. More commonly, however, subcomponents will be involved, and the average American or West European is unlikely to explore the interior of his purchases to find out whether Taiwan, Hong Kong, or East European parts have been included.

2. Types of Market

There are well over a hundred nation states in the world. Each represents a distinct market with opportunities and problems of its own. Some of the largest and richest nations contain several geographically distinct markets. To complicate the picture further, many are grouped into economic and political alliances, common markets, free trade areas, and the like, which are effective in varying degrees.

Several methods have been devised to group these national economies according to their degree of economic or political development. A criticism of such classifications is that often detail and precision in the groupings is achieved at the expense of reality. The classification attempted here is very rough and ready. But it does bear some relevance to the problems of international business, namely, to identify those areas in the world which will best repay direct investment or an exporting drive.

The first grouping is of the Western developed nations. This is an economic and political, rather than a geographical or racial description, including most of Western Europe, the United States and Japan. These are nations operating mixed economies largely dominated by private enterprise and with a distinct consumer orientation, but with large and growing public sectors. Such countries have enjoyed a generation of postwar prosperity, are politically more stable than most, and, short of a world war, are likely to go on enjoying an increasing measure of affluence. Because of these characteristics they represent the most promising markets of all for their domestic industries, for exporters elsewhere, and for international investment.

The next two groups are conventionally regarded as the developing world, i.e. countries which hope to develop from economies based on agriculture or raw material production to industry. They aim to become high production, high consumption societies enjoying the visible material success of the West although not necessarily subscribing to Western political or cultural ideals.

Confusingly, however, the phrase 'developing economy' can cover at least two fairly distinct groups.

The first of these comprises truly developing nations such as Australia, New Zealand, possibly even Canada, South Africa, Israel and one or two South American countries, often with a relatively small population in relation to their national resources, which are trying to lessen dependence on agricultural or raw material exports. These nations enjoy a high standard of living now, and provided they can avoid political or racial strife, are likely to succeed in the material sense. They provide a rich but limited market to exporters. Most important in the present context, they are by and large anxious to attract the activities of international manufacturers, if necessary by investment grants, tax concessions and tariff policy.

The term 'developing nation' is also applied, sometimes with more charity than accuracy, to that one third of the world's population, living in largely pre-industrial societies, many in a state of near or actual starvation. The plight and problems of these nations are immense and in many instances growing worse day by day. In the long run the actions of international business may help to alleviate some of their economic problems. But looking at them cold bloodedly in short term market prospects, two factors stand out: the very low standard of living and hence of purchasing power in many of these nations make their potential as consumers, either of Western imports or locally produced Western-type consumer goods, dismal: secondly, unlike the earlier group of developing nations, it is difficult to be sanguine about their prospects of achieving a rapid improvement in living standards. Their desperate need of the products which the industrial nations can supply is not generally matched by their ability to pay for the goods. International business has tended to by-pass many of these nations except as possible sources of raw materials. Most, however, do not have the raw materials in quantity, only millions upon millions of men, women and children on the verge of starvation.

The term 'developing' replaced 'underdeveloped' and is in the process of being replaced in turn by 'emerging' 'less developed' nations. This polite gloss has come about because the earlier terms have been regarded as derogatory. The difficulty is the more polite the term the easier it is to assume that all of these nations are progressing in economic terms. It might indeed be more accurate but offensive to use the phrase 'poor and backward' for in brutally realistic terms that is what many of them are, with faint hope of breaking out of their misery without really massive international aid. In general the term 'underdeveloped' will be used in this book to distinguish them from the more obviously Western oriented 'developing' nation described earlier. This is the group which is conventionally known as the Third World.

The fourth type of market is perhaps the least exploited of all in terms of international business: the countries of the Communist world. With a population again about one-third of the world, their market potential might appear to be vast. A closer inspection of the problem of doing business with these societies, either in terms of straight exporting or by some more involved process, suggests that the difficulties are formidable. Nevertheless for the company which produces the type of goods or has the expertise the Communist economies require, the rewards can be great.

THE WESTERN DEVELOPED NATIONS

The richest and most important of the world's markets are in the developed nations of the Western world: in those economies which are industrial rather than agricultural or raw material producers, and with a high and rapidly growing standard of living. The best export markets for an industrialist in such a country, the most promising areas for direct foreign investment in production facilities outside his home country, are quite likely to be in those countries which are economically and technologically very like his own. The developed nations are at once the major source and recipient of each other's foreign investment. In the nineteenth century much of America's industrial development was financed from European investment: now the process is operating in both directions, the European stake in the U.S.A. rising steadily, the American stake in Europe rapidly.

The major characteristics of these nations is that they are both rich and technologically developed. Any one of them can rapidly absorb and adapt new industries wherever in the world they originate. Not only do they have this vitally necessary technological infrastructure, they have the legal and financial frameworks, initially to protect new industrial concepts, but ultimately to force their exploitation, if not by their inventors or originators, then by others.

That simple fact explains much of the driving force behind international business and direct foreign investment. A European or American enterprise which develops a new idea can patent it or protect it throughout the world for a relatively limited period. That length of time may be expressed legally in the lifetime of the patent or licence, or less exactly in terms of the technical or marketing expertise of the enterprise. But unless the originator is prepared to make the results available in every other technically developed country, either by producing locally, or by licensing out the process, it cannot, in the long run, stop other companies using it. An international enterprise has often emerged from a domestic company simply because the latter has developed its own technological or managerial expertise to a virtually unassailable position in its home market, and then realized that if it did not exploit that experience in similar markets elsewhere, someone else would be able to exploit much of its knowhow at little of no cost.

It is often a matter only of academic interest where the key concepts of modern industry developed, for example the transistor and all the other aspects of electronics: or at an earlier stage the jet engine, or even the internal combustion engine. The point is that once the concept had been translated into reality in any of the developed nations, and a commercial or industrial application could be seen, it was only a few years at most before the process could be duplicated or adapted elsewhere. Indeed the transistor is almost a classic example of what can happen. Within twenty years of its development in the U.S.A. a large section of the U.S. electrical and electronic industry had been wiped out by Japanese imports based on the concept.

Companies cannot in practice control their own product concepts. But if a company which does make a significant contribution to any industry is to reap anything like the full benefits, it may have to think internationally almost from the start. This is a factor which will loom even larger in the future. Increasingly a good deal of Research and Development of new products involves longer periods of time, and more expense. Indeed the actual exploitable life of the product in the home market can be less than the gestation period. Products of this nature cannot be allowed to stay comfortably in suspense until the home market is saturated, and it becomes convenient to release them elsewhere. This means that any company in any Western developed economy, which has made a substantial technological breakthrough has an immediate incentive to consider its exploitation on an international, indeed a world, basis.

WESTERN EUROPE

The dominating factor about the West European economy is the existence of the European Economic Community, the Common Market. The Rome Treaty which created the Community was signed in 1957, the Community came into existence the following year. The original six founder members were increased to nine in 1973 with the accession of Britain, the Republic of Ireland and Denmark: the end result was a community of some 250 millions comparable in size and economic importance with the U.S.A. or the Soviet Union.

The Community has proved on the whole to be an economic success, though its political achievements have been less marked. Every other nation in Western Europe had to take account of its existence, to formulate economic policies accordingly and, if necessary, bargain with the new body to obtain acceptable terms: so too had many of the developing nations, having former colonial links with members of the Community. And most important of all perhaps, the super powers, the U.S.A. and the Soviet Union, have had to bargain with it as an economic equal.

In the early years, particularly, the economic potential of the new grouping was most successfully exploited, not by European companies but by the giant U.S. corporations who in the 1950's were already going international and who were readily able to plan on a continental scale—their home market being effectively on the same scale as the new market.

American business was able to operate on a European scale. U.S. car factories were able to manufacture the same model in different countries, indeed to assemble spare parts made in two or three countries. Other American companies were able to supply their home market from European plants leaving what was largely an administrative and market framework in their home ground. But European companies were able to follow the same pattern. Even while the Community moved towards free trade, increased trade between member states was matched by investment in each other's economies.

The legal structure of the Community favoured such movements. Apart from the obvious liberating effects on trade of the dismantling of trade barriers between members and the creation of a common external tariff (the CET), the whole legal framework of the Rome Treaty and its subordinate legislation favoured the internationalization of industry. The rules of competition, monopoly and restrictive agreements embodied in Clauses 85 and 86 of the Rome Treaty were likely in the long run to become as important as the U.S. anti-trust legislation which in many ways they resemble. Certainly they ran contrary to the instincts towards cartelization and protection which in the past had been characteristic of some of the major partners.

The harmonization of corporation law was a longer term and perhaps less spectacular move in the same direction. The forms of incorporation devised by the European economies, the Joint Stock company, the Société Anonyme, the Aktiengesellschaft and their variants had been the models for similar legislation in many other parts of the world. Harmonization, if it succeeded, could mean that the structure of commercial enterprises within the Community might differ no more than U.S. corporations registered in different U.S. states.

In spite of the spectacular economic advances and the ambitious plans for further economic and legal integration in the future, it would be an exaggeration to say that the Community in the 1970's was a single market. There were still enormous variations of standards of living and tastes. But at the very least Europeans were beginning to think European in the sense that they were more willing than ever before to consider buying goods from other countries than their own on a greater and greater scale.

International Trade or International Production

A major intention of the European Economic Community had been to establish free trade between members and a common external tariff against the rest of the world. The prospect of a common external tariff might seem to justify direct investment within the Community by outsiders such as the U.S. corporations, even though the CET, as the average of former individual members' tariffs, was in practice being cut so that it was becoming cheaper and cheaper to export to the new markets. But an American corporation, instead of investing in only one country within the CET and using it to supply all the rest, tended to spread investment into two or three of the member nations.

Partly this was historical. For example, Britain had been a traditional area of investment for American corporations. But as long as Britain was not a member of the Common Market, i.e. for the first 14 years, it made sense to invest both in the British and continental markets which might remain separate. After all, the Europeans were doing the same. British companies invested in manufacturing facilities in the continent in pre-membership days. The French, German and Italians did the same in Britain.

But even after Britain became a member of the Community and was thus absorbed into the CET the practice of investment by the same enterprise in more than one of the member states continued: in some respects it accelerated.

There were of course some obvious reasons: different skills, costs and the like existed to be exploited. But the reasons probably went a good deal deeper.

In an increasingly competitive and market oriented community, customers could and did insist on as good delivery conditions from foreign suppliers as from domestic. In some industries— processed foods or soft drinks for example—nearness to markets was more important than nearness to suppliers. These, as it happened, were already heavily infiltrated by U.S. enterprises, for the simple reason that the processed foods and drinks had originated in the U.S. domestic market. In the more durable products the location of manufacturing plants was less important but fast and reliable servicing was vital. Ford (U.K.) might be willing to rely on Ford (Germany) for components. But the Ford organization would be less happy to depend on an independent British component supplier to meet the needs of say their Belgian production lines, unless that supplier was willing to set up manufacturing facilities on the other side of the English Channel.

Much the same argument applied to capital goods. If a British manufacturer were competing to supply an Italian customer against competition say from German and Italian firms, it would be fool-hardy merely to quote a price and offer delivery to an Italian port against door to door delivery by the continental suppliers. The British company might not have to go as far as setting up manufacturing plant in Italy. But at the very least it might find it expedient to have an Italian registered company to undertake door to door delivery, installation and servicing. The existence of a highly competitive common market means that any customer can demand the same service from a foreign supplier situated outside the market as he gets from a supplier within the market. And that means that enterprises which have serious pretensions to serve a European market may require to have a national and legal presence in other countries within the market, to manufacture, assemble or even perhaps merely to sell on a local basis. The European Economic Community means not only increased exports and imports between members. It means that even medium and small national enterprises may have to incorporate, i.e. have a legal personality, in their major markets elsewhere within the Community.

THE UNITED STATES

The U.S.A. is the largest and richest national market in the world and is likely to remain so for most of the remainder of the century. More strictly perhaps it is several relatively distinct markets, but it is geographical rather than political or economic factors which produce this effect. The areas best represented in the international business scene by non-American enterprises are the Atlantic sea-board from Virginia north to New England, and the Western seaboard, particularly California. International subsidiaries of non-American enterprises are not perhaps so common elsewhere—in the mid West, for example. American multinationals on the other hand originate from many, if not most, of the fifty states with perhaps the Eastern states predominating in the more traditional industries and many of the high technology industries in the West.

The American situation is evolving very rapidly, at least as rapidly as the European scene. American enterprises were not traditionally concerned with overseas operations: their prospects at home were adequate for nearly a century after industrialization and it was not until the 1950's that really large scale investment began. The traditional U.S. attitude to the rest of the world was therefore of relative detachment, a business version of isolationism. Imports were very small; so were exports apart from foodstuffs and raw materials. There were few important political interests concerned with international business and political problems with a foreign dimension were solved with little regard to the opinions of foreign governments let alone foreign companies. The real offence of American political decisions of that nature up to the 1930's was not that they were made in a manner inimical to other national interests: what was worse, the latter were merely ignored. The Second World War and postwar events propelled the U.S.A. into the leadership of the free world. But in a sense the same criticism could still be made by America's foreign critics, of decisions made, with little or no concern for the consequences elsewhere. The U.S.A. was an economic giant and even a well meaning giant can do a good deal of harm merely by careless or ill-considered movements.

The situation has changed significantly since the 1960's in that the American government is paying rather more attention to the effects of its actions on the international business community for a number of very good reasons.

Firstly, the U.S.A., through its very large investment overseas over twenty years, has given a very substantial hostage to fortune. American industry, conscious of the possibility of tit-for-tat, urges moderation on ill-considered actions by Congress or the Executive.

Secondly, the dramatic improvement in the European economic situation, together with the existence of the Common Market, means that negotiations are no longer between an economic giant and individual medium or small sized states. Bargaining power is a good deal more equal, and while the U.S.A. has justifiable grievances about the actions of the EEC, the American government is certainly in no position to demand rather than negotiate for redress. The position of Japan, a new economic giant, is as yet more vulnerable, in that American markets are far more important to Japan than vice versa. But it is probably a matter only of a few years before Japanese economic bargaining power matches that of the U.S.A.

Finally, the growing economic dependence of the U.S.A. on raw material imports, while not directly affecting her relationship with the other economic giants of the developed world, is likely to make her more aware of the nuances of international business.

So far as international investment is concerned, the U.S. government is as anxious as any other to persuade overseas manufacturers to set up production facilities.

The large and persistent U.S. balance of payments defects in the late 1960's and early 1970's made the Federal Authorities anxious to bring in capital investment from abroad which as well as immediately providing foreign exchange, in the long run might cut down the demand for imports. In passing, however, it might be remarked that the U.S. balance of payments situation was never, in reality, as critical as its sheer size might suggest. A very large proportion of the payments for foreign imports was in practice likely to go to the subsidiaries of U.S. firms, who, better than most, knew how to sell in the U.S. market. Such overseas payments depleted the U.S. foreign exchange reserves and helped to nullify the efforts of the U.S. government to control the growth of U.S. capital investment elsewhere. But they could hardly in a real sense weaken U.S. economic power in the way that say heavy imports of Japanese products from factories which are not U.S. subsidiaries, did.

Another very sound reason for putting out the welcome mat for foreign investment is that it tended to blunt the criticism of very heavy U.S. investment in other countries. It could be demonstrated that the American government did not place restrictions on similar activities by foreign enterprises wishing to set up business in the U.S.A.

Thirdly, and less creditably perhaps, is the allegation that American political conditions made it very difficult to sell a wide range of industrial and even consumer products, unless they were produced within the frontiers of the U.S.A.

Sometimes the methods of discriminating against imported goods were overt. 'Buy American' legislation was designed to favour local products even where the prices were significantly higher than imports. Sometimes the methods or alleged methods, were more subtle, e.g. Certificates of Safety, or any type of safety legislation which bore down harder on imports than home production. Such activities were of course by no means unique to the U.S.A. but the complexity of the American system of government, the separation of powers between the executive, i.e. the Federal Government or State Government and the legislatures, meant that legislative action could produce barriers which were not particularly condoned by the U.S. government; or that state governments could follow policies contrary to the wishes of the federal authorities.

Anti-trust Legislation

One of the pitfalls for the successful American corporation and even more for the unwary foreigner is the existence of a mass of anti-trust legislation designed to make competition more effective by inhibiting monopoly and restrictive practice. Such disapproval of action which smacks, however remotely, of attempts to reduce competition, is foreign to the tradition of several European countries —even though the Rome Treaty provisions are moving nearer American practice. But the immediate implications on the international business man, and his home government, can be curious. In the first instance the American legislation ensures that it is safer to have a wholly foreign owned subsidiary operating in the U.S.A. than a Joint Venture, either between an American and a foreign company, or even two foreign companies, on the grounds that a Joint Venture means one company instead of two competing. This is not to say that Joint Ventures are illegal, merely that Joint Ventures of any size can attract suspicion.

Are 'Imported' Goods Superior?

There are parts of the world where 'Made in Britain', 'Made in Germany' or 'Made in Japan' would carry an automatic assumption that such goods were superior in quality to locally produced goods. That is hardly the situation in the U.S.A., but there is for a limited range of goods a cachet in having the designation 'Imported'. 'Imported' in the U.S. context is synonymous with quality, largely because of the comparative rarity (and implicitly, high price, high quality image) which goes with certain consumer goods. Certainly one would find it hard to imagine a British retailer using the equivalent tag 'Foreign' in his advertisements, although he would certainly be prepared to use certain national origins to establish a quality image.

The imported cachet however depends on the market segment being relatively small. As in any other developed country, large scale marketing of consumer non-durable goods depends on local production facilities being available. The American multinationals with their substantial production facilities in Europe and Asia are better able than anyone else to break into their home market with consumer goods manufactured overseas. But the prospects of non-American companies achieving this are limited. Even in the consumer durables, like cars and televisions of German and Japanese origin, they are very newsworthy precisely because they are so exceptional.

The Role of Sales Companies

In a paradoxical way the relative rarity of the imported product, save in well defined areas like cars and electronics, may be accelerating the development of international enterprises in the U.S.A. The foreign supplier is a novel and at first glance unattractive proposition for the U.S. wholesaler, who is used to ordering from a domestic supplier and getting door to door delivery. If, however, his supplier is several thousand miles and an ocean apart, this causes problems of delivery, payment, etc. He may be willing to buy imported goods, but less willing to go through the rigmarole of collecting them as they unload in a ship perhaps thousands of miles away.

The solution, in many instances, is for the foreign manufacturer to set up his own sales office in the U.S.A. which can handle customs clearance and door to door delivery. Once such a sales company is set up it may be possible to use the fact of multiple legal personality to save on tariff or taxes; and this is, as has been suggested, a key characteristic of the international enterprise.

JAPAN

The Japanese economy is unique: in one sense a Western industrial society which has adapted to Western technology and then surpassed many of its mentors: in another a profoundly non-Western culture with its own mores and values quite unlike anything in Western society.

Above all from the point of view of international business, Japan has been one of the fastest growing economies in the world— certainly the fastest growing of all the major industrialized countries and already talked of as one of the coming superpowers. Since the end of World War 2 it has steadily grown, overtaking a substantial part of Western Europe in terms of standards of living, and on the basis of simple projection likely to overtake the U.S. well before the end of the century.

In part the Japanese success has been attributed to its 'low profile' policy, which is now at an end. For a quarter of a century in the postwar world, Japan played only the most minor political role under the aegis of the U.S.A. The low profile helped in several directions. With only nominal expenditure on defence, its level of investment was indeed formidable: with an undervalued currency, its export successes remained virtually unremarked for years, as did the severely restrictionist policy towards imports and foreign investment. As long as the Japanese remained inconspicuous they were able to claim virtual freedom of action in the West while preventing reciprocal action by Western exporters and investors. It was only when economic power grew to the point that it caused grave embarrassment to much U.S. industry and the dollar as an international currency, that, most unwillingly, the strength of Japan began to be appreciated. In the future the low profile posture will be impossible. An economic giant cannot remain inconspicuous. But it is still doubtful whether the Japanese market will be as open as the international business man would like. Some very substantial barriers remain.

The first of these is that Japan remains profoundly alien to the West. For every Westerner who speaks or understands Japanese, there are probably a hundred Japanese who can speak English or any other of the key languages of the West. At a deeper level the culture and traditions of the country are almost incomprehensible to the Western businessman. As a very crude analogy Japan is a culture where the move from feudalism to industrial society has blended, indeed jelled. It may be that in time Western industry will produce Western values and Western stresses: so far, however, the synthesis of tradition and industrialization has produced a unique society where feudal loyalties often appear to be more important than the conflict of interests between employers and employed in the West, and where too the whole style of management with its emphasis both on consensus and respect for age and seniority seems to refute many of the received truths of Western industry and management.

A second barrier has been the powerful combination of government, banking interests, and industry in advancing national interests and absorbing all that was to be gained from Western technology. Considerable government pressure was brought to bear to ensure that little would be imported or manufactured by a foreign owned subsidiary which could be manufactured under licence: with the result that foreign companies had to license out new techniques to local firms, or at the most, enter into a Joint Venture with a local firm rather than be permitted to manufacture on their own account. It would be unjust to Japanese genius to claim that they originated little. But more than any other nation they have been able to absorb other nation's technology on their own terms and then improve on it. The policy has been relaxed relatively in recent years, but even the most technologically advanced foreign enterprises have found it very difficult to get a manufacturing foothold without paying a very high price in terms of transfer of knowhow.

Even now, the fact that legislation limiting foreign investment in Japan has been substantially modified does not mean plain sailing for the non-Japanese international enterprise. Over and above the legal situation there is in Japan the concept of 'administrative guidance' which may produce a situation where what is legal is still not in practice permitted.

There is some evidence that the very success of the Japanese economy has now limited but not stopped the rate of development. One obvious example has been the rapid rise in the standard of living, and hence of wages and other costs: the rapid rise in costs has been accelerated by the reluctant revaluation upwards of the Yen as the U.S. dollar has declined in value, and it is unlikely that Japan will be able to go on for years with undervalued currency in the future. In other respects too Japan is showing many of the characteristics of a mature and prosperous economy. More public expenditure on raising the quality of the environment, more leisure, more tourist expenditure overseas, more purchase of luxury goods. But if Japanese economic growth is decelerating, it still represents prodigious growth by the standards of most other nations.

As a market for the international businessman, Japan is probably improving all the time. A vast and growing demand for imports, manufactured as well as raw materials. More significantly, the prospects are slowly appearing of more direct investment by overseas businessmen in a very prosperous market. And by the same token, with labour shortages turning Japanese industry towards its own overseas investment, not only in the underdeveloped regions of Asia, but in Europe and the U.S.A., it is eminently possible that the Japanese controlled multinational will in time rival the American on the world scene.

WESTERN DEVELOPING NATIONS

The phrase 'developing nation' as used here means those societies outside Europe which are nevertheless European in culture and outlook, and do not yet possess the massive industrial base of the developed nations of the first group, but have substantial national resources and the determination to industrialize and so lessen their dependency on raw material exports. Although these areas have been colonized from Europe, sometimes very recently, there may also be large indigenous populations with the possibility, in some cases, of racial strife. But whatever their internal problems, they are, so far as the ruling societies are concerned, prosperous and likely to remain so.

The legal and commercial structure generally derives from the European model, since they are often ex colonies. Commercially the major influence in the past has been the European and par-

ticularly British connection. Some, like Australia, New Zealand
and South Africa were members of the Sterling Area when that
monetary bloc effectively acted as a discriminatory trading area
reinforced by Commonwealth Preference tariffs. The practical effects
on day to day trading of these historical ties is clearly fading
but in the case of these countries it still produces a society and
economy resembling that of the U.K. The fact that a very large
proportion of the community have fairly recent ties with the U.K.
plays its part in creating such a society. The same is not the case
obviously with Israel or the emerging countries of South America
such as the Argentine and Venezuela. But here as a reaction to
the almost overwhelming power of the Northern giant, they tend
on occasion to emphasize the European origins of their cultures
and use this, and European investment, as a counterweight to North
American dominance of the continent.

These societies are often embedded in the underdeveloped world:
consciously or unconsciously they may fear absorption by poor
but more populous societies with far higher birth rates. But the
major distinction between these societies and the first group discussed, i.e. the developed, is that they are often even more anxious
to attract investment and industrialization. They will actively encourage such investment by grants, tax concessions and the like,
as indeed will the developed countries in some selected regions
of high unemployment. But more importantly, they will often back
up these incentives by imposing high tariffs, quotas, or import
controls, once an international enterprise or local interests have
been persuaded to set up local production.

The only qualification on this welcome for overseas investment
is a desire to avoid excessive dependence on any one source.
Australia and New Zealand welcomed American and Japanese
investment as an alternative to British investment, but are now
perhaps nervous of the extent to which the latter souces have
grown. The Israeli situation is a unique one but there is little
doubt that the Latin American countries within this group would
be happier to see more European or Japanese investment as a
makeweight to the dominance of their industries by American
capital.

Such societies then are rich if limited markets: provided they
do not succumb to racial or political troubles internally or with
their neighbours they are likely to be very prosperous indeed. The
major problem for the businessman who supplies these markets
from production plant elsewhere, is that sooner or later he is likely
to find the market being closed to his exports, once local production
commences. In developed societies tariff barriers are more likely

to fall than rise. In developing societies the reverse is more probable, and this is a factor which must weigh with the international enterprise contemplating investment in these areas.

THE UNDERDEVELOPED WORLD

A third of the world's population lives in the relatively underdeveloped areas of the world. With a rapid rise in population, that proportion is rising rapidly and for the three broad areas of the underdeveloped world, Latin America, Africa and Asia, are the areas with the fastest growth in population if not in prosperity.

There are now over a hundred such countries in the so-called 'Third World', varying widely in size and social structure but with similarities which outweigh their economic and social differences. Many of them are overpopulated in terms of their resouces, and, with population rising faster than national product, may actually be becoming even poorer per head of the population. In attempting to break out of the vicious spiral of over-population and poverty, many or most are trying to industrialize to move away from subsistence farming and the export of raw materials to a measure of industrial development. The first result of this move is all too often a balance of payments problem externally, and uncontrolled inflation internally, as their industrialization policies pull in imports of equipment, and even of consumer luxuries for populations, realizing for the first time the measure of consumer luxuries available in other parts of the world. Only a handful of these countries are relatively free from these problems on account of substantial raw material endowments which enable them to sustain a drive towards a Western technological society without running into foreign exchange problems.

These nations almost invariably wish to adopt Western technology, if not ideals and culture. But most of them are very ambivalent about the idea of attracting investment, possibly the most direct method of achieving a Western type technology. They want investment in many instances but simultaneously they fear foreign domination of their industry and commerce. A country in consequence may officially welcome foreign investment while at the same time display an almost paranoiac suspicion.

It is not absolutely essential to pay the price of foreign economic domination, 'neocolonialism' in the fashionable jargon, in order to industrialize. Legislation can be used to limit foreign participation, to prevent outright foreign ownership, and insist on Joint Ventures with local interests, or licensing of technology.[9] The problem for many of these countries is that on the conditions they are willing to permit investment by an international enterprise, they are not all that attractive as markets. It seems to be a characteristic of many of the most recently independent states, that they overestimate their attractiveness to the foreign investor. Nevertheless it is becoming clear that without a certain minimum of technical educational, legal and administrative infrastructure, the choice may lie between foreign investment, stagnation, or a corporate state approaching totalitarianism.

The major exceptions to the bleak outlook facing the underdeveloped countries are a comparative handful which have substantial mineral wealth—oil being the most obvious example. At first sight, wealthy underdeveloped nations ought to attract investment by the international enterprise, in productive capacity. Unfortunately most of these countries have little to offer but their wealth from raw material exports. They are often areas of relatively small populations and therefore unattractive as domestic markets *per se.* [10] Except for the *Category I* extractive industry, the enterprise requires a substantial domestic market, and only a handful of countries fill the bill—Iran, Indonesia, Egypt and Nigeria, perhaps. Such countries have an opportunity of developing industrially, using the international enterprise as the medium of development if they so choose. The others, in spite of their wealth, find it difficult to move beyond the import stage. At most, they may achieve assembly operations, e.g. in motorcars, using imported components, but without a substantial home population their prospects of industrialization are limited. Ironically, their very wealth may act as a barrier to industrialization via the international enterprise. Their governments do not face foreign exchange problems which would force them to encourage local production, while their relative affluence destroys the prospect of low labour costs which might attract the international enterprise.

A. INVESTMENT IN THE THIRD WORLD—EXTERNAL ISSUES

There are two external political factors which affect the operation of international business in the underdeveloped world. The first is rivalry between East and West, competing for influence in the Third World. In its earlier stages this was a straight conflict between the U.S.A. and its allies and the U.S.S.R. The situation is now a good deal more complex.

In one sense, East/West competition has weakened, largely because of disillusion about the political dividends to be won. The U.S.A. has gained no gratitude from most recipients of aid. It almost appears to be a point of national pride in some quarters to repudiate any sense of obligation or gratitude for such aid as a demonstration of national independence. The experience of America's allies has been rather similar. The extent of Commonwealth Aid by Britain has neither prevented the erosion of the Commonwealth nor enamoured either donor nation or recipient to each other. Only France, with a more rigorous attention to her own national interest in distributing overseas aid has received much political advantage, and even this appears to be eroding.

If the West has little to show for a generation of giving aid, the Russian experience has been equally disillusioning. Here again, past aid brings little present gratitude.

Before looking at the more complex situation existing today, it would be useful to relate this East/West competition for favour to the situation of the foreign enterprise operating in the Third World. Briefly, in the event of a conflict between an international enterprise and a host nation in this group, it is fairly certain that the latter will receive assistance, technical or financial, by one side or the other in the major power bloc.

In pre World War 1 days trading and industrial nations could defend their overseas interests, including the commercial interests of international enterprise, by variants of 'gun boat' diplomacy. This option is simply not open any more where the other major power bloc is ready to weigh in for its own advantage.

In the 1970's the situation was much more complex than the simple East/West rivalry. Both blocs had to some extent splintered. In the West, U.S. supremacy was no longer unchallenged and national interests, even between allies, were no longer even nominally uniform. Even in the coldest of cold war days the relationship between American, British and French oil interests in the Middle East were hardly compatible. As time went on the conflicts between different countries in different areas increased; certainly France was able to exploit anti-American feeling in Arab countries and Latin America.

The same situation was true of the East, most notably in the schism between the U.S.S.R. and China, each of whom in the early 1970's appeared to detest the other more than their ideological enemies in the West. Even within the Soviet bloc it was remarkable how readily, for example, Czech arms were made available to regimes which had expressed their detestation of the U.S.S.R.

None of this splintering makes the problem of international business easier. Now, when a host government in the Third World is in conflict with an international enterprise, it can find aid and a replacement without having to compromise its ideological stand.

The second political factor particularly affects American international enterprises in Latin America and European enterprises in Africa and Asia. This is a sustained attitude of suspicion directed against the commercial and industrial representatives of these powers which have dominated the area politically and economically in the past. This suspicion, indeed hostility, derives from fear of continued economic domination: it may however be accompanied by a very considerable respect for the technology of the country.

In Latin America, where it might be said that the U.S.A. is on the defensive, the situation is rendered more complex by the appearance of Common Market and Free Trade areas modelled on the EEC and the European Free Trade Association. The two major groups are the Central American Common Market, which has had a measure of success bedevilled by political quarrels among members: and the American Free Trade Area which is in a state of suspended animation. The smaller members of the latter have continued the process of integration through the Andean Pact.

In Africa the common market arrangements are even more tenuous and are complicated by French or English speaking rivalries as well as by racial tendencies. International enterprises in this sense are increasingly having to choose between investment in the Union of South Africa, which is economically powerful but politically ostracized, with an uncertain future, and those African states which are in a relatively primitive condition now but which may be far more important in the future. It is probable that the political future for American companies in Latin America and European companies in Africa is somewhat uncertain at least in the short run. But whether this really means that in the long run these areas will be able to dispense with the international business enterprise as a means of acquiring technology and gaining access to the lucrative markets of the West, is doubtful.

The Asian situation, again, is different: in many instances highly developed cultures exist whose aspirations and values may make it difficult for them to absorb Western practices, in spite of the deep rooted influence of English culture and the English language there.

The external political situation of the Third World might be summed up thus: a suspicion of the West and an hostility which may be the conventional clichés of politicians in some instances, yet much more profound in others.

The underdeveloped world has a well publicised platform in UNCTAD, the United Nations Conference on Trade and Development.[11] This conference is in the main a four-year affair, and generates a good deal of hostility in public towards the West.

Increasingly however the hostility is now being directed in part
to the developed nations of the Communist world also. They are
seen as unsympathetic to their problems as the developed nations
of the West. Potentially then the East/West conflict may be sub-
merged into a North/South conflict, i.e. the 'haves' of the Northern
hemisphere being drawn into conflict with the 'have nots' of the
South. The sinister nature of such a conflict with its racial overtones
can hardly be exaggerated. In a book of this nature, however,
it will be necessary to consider the implications basically in relation
to international business: to consider for example, how this potentially hostile environment can be coped with by the international
enterprise, and incidentally, to consider the extent to which these
operations may exacerbate or ameliorate the problems. But at the
moment it is important to make two very obvious points.

The first is that even where there is general hostility to international enterprises, it is often most concentrated on those of one
nation. There are parts of the underdeveloped world where, if an
enterprise is foreign owned, it is expedient to be manifestly not
American owned, e.g. in parts of Latin America. The same
phenomenon occurs in parts of Africa in respect of British, French
or Belgian enterprises.

The second point arises from the first: there is very little unity
of purpose, except on ritual occasions, e.g. passing resolutions at
the UN or at UNCTAD conferences. The nation state of the
Third World presses its quarrels with other Third World states
as enthusiastically as the most thrusting nation of the West.

B.   INVESTMENT IN THE THIRD WORLD—INTERNAL ISSUES

Internal problems of Third World nations are extensions of their
external political problems. One political factor however is particularly worthy of comment. The great majority of Third World nations
profess Socialism as an ideal. Socialism in the Third World is
like Democracy everywhere, a useful catchword that has in places
been so debased in meaning as to cover anything.

Socialism, however, whether Marxist inspired or not, presumably
has something to do with the public ownership of the means of
production: public ownership in many instances of exactly the type
of enterprise in which international business is directly interested.

How important then is the implication that in the long term,
nationalization or outright confiscation is apparently inevitable?
It is frankly very difficult to give an answer but the question
must be faced. For those governments which adopt an increasingly

Marxist form of government, nationalization is the inevitable result
—witness the fate of U.S. investment in Cuba under Castro and
Chile during the Allende period. For many others of course the
gesture to Socialism is as meaningless as gestures to Democracy.
The extremes of affluence and poverty in many of the overtly
socialist economies of the Third World are far more acute than
in the capitalist West: and certainly the profession of Socialism
is not accompanied in many instances by much display of concern
for the old and poor.

Socialism may remain an abstract ideal in many countries of
the Third World. It may be modified into the somewhat mild
variety of Social Democracy of Western Europe which does not
seek to own so much as moderate the activities of the means
of production. It may lapse into the stultifying bureaucracy which
seems to be the fate of the Indian experiment, or it may blossom
into a full scale revolutionary Marxist style. In the first two situations, international business can operate, in the latter two, it either
withers or is killed off.

One of the intellectual triumphs of socialist thought is that it
has convinced many thinking men that in fact Socialism is inevitable,
and this conviction remains in spite of the manifest failure of most
socialist economies to deliver the goods with anything like the
competence of the capitalist system. Whether or not the theory
is valid is not likely to be settled for many generations, but the
assumption of inevitability has to be challenged in so far as it
paralyses initiative by international business. There are at least
two good reasons for arguing that although Socialism has to be
taken seriously by the privately owned international enterprise, its
inevitability as a barrier to overseas manufacture cannot be taken
for granted.

In the first instance many underdeveloped nations having flirted
with Socialism, even Marxist Socialism, may discard it and go
back to a more free-wheeling capitalist style if failure and corruption
become too rampant. The Indonesia of Sukarno in the mid 1960's
looked like a transitional stage to a fully Marxist revolutionary
state but it was replaced by a largely non-ideological government
which welcomed Western investment and was manifestly dis-
illusioned with its former Russian and Chinese friends. Arab Socialist in the Egypt of President Nasser had become a remarkably
watered down doctrine in the 1970's with foreign investment being
encouraged and even the establishment of a Stock Exchange, the
arch symbol of a capitalist system, being actively considered. There
is almost a cycle, rather than a Marxist dialectic. A manifestly
corrupt and inefficient regime may be overthrown by the sea green

incorruptibles, the young officers or intellectuals and veer towards a puritanical Socialism; in turn this regime will become as corrupt as its predecessor and be replaced by a non-ideological, probably military, government which may turn to the West: in time it too may be overthrown by the next generation of left wing idealists, and so on.

The expulsion of international companies is rarely an irrevocable act. Dramatic nationalization is often quietly reversed.

This might seem a rash claim in dealing with Marxist states whose governments are remarkably resilient at retaining power. Certainly in the first few years of ideological purity, international business is anathema. But, as will be observed later, mature Marxist states, not least the Soviet Union, are ready and eager to do deals across ideological barriers. International businessmen operating in the Third World have to take account of Socialism, and learn to live with it, but socialist governments in their turn learn to accept the persistence and usefulness of international private enterprise and trade with it on non-ideological terms.

THE COMMUNIST WORLD

In the present chapter the relationship between international business and the Communist countries will be dealt with mainly in terms of trade. The rapidly emerging problems of the so-called transideological co-operation in manufacture is the subject of a latter section; it is at the moment in its infancy, while trading with Communist markets has been an established fact of international business for over half a century.

Like the underdeveloped world, the Communist nations comprise one third of the world's population. In degrees of development they cover the complete range from countries with standards of living comparable to some countries in Western Europe to the really underdeveloped. Most of them, however, are progressing and their apparent demand for the consumer goods of the Western world—and the technology which supplies it—may be almost insatiable for the rest of the century.

The contrast however between the vast potential demand and the actual level of imports from the West is painfully obvious. The reasons for the gap between potential and reality can be understood partly in terms of economics, partly in terms of politics.

To consider firstly the U.S.S.R. and its allies in Eastern Europe, the main problem is that these countries generally trade with the outside world on the basis of bilateral currency quota arrangements, i.e. a sophisticated form of barter. In an emergency, such as a harvest failure, Communist governments will go well over the currency quotas and sell gold to buy grain. Normally, however, they will tend to balance their trade with individual countries as far as they can.

Eastern Europe has its own trading bloc, the Council for Mutual Economic Assistance, the CMEA or more commonly known as Comecon.[12] This comprises the Communist nations of Europe, less Yugoslavia (which has closer trading links with the West), and Albania allied to the Chinese. Outside Eastern Europe, Comecon now includes Mongolia and Cuba, but for practical purposes it can be regarded as the trading bloc of Eastern Europe.

The original objectives of Comecon were to divert the trade of the smaller countries of Eastern Europe from their traditional links with the West, towards the U.S.S.R., and ensure that member countries would buy from their Comecon partners, rather than outside, except when it was difficult or impossible to do so.

Comecon has been loosely equated with the EEC as a trading bloc. Like the EEC it has had its vicissitudes, the greatest of which has been the growing, if still limited, independence of other Eastern European countries from Russian control. This has in part frustrated an original political aim of its Russian originators to create a system of division of labour on an international scale by an increasing tendency towards economic nationalism and self-sufficiency. An original concept of specialization by countries has been replaced by a degree of independent national planning. This has increased the prospects of sales from outside the area.

It would be unwise however to push the implications of revived nationalism too far. Comecon still exists, accounting for about two thirds of all the international transactions among its member states. The trade channels to the West have been diverted, probably permanently, and no Western manufacturer is likely to find himself competing on equal terms with state organizations within the group for markets also within the group.

The opposite pole of the Communist world is China, currently on worse terms with the other Communist giant, than with the West. China does not operate a trading bloc on Comecon lines though her influence in the Communist areas of South East Asia and Albania are obvious.

In spite of political quarrels, the general methods of trade in Communist countries is much the same everywhere with the exception of Yugoslavia. What then are these methods of trading? What are the types of goods which can be sold? And what sort of Western enterprise can have reasonable prospects of doing business with a totally different ideological system to that of the West?

There is, in general, little if any chance of selling Western products to private firms, or even in many instances to the state owned industries. Foreign trade in most Communist countries is in the hands of state controlled foreign trade organizations (FTO's), which generally have a monopoly of the import and export trade in a particular industry. Thus, for example, Autoexport is the Russian trading organization which covers all types of cars and ancillaries. The name gives away some of the emphasis. Often they are more interested in exporting than importing.

So far as the Comecon countries are concerned the situation is neither uniform nor static. In some instances direct access to customers is possible, and the ease or difficulty will vary from time to time and country to country. Nevertheless, having said that, the newcomer to the market is likely to find himself dealing initially at least with the trading organization, rather than the ultimate user.

There are several advantages as well as disadvantages to the international businessman in this situation. The main advantage lies in the fact that once an order has been secured, (and the specification can be exceedingly rigorous) then the record of payment is good. There is a minimum credit risk, short of an absolutely disastrous diplomatic breach between the Communist country and the parent government of the international enterprise: in spite of the political difficulties of the postwar years, no established Communist regime appears to have repudiated a commercial payment because of a political quarrel.

The fact that payment, provided the contract is rigorously met, is assured does not mean that credit is not a problem—it is only credit-worthiness that is satisfactorily disposed of. The almost chronic shortage of foreign exchange which is a characteristic of Comecon countries, allied to the powerful bargaining position that a sole buyer has in the market, means that sales have very often to be negotiated on the basis of medium or long term credits. But, in general, provided that no difficulties arise because goods are on a strategic embargo list, the problem of financing exports to Comecon countries by orthodox export credit methods is not as great as exports to areas where the creditworthiness of the individual buyer, as well as the whole economy, is an issue.

It is worth emphasizing that the question of credit is important in Comecon trading, much less so with China. The latter country is a good deal less willing to buy unless it can pay immediately. The situation of course may change but at the moment it appears that the Chinese government has a very puritanical objection to living beyond its means in the international market. But with this reservation, what is true of Western Communist states is broadly true of the non-European ones too: the state trading organization is the key institution in the business deal.

The practical disadvantages of the system are great, from the point of view of the international business enterprise, and, arguably, from the point of view of efficient use of resources by the Communist governments.

From the businessman's point of view the most obvious disadvantages are the difficulties of dealing with any opportunity expeditiously, or of selling anything for which specific provision has not been made in the current development plan: and also of getting through to the ultimate customer to determine what exactly his requirements are.

A certain amount of advertising can be achieved in technical journals; it appears to be normal for the potential user to learn of the available Western products through advertising or trade fairs, and then for him to make out a case for the purchase with the Trade Organization—presumably in the case of a Comecon country, proving that equivalent equipment was not available from a trading partner within the bloc.

The result of this use of a state owned middleman in the form of the Trading Organization is that negotiation may be clumsy and lengthy. It may be a considerable time before face to face discussion between the seller and the ultimate user takes place. It is not uncommon for some industrial equipment which requires elaborate installation to be accepted for delivery, without the seller being allowed to know exactly where the plant is located let alone being able to supervise installation in the factory. Some of the Soviet Union's difficulties with electronic data processing equipment bought from the West may have arisen from this unwillingness to accept the presence of on-the-spot advisers.

Even from the point of view of the Communist country the situation may have as many disadvantages as advantages: FTO's depend for their existence on ideological as well as commercial considerations. The situation is not eased by the fact that the FTO has taken over what would be regarded as procurement problems in the West and, unlike a procurement division, its interests need not coincide exactly ·with those of the ultimate buyer, for the FTO, although acting under the general direction of the Ministry of Trade is for some purposes a legal entity with its own resources and its own aims which place at least as much emphasis on selling as buying. The result of this is that though the ultimate user, say in the Soviet Union, and the exporter in, say West Germany, may be agreed on all specifications, and price, the FTO may have its own ideas on what credit terms it seeks and indeed on whether it can tie in a sale of some of its own products to the purchase of the German equipment. In consequence, the German buyer who believes he is virtually home and dry for the order, might then be presented with conditions involving part payment in the form of a product which is of no particular interest to him, or for that matter, to his Soviet customer. In the event, an attempt may be made to barter, in part linking the purchase of the German export with the sale of another commodity which that particular trade organization happens to be trying to dispose of.

The value of this so-called 'contra sale' is however likely to be only a fraction of the value of the original sale, the remainder being in an agreed Western currency. The proportion of barter involved in the counter order may bear some relationship to the scarcity or otherwise of the currency required to pay for the original order, or to the degree of urgency with which the product is wanted in the U.S.S.R., or even to the success or failure of the FTO in achieving its target for export sales. And, of course, the result of refusing to entertain a contra sale, whether it causes the sale to be lost, will depend on which of these factors has been uppermost in the mind of the FTO negotiators. To use modern managerial jargon, the FTO may suboptimize its aims at the expense of the ultimate user and arguably of the whole economic system. Indeed the personal career prospects of FTO negotiators may be measured in their ability to earn foreign exchange (or at least to conserve it) by barter deals and displays of toughness in bargaining with foreign businessmen, rather than by their ability to get the best equipment available.

The role of barter is of considerable consequence and is likely to remain so as long as Communist countries are short of foreign exchange, and committed to the FTO system. In a later chapter on more general transideological deals it will be necessary to examine the issue in far more detail. But at the moment it may suffice to say that an enterprise seriously interested in trade with the Communist countries must consider very seriously whether it wishes to get into the barter field, with the advantages and disadvantages which follow. As often as not the issue of barter deals comes down to one of attitudes, whether one regards a barter deal as a necessary evil to be dealt with as expeditiously as possible, or as another opportunity to make a profit by accepting delivery of perhaps raw materials at a discount over the prevailing world market price.

It is of course a relevant factor to bear in mind that since the FTO's are organized on an industry basis, any barter deals are going to be in broadly related products. A Western exporter selling machinery might be faced with the possibility of having to accept in part payment a few hundred tons of metal ingots. He is not so likely to be offered timber, dried fish or cotton.

Assessing Future Trends in Communist Markets

There is a very considerable uncertainty in day to day exporting to Communist countries in that future demand can rarely be forecast once the current order runs out.

Firstly, certain large capital items may be purchased for a specific project with no great prospect of a repeat order. Secondly, an order may be given because some plant within the Communist economy has unexpectedly failed to deliver on time, i.e. a particular component which would usually be available locally was held up in circumstances where the national plan could not afford to wait for the usual Comecon supplier.

Both situations result, in a sense, in the 'one off' job situation, where a repeat order is less likely than in other markets where the quality and price might be attractive enough to secure any subsequent orders. Outside buying in the Comecon system is the exception, rather than the rule. To some extent needs in Communist countries might be anticipated by a study of the current development plans, although these will certainly not specify in advance what types of commodity will be purchased overseas. In general, the requirements of Communist countries cannot be foreseen, there is little prospect of market research by on-the-spot surveys, and little prospects of stimulating demand by extensive advertising.

Finally, it should be remembered that there is no general convertibility of currencies among countries of Comecon for trading with the West. Even those countries which have trading surpluses with their Comecon partners and are unable to satisfy their import needs from other Communist countries, are generally unable to convert their surplus into Western currencies. The non-convertibility system has undoubtedly worked to the advantage of the U.S.S.R. and to the disadvantage of, say, Poland. It may be that growing independence by the non-Russian members of Comecon may compel these countries to make concessions by paying them in gold or convertible currency.

All Communist countries, not merely Comecon members, are interested in the main in capital goods—or more strictly perhaps in Western technology. Consumer goods have a relatively low priority in home production plans, and scarce foreign currency will rarely be used to purchase luxuries. In view of the relatively

poor quality of much of the consumer goods produced, compared
with those of the West, it is scarcely surprising that comparison
is often not invited. There are perhaps two market segments for
such consumer goods. The first of these is the shopping markets
which are available only to those with foreign currency from the
West, i.e. diplomats or other foreigners, and local nationals who
have acquired such currency perhaps by remittances from abroad.
The acute shortage of foreign exchange in many of these countries
has encouraged the authorities to create, what is in effect a privileged
market place to mop up any foreign currency available. Secondly
the authorities have been known on occasion to import consumer
goods which are then retailed locally at a very high price, apparently
to mop up purchasing power in a situation where the problem of
inflation is regarded as more acute than the foreign exchange
shortage. Both these segments however are relatively small, and
the thinking behind them is ideologically suspect, i.e. they appeal
to the large established and less orthodox Communist countries
of the West; an improvement in local production methods, or a
reversion to more political orthodoxy is liable to wipe out these
market segments.

The Trade Salon, Joint Ventures and the like

It was emphasized at the beginning of this section that it is a
mistake to assume uniformity of policy in Eastern Europe, let
alone in the entire Communist world, for there has been a great
deal of experimentation, which has at bottom a political or an
economic motive, and which in some cases may affect even the
ideology of the countries concerned. The instances of these
developments in the early 1970's are perhaps worth noting.

The first of these is the creation of a new type of trade exhibition
in the U.S.S.R. Trade Fairs in the absence of other lines of com-
munication, have always been an important means of securing
orders. What is unusual about the 'Salon' type of Trade Fair is
that it is very specifically designed round the requirements of one
particular industry which is due for rapid development under the
economic plan which happens to be current at the time. The general
public are not admitted to these fairs and the visitors are therefore
clearly the potential customers. Finally, foreign firms exhibit only
by invitation, normally based on the satisfactory supplying of
products in the past. A trade fair of this nature and an invitation
to display means therefore a reasonably good chance of a sale
if the terms are right.

Secondly, so far as other members of Comecon are concerned,
there is a good deal of economic experimentation which implies

a closer approach to Western costing and pricing practices. The Soviet intervention in Czechoslovakia in 1968 has indicated the dangers to the smaller members of Comecon of pushing reform into the political side, but, by and large, the ground rules which seem to be emerging, are that as long as political orthodoxy and in particular the supremacy of the Communist party in government is not challenged, the U.S.S.R., while rarely approving of economic change, is not likely to intervene militarily. Political orthodoxy may be the price of economic heresy in the Comecon world, and areas which look least promising in the political aspect may afford good opportunities. Within Comecon for example, the most rigid resistance to political changes is to be found in a country like Rumania, which is nevertheless tolerated in a more venturesome external policy, which obviously irritates the U.S.S.R.: and is now even experimenting with joint ventures with Western companies to build new factories and industry.

Finally it is well to remember not only that some Comecon members may wish on occasion to challenge economic orthodoxy, but there are other Communist states which are neither Comecon members nor indeed on particularly friendly terms with the Soviet Union. The obvious example is the one already mentioned, China, whose relationship with the U.S.S.R. at the time of writing is a good deal worse than with the U.S.A., the arch capitalist, and which approves of the European Economic Community, precisely because it strengthens Western Europe against the U.S.S.R. But the same applies to other smaller countries whose relationship with their larger protectors can switch with remarkable volatility. Cuban relationships with the U.S.S.R. have had their ups and downs, as Western European exporters, if not American, have found to their benefit.

The problem about the latter point is in the word 'volatility'. Present ideological differences in the Communist world may close again, to the political detriment of the West, and the economic disadvantage of its businessmen: or yet more fissures may appear. In general the Communist world is no longer, if it ever was, monolithic and new stresses and strains open up footholds for merchants and industrialists outside the system. The only thing which can be taken for granted for the outside industrialist, however, is that the economic and political scene within the Communist world has changed vastly in a decade, is still changing, and is likely to go on changing, for good or ill, for the rest of the century.

3. International Business—Degrees of Commitment

Figure 1 sets out in schematic form degrees of commitment to an international status. The 'International Enterprise Condition' is flanked on the one side by methods of exporting which do not involve going international and on the other by an alternative, namely licensing. The two flanking conditions are not however rigidly designated. In a real life enterprise the situation can be rather fuzzy.

Apart from the extractive industries defined in the first chapter as *Category I*, virtually all international enterprises go through a phase when they simply export. Exporting, however, does not automatically lead to international status: even these enterprises which do get to the point of setting up sales companies in foreign markets and are therefore, potentially at least, international, do not always attempt to exploit the extra dimension created by multiple legal personalities.

It is difficult, particularly in hindsight, to account for the fact that some enterprises achieve international status relatively easily, while others do not. The phrase 'in hindsight' is particularly important because when company histories are written up, or even when businessmen recall events of a few years back, they are liable, unconsciously or otherwise, to rationalize some ad hoc initiative, or downright casual decisions, in terms of the long term results. But it is at least as likely that the most important decisions affecting the long term international prospects of the enterprise may have been taken, for good or ill, for very short term reasons.

It might, for example, seem merely commonsense to say that a company's marketing policy will determine its methods of exporting, by agent, sales company, etc. But it is apparent that in many instances it has been the method of exporting which determined policy, and the whole pattern of international development. A snap decision to choose one man as an agent instead of another, or possibly to use an agent because a sales company

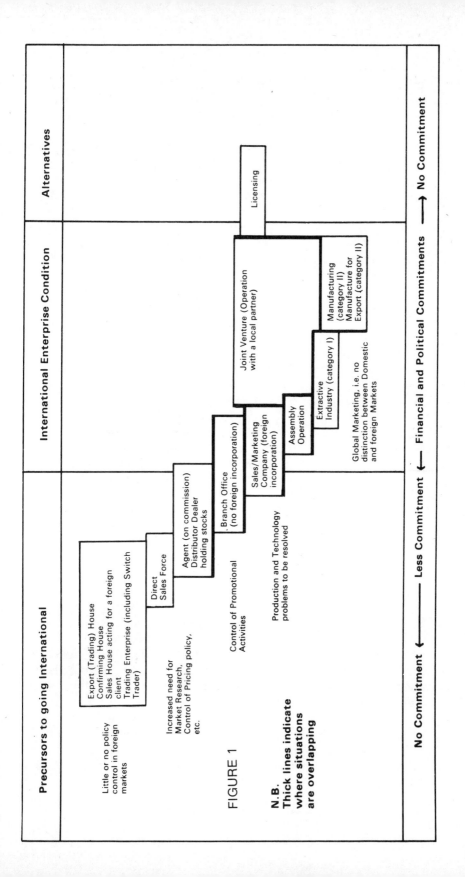

Precursors to going International | International Enterprise Condition | Alternatives

Little or no policy control in foreign markets

Export (Trading) House
Confirming House
Sales House acting for a foreign client
Trading Enterprise (including Switch Trader)

Direct Sales Force

Increased need for Market Research, Control of Pricing policy, etc.

Agent (on commission)
Distributor Dealer holding stocks

Branch Office (no foreign incorporation)

Control of Promotional Activities

Sales/Marketing Company (foreign incorporation)

Production and Technology problems to be resolved

Assembly Operation

Licensing

Joint Venture (Operation with a local partner)

Extractive Industry (category I)

Manufacturing (category II)
Manufacture for Export (category II)

Global Marketing, i.e. no distinction between Domestic and foreign Markets

FIGURE 1

N.B.
Thick lines indicate where situations are overlapping

No Commitment ⟵   Less Commitment ⟵   Financial and Political Commitments ⟶   No Commitment appeared to be too expensive, can affect the size of the market which develops. Indeed, by determining the size of the market, it can appear to confirm the wisdom of a rather casual decision, and make it in hindsight appear much better thought out and logical than it really was at the time. And on the basis of the market size which is so decided, an enterprise will, a few years later, make a decision whether or not to go international.

This is the main justification for devoting much of this chapter to the precursors or alternatives to international business. An enterprise has to go through an export phase before becoming international. The decisions made then on how to export either create opportunities or impose constraints on whether or how an enterprise will go international.

EXPORT DISTRIBUTION CHANNELS

All marketing involves a chain of distribution. Depending on the product, the conditions prevailing in the market, and his own inclinations a manufacturer has to decide how far along the chain he wants to control the product. He may choose to sell literally at his factory gate, and let others take over the distribution from there. Or he may try to get to the ultimate consumer himself. Generally, at the risk of vast oversimplification, it will be easier for a manufacturer of a branded differentiated product to move further along the distribution chain, if he chooses. A producer of raw materials or an unbranded product does not have quite the same choice, unless he is also a user of the product.

Exporting, as opposed to domestic marketing, lengthens the chain, increases the number of links. It may therefore give the manufacturer a wider choice of how far along the chain he wishes to try to retain control. This element of choice is greatest in a developed economy because he is more likely to be dealing with branded goods.

Prima facie there are two good arguments for an exporter in this situation extending his operations along the distribution chain.

Firstly, although every link in the distribution chain involves additional cost and administration, it also represents a mark up, a commission, or a discount; and the further along the distribution chain he retains control the more say he has on marketing, advertising, pricing, etc. Any consumer loyalty built up accumulates to his operation and will persist even if he changes his method of distribution. Secondly, the further he has penetrated into the market, the better he is able to judge its potentiality instead of receiving information passed back through links in the distribution chain, which, to mix a metaphor, have their own interests or prejudices in interpreting the market situation.

This is of course a theoretical ideal. Any new marketing operation is hazardous: a foreign market operation is particularly hazardous and expensive. There is a natural tendency therefore not to press forward too far, but rather to settle for the inexpensive option, i.e. to use a trading house with its own expertise or an agent or a distributor who will take over the distribution. Such a solution may seem to be relatively simple, and capable of being amended later. But that initial and tentative decision may affect future developments profoundly. Why this should be so is the subject matter of this chapter. It is worth repeating the point made at the beginning of this section, namely the subtle danger for a potential international enterprise is that its fate may be decided, almost as soon as it begins to export. The tentative arrangements to break into an export market may harden into a permanent arrangement without the long term implications being considered. Instead of determining an overall marketing strategy, including estimates of what level of sales could reasonably be expected in a market, and choosing the appropriate method of coping with the scale of business, the enterprise may proceed in the opposite order by choosing the simplest and cheapest distribution chain and letting that decision determine the market size.

Such an arrangement is not obviously disastrous. It is just as likely to work well enough in that if the export venture does take off it will generate a volume of orders ideally suited to the distribution chain. The self-fulfilling element of the situation guarantees that more often than not an acceptable result will be produced. But whether a much larger volume of sales could have been achieved by another distribution method may not be obvious. And an enterprise which might in other circumstances become a larger and faster growing international enterprise, can thereby remain confined within its own domestic boundaries and its traditional methods of doing business.

THE EXPORT (TRADING) HOUSE

There is a variety of terms covering organizations performing virtually the same functions — 'export house', 'trading house', 'confirming house', etc.

In its simplest form this type of organization makes its money from its expertise in foreign markets — generally markets in under-developed countries. It will either buy directly and export on its own account, or undertake to export on a commission basis, generally specializing in particular markets or products.

In the role of buyer, i.e. as an export merchant, it creates for the manufacturer the first and earliest link at which he can opt out of the distribution chain. The manufacturer can sell 'ex factory' or 'ex warehouse' receive payment in his own currency, and treat the whole operation as indistinguishable from any other sale in the home market.

Three illustrations show appropriate occasions for the use of the export house, particularly as a buyer: a) the small manufacturer who lacks expertise in exporting, knowledge of the market and the financial strength to take on credit arrangements; b) an established exporter may choose to sell to, or use the expertise of the export house in a new market where the expected return does not appear to warrant heavy expenditure; c) where a firm has only a marginal interest in exporting, i.e. to get rid of surplus production, and does not contemplate further developments.

Most products can be handled by export houses, the major difficulty being products which are likely to require extensive after-sales servicing by the manufacturer.

There are obvious problems arising from the use of an export house for the manufacturer who has any serious intentions of going international in a big way. It represents the least penetration of the distribution channel in that the manufacturer has no real control of the situation or even knowledge of the market; it is not even possible to ensure that the export house will not end the transaction at its own convenience if it can find a more profitable source for the same product. If the product does require after-sales service, the manufacturer may have more security; and where goods are branded and their source readily identifiable, consumer loyalty of a sort may be created. The point remains, however, that there are limitations in using an export house simply because the latter has no incentive to help the manufacturer to dispense with its own services. It has, on the contrary, every reason to keep him from getting to know anything about the market let alone going international.

A further complication is that the export house as buyer of the goods is likely to have complete control of price, advertising and distribution in the foreign market—a situation which may limit the freedom of action of the manufacturer who may wish a wholly different marketing policy, if he subsequently enters the foreign market by more direct methods.

Most of the objections discussed so far arise only when the export house is the buyer. Export houses can, however, be used as a ready made export department. On a commission basis an export house will take care of most of the problems of marketing goods abroad, as an agent rather than as a principal. The role of an agent *per se* will be discussed in the following section, and much of what is said there is also appropriate to the export house in this role except that the latter's agency activities in part at least are carried on at home while the agent, as the term is normally used, works and resides in the foreign market. Additionally, the export house can be used to handle much of the mechanics of exporting, arranging documentation, shipping insurance, etc. as well as the more direct marketing function. On occasion too it may be used in a factoring role, i.e. to handle the details of credit finance and collect payment on behalf of the manufacturer.

When the use of the export house is on a commission basis, the long term results may be more satisfactory if it is the intention of the manufacturer to move on later to methods giving closer direct contact with the market. Prices can be controlled; brand loyalty can be better safeguarded. Even so the probability is that rather less direct information on the market will accrue to the manufacturer, than by the use, for example, of an agent. The export house deals with the manufacturer from an address in the manufacturer's own country, while the agent is resident in the foreign market. This means that there is even less incentive than with an agent to go out regularly and look at the market.

What criteria can be established to determine when an export house ought to be used? Realistically, if the enterprise is small and likely to remain so, the case for an export or international division becomes hard to justify, unless exporting is limited to one or two markets which can be studied thoroughly. Otherwise the use of an export house as opposed to an international division is a matter of the degree of risk the enterprise is prepared to take.

Thus far, comments on the role and appropriateness of the export house have been confined to the buying of goods for export and the hiring out of expert knowhow. The same organization can use its expertise in the opposite direction by its knowledge of producers as well as markets, i.e. it may act as a buying agent for a foreign customer negotiating and purchasing from a foreign firm designated by the buyer or selected on his behalf by the organization. The main function is to confirm financial arrangements so that the export house, or more strictly the confirming house, although acting only for the buyer and paid a commission by him, can be regarded as a domestic buyer. Once again, so far as the manufacturer is concerned, an export sale has become another home sale.

From the point of view of the manufacturer the advantages or disadvantages of dealing with a confirming house are much the same as with the export house, except that the initiative has come from the buyer's end: it has the additional advantage that *del credere* provisions can be made, i.e. payment can be guaranteed.

A rather specialized example of the confirming house pattern is the use of the so-called buying house by large departmental and chain stores. These undertake the purchase of consumer goods for their principals. They are of limited use to the prospective international enterprise.

By and large, the tendency has been for confirming houses to decline in importance. They reached their heyday in the nineteenth century in aiding exporters to sell in colonial or underdeveloped territories. Today, although the uncertainties of selling in some of these regions is still great, help and advice is generally available from official sources since most national governments are only too willing to help exporters.

There are possibly three areas where the export houses may still flourish: firstly in dealing with Communist markets where special rules apply, a large number of small organizations, often started by former nationals of Communist countries, offer advice on dealing with the market; secondly in many Japanese Corporations, the so-called Sogo Shoshas, function as export houses as well as manufacturers, not only handling Japanese exports but offering their services to prospective exporters to Japan; and finally there are the various switch traders, who in a sense also function as export houses in a situation where trade involves payment by barter rather than straight currency transactions.

THE AGENT

The overseas agent is the most widely used and probably the most satisfactory method employed by exporters. It is, incidentally, the final stage before an enterprise can be classified as international.

There are several types of agents and a considerable variety of circumstances under which they are used. Many countries lay down stringent conditions relating to the functions of agents, and in this respect, as in so many others, each market is subjected to different conditions.

Essentially an agent is a person resident in the foreign market who is used by the exporter to solicit orders. He is not an employee of the manufacturer but is paid on commission. Generally the orders will be filled directly by the manufacturer and the agent's commission is paid when the manufacturer is paid.

The advantages of using an agent are considerable. The most important is the extension of control further along the distribution chain right into the foreign market; marketing policy remains under the control of the manufacturer. The agent will be able to relay information on market conditions, and he can be visited regularly from the home office so that information feedback is not always at second hand.

There are other advantages, particularly if the manufacturer is not considering extending his commitments towards international status. As compared with the establishment of an overseas sales office, an agent is relatively inexpensive. The main costs are his remuneration and since this is normally on a commission basis he costs the exporter little or nothing when he is not bringing in orders. If the agent employs his own sales and office staff the costs are his alone.

Since the agent's commission depends on sales, his interests are to a large extent identical with those of the manufacturer. However, the embryo international business enterprise depending on an agency system in exports has to recognize certain limitations. The major one is simply that a good agent is in considerable demand and will almost certainly be representing other lines for other manufacturers. His attitude to one line can be conditioned by the other lines he carries. Three situations may occur:

a) The ideal situation is where the agent carries complementary, but not competing lines of products, for his other principals. This is likely to be most common when a certain degree of technological expertise is required. The products tend to support one another and one line provides an entrée for another. The main problem here may lie in the future, if and when one of the principals decides to extend his product range and in so doing creates difficulties for the agent who finds himself representing competing products. It may well be that his agency agreements effectively prevent him from doing so, and one principal or the other is going to find his product dropped. This type of unforeseen check may hit the unwary exporter who has taken it for granted that once a good agent has been found he can handle any product which later becomes available.

b) The second possibility is where the agent represents competing lines from the outset. This, on the face of it, may seem a completely unacceptable situation, but in some industries or markets where technically qualified representatives may be few and far between, it may be the only answer. Possibly the worst situation is where the agent accepts a line merely to prevent someone else taking it and in so doing, extends his domination of the market. In such a situation sales will probably be the minimum the agent can get away with, without losing his franchise.

c) The third situation occurs when the agent has a variety of totally unrelated lines. In this situation there is not likely to be a conflct of interests between one line and another but in some of them at least the agent may be less than an expert, and this may be vital. The other drawback about representing other principals is that the agent may concentrate on the easy sales and simply become an 'order taker'. In most instances the agent will pay more attention to a product line from a manufacturer who shows him an active interest than to one who leaves him undisturbed. Thus, regular visits by executives from the principal and keeping the home office acquainted with market conditions are important functions. So too is readiness to back up an agent's initiative by following up a line of enquiry opened by him with a sales or technical team.

There is no particular financial reason why an agent should respond more vigorously to the principal who keeps constantly in touch, than the more passive, but possibly equally profitable principal. The fact that he normally does so simply illustrates that personal contacts are far more important than in a more formal employer-employee relationship.

This human factor is also important when one considers the problem of conditions and relationships changing through time. There is sometimes a tendency to assume that the conditions which prevailed when an agent was appointed will continue. Generally they do not. There is no automatic assurance that the relationship between principal and agent will adjust accordingly. Often, for example, the situation develops that a young agent gets his first few agency agreements and works long and hard to satisfy his principals. But in time his very success makes him more attractive to other principals, and his efforts are thereby diluted, as he acquires more, and possibly competing, products. For this reason it pays the principal to keep a check on new lines which an agent may acquire after his initial appointment. Not only are visits and regular information from the head office of the principal desirable but many enterprises operate what amounts to a newsletter service throughout their agency network so that agents are not only appraised of what new developments are taking place in the enterprise, but also of the experience of other agents operating in different territories, handling the same products.

Ideally contacts work both ways. Obviously, not all agents generate enough business to make it an economic proposition to have them regularly attend conferences at the enterprise's head-quarters. But there is a very strong case for having regular conferences where agents can not only be brought up to date on new products and techniques developed by their principal, but also have the chance of personal contacts with production and finance as well as marketing personnel. Not the least of the advantages to be gained are the personal contacts and comparisons of methods used by the other agents attending such conferences.

A good agent is worth treasuring. Some of the problems which arise from conflicts of interest will arise because an agent is good enough to attract other principals. An inefficient agent can be a considerable problem — in some countries an agent, once appointed, tends to be in a relatively strong position *vis-a-vis* his principal who may not be able to remove him easily if he chooses to claim his legal rights.

When the relationship between agent and principal begins to go sour both sides are often ready enough to call off the arrangement. Since it is easier for the agent to do so, it pays his principal to have some contingency planning for an emergency — the names of potential replacements, for example, who could be approached if the need arose.

THE AGENCY AGREEMENT

Much in the relationship between manufacturer and agent will turn on the agreement defining his duties, territory, etc. Ideally, if an agent's worth is relatively unknown, or the agency method is being used as a stopgap measure, a short-term agreement which can easily be terminated in a year's time meets the situation. This, however, gives the agent no guarantee that he will not be dropped without compensation at the very moment he has developed the market. Unless he is sure both of his own abilities and the company's goodwill, a confident agent is not likely to be interested in such a one-sided arrangement. He may demand a longer term contract, and may have to be compensated if the enterprise decides to move into more direct distribution.

Other important points in the agreement are exact definitions of the territory in which an agent has exclusive rights, the circumstances under which he will be remunerated, and methods of arbitration in the event of a disagreement. Thus, for example, it may be clear from the outset that certain customers are excluded from the agency agreement because a direct link has already been established by the principal. But the sort of situation where some dispute may arise is when the principal receives an unexpected order directly from a customer in the agent's territory without it being clear whether or not the agent's activities contributed to the order being received.

The recent tendency towards customs unions, common markets, or free trade areas can cause problems, not so much as between agent and principal, but as between one agent and another. Even where an agent has an entire country as his territory, it is increasingly possible that goods may enter his area from elsewhere, for the reduction or abolition of customs barriers makes it difficult to impose an absolute check. Not only must the agent be protected but it is necessary to ensure that he in turn does not supply customers in an adjacent territory. Such problems sound relatively simple to solve, but where a local headquarters buys for a wider area, say all of Western Europe in the case of a U.S. owned enterprise, the situation becomes complex.

Problems may arise over details of expenditure. If, for example, an agent considers it necessary to make gifts to secure an order, he must know whether the enterprise is prepared to accept such business methods as permitted expenses. The whole problem of business morality in different nations and cultures is involved here: an agent will almost certainly conform to local standards. If bribery is the norm, he will bribe. And the principal may have to decide whether to accept practices that he would regard as quite unacceptable in his own country.

In discussion of the agency system, it is one of the paradoxes of the situation that an agent can be too successful if his efforts have convinced his principal that there is more potential in a market than he had realized. Generally, however, the very fact of an agency arrangement can impose a limit on market growth, not only because of the temptation to 'skim' the market for a wide range of products, rather than exploit fully any one. Sales can be determined by the amount of effort agents or their employees put in for each line, and an agent who likes his independence may choose not to push one line too hard. In this respect an agent may be a hindrance to an enterprise going international.

There are obvious complexities in operating an agency system, particularly if this is seen as a stop-gap measure preliminary to going international in a systematic way. There is no doubt however that it is a good way of opening up a market, provided it is accepted that the volume of business generated may be dictated by the fact that an agent is being used. If, on the other hand, the exporter does not intend to go international in one or two markets, but instead chooses to spread his risks by relatively small scale exports to dozens of different markets, then the use of an agent is almost probably the best method even on a long-term basis. In any event, more than in any other situation, the system stands or falls on the personal ability of the agent.

THE AGENT AS DISTRIBUTOR

The role of the agent can extend into the distribution field. Basically a distributor will have the franchise for a particular product and will buy directly from the exporter with a view to selling thereafter on his own account. In this situation the distributor is one of the principals in the transaction and clearly is likely to use a great deal more initiative. He will in many instances have control over pricing, and possibly over advertising and sales promotion. Indeed he may be able to prevent the manufacturer from finding out much about the mark up he charges, and the ultimate customer.

There are two situations in which an agent acting as a distributor may be a better proposition than an agent acting purely on commission. The first is in a very big market, where the distributor himself has a very large organization and is able to meet market demand with far more efficiency than the one man agency system. The second is where the product requires initial installation, and subsequent servicing and where the distributor is better placed to install the product, hold spares, etc.

A good distributor will be able to make a case for an exclusive franchise if he can provide a ready made distribution chain. Strictly speaking, if a distributor is buying on his own account, he is not an agent in the conventional sense. The use of the term 'agency' as a substitute for 'franchise', however, creates a situation where the term 'agent' is applied loosely to this situation. The case for a rather loose use of the term 'agent' to cover the distributor situation is strengthened by the fact that the principal will often supply the same services as he would to an agent, regular visits on the same basis as an agent, including visits to the home county factory. Another example of the hazy territory between agents on commission and distributors is that the latter may be deliberately built up by the manufacturer, i.e. by giving extended credit on products to finance his distribution chain.

In some circumstances the role of the agent on commission and distributor can be performed by the same person. He may be an agent on commission for a whole territory and simultaneously a distributor with a franchise for part of it. The situation has its advantages, but it does mean that there is a conflict of interests between the two roles which cannot be ignored by the manufacturer.

CHANGING FROM THE AGENCY/DISTRIBUTION SYSTEM

The major problem for the potential international enterprise, relying on the agency or agency/distribution system for more direct control of a market operation in a foreign market, occurs when the time comes to move on to a sales company system.

Sometimes, it may happen that the principal has entered casually into an agency agreement without realizing that there may be practical legal difficulties about ending the arrangement inexpensively. Even where there are no particular legal difficulties there may be a certain loss of goodwill which the principal is anxious to avoid. Some enterprises try to ease the situation by offering the agent a key post in the new set up.

This may be acceptable to the agent or distributor. On the other hand, an agent who values his independence (as well as his agencies or franchises from other manufacturers) may be less than enthusiastic about such a proposal, which turns him from an independent operator into an employee.

A possible compromise solution which may be acceptable is to enable the erstwhile agent to take up an equity share in the subsidiary company which becomes in effect a joint venture with the majority shareholder retained by the erstwhile principal with the agent now running the operation as part-owner. Whether such an arrangement can satisfactorily deal with the other interests of the agent depends on the individual case. The same sort of deal can sometimes be made with the distributor who in effect moves on to joint venture status.

A solution on these lines may be quite acceptable, but the acid test is whether it was contemplated from the outset or whether casual ad hoc decisions about agents or distributors a few years back are now acting as a constraint on freedom of action at a time for development. The ironical part of any such deal is that if the agent or distributor has to be bought out, his asset value may be as high as it is because of the benefits the agency franchise brought him. The principal is therefore 'upping' the bill that he is ultimately going to have to meet himself.

DIRECT REPRESENTATION

The agent is in general dealing with distributors—probably wholesalers, if he is handling consumer goods, or industrial buyers if he is handling other types of products. Sometimes it is better policy for an exporter to bring the role normally undertaken by the agent more directly into line with company policy, by the use of a company employee: certainly it is necessary if the company intends to 'go international' to the extent of becoming an international enterprise.

The person concerned may be a visiting salesman, or an employee resident in the market area. A salesman is likely to be employed if the amount of sales generated on each visit seems likely to cover expenses. The advantages of having a company employee, with the right technical background, seems obvious: so too are the possible disadvantages of unfamiliarity with the market and possibly even with the language.

The advantages of a locally resident employee are clear: he can be trained in company policy, be technically competent, is more clearly identified with company interests, and presents no problem if the company policy on marketing changes. Local manufacture, a logical step for the potential international enterprise, or complete withdrawal from the market, can be achieved without the representative proving an obstacle. He can be moved elsewhere or back into the home market. The main difficulty is to find someone with the right temperament and background, whose family will be willing to put up with a move to a perhaps uncongenial part of the world, and who may feel that he is out of the mainstream of company activity when it comes to promotion.

Single representatives of this sort are often merely a preliminary to the creation of a more elaborate structure, namely a branch office, employing a mixture of executives from the home company, and other staff recruited locally. The branch office may have to be registered as a local company in order to achieve separate legal personalities, and attendant problems of operating an establishment in a new area may arise. Where the scale of business is large or the problems of distribution and servicing require fairly continuous contact with the distributors, instead of the occasional personal contact via the salesman, and for the rest contact by mail, then the branch office is the best long term solution, even for the enterprise which does not intend to go international. The branch office represents a considerable investment, and so is a stepping stone in the company's development. A branch office abroad, scarcely makes a company a truly international enterprise: but once this step has been taken, it is psychologically easier to consider a more wholehearted approach to international marketing through assembly plants or local production.

LIMITATIONS ON DIRECT EXPORTING

This section will concern itself with the sales company, in terms of its legal existence outside the home territory of the enterprise,

and the room for manoeuvre this implies. Regardless of whether
the sales company is used to give this room for manoeuvre it
is a significant alternative to dealing directly with and exporting
to the customer.

The most obvious disadvantage is the cost. To cover overheads
the sales company must generate many more orders than an individual agent: and this is one major reason who so many enterprises
hesitate to move away from direct exporting to exporting via a
sales subsidiary resident in the country. Nevertheless, there are
substantial considerations favouring a sales company as an intermediary in the export process, or as a first stage in moving to
international enterprise status.

Delivery problems

A major advantage is that it is possible, if the enterprise so chooses,
to convert the export deal into another domestic transaction so
far as the buyer is concerned. The latter can order the product
from a company registered under his own national law, pay in
his own currency and expect the same delivery conditions as he
would obtain from any other local enterprise.

Conventional exporting at least so far as the U.S.A., Britain
and Japan are concerned has meant normally export by sea, with
cif (cost insurance freight) or fob (free on board) export clauses.
In other words the buyer had to make arrangements to pick up
goods when they arrived at a designated port, clear customs duty,
and arrange delivery from there to his own premises. Even in
North America, outside the U.S.A., or in the mainland of Europe,
rail transport often sufficed, with the buyer picking up goods at
a railhead.

In exporting, much of the costs of transport, and probably most
losses through damage or pilferage occur when products are loaded
or unloaded.

The advent of the container and the pallet has done much to
revolutionize the situation. Containers can be loaded at the manufacturers, moved from road to rail to sea transport without being
unloaded (unless perhaps for customs inspection) and delivered
literally door to door. Palletization, though a more vulnerable form
and particularly adapted to air freight, means that once again goods
can move from manufacturer to buyer without leaving their pallet,
thanks to fork-truck lift operations in the intermediate stages.

In many of the major industrial areas, Western Europe for
example, customs conventions means that TIR vehicles (Transport
International Routier) may pass through customs in intermediate
points on the route without being searched.

These developments mean that importers can in many instances expect to get delivery from foreign manufacturers with exactly the same delivery arrangements as from a domestic manufacturer. While it is possible to arrange through delivery via a shipping agent in the market who will pick up products delivered by rail, sea or air, clear customs and deliver to the customer's premises, the argument for a sales company as an intermediary becomes much stronger. Certainly an American or British based enterprise selling to an inland customer in continental Europe, in competition with an enterprise operating in the mainland of Europe, is at a tremendous disadvantage if it is not prepared to deliver as efficiently as the rival, instead of merely to the nearest sea or air port. Japanese exports are less exposed to this disadvantage because of the double role of many of their enterprises as export houses as well as manufacturers.

In an increasingly buyer's market the case for a direct representation in the market instead of operating at long range via agent or shipping agent becomes formidable.

TARIFFS AND OTHER RESTRAINTS ON TRADE

There are two basic types of tariff, specific and ad valorem. Specific tariffs are a fixed amount per unit imported, ad valorem vary with the value of the product. There is little which can be done to mitigate the effects of specific tariffs but the use of a sales company may in certain circumstances enable an ad valorem duty to be reduced.

There may be a case therefore for a local presence in the market simply to deal with ad hoc tariff or quota problems, e.g. to supply continuous information on changes in import regulations, advice on the description of imports on the bill of lading or airway bills. In general there is no real substitute for personal contact with the officials concerned and this is a role best played by a local resident representing a locally registered company.

Finance

The problem of finance and credit for exporting is immense and shows few signs of easing. The basic problems are not resolved by a decision one way or the other on a sales company. In fact in some countries where inflation is rampant and it would therefore be unwise to quote in the local currency, a local sales company would have to make it clear that payment in a hard currency was essential. Nevertheless, there may be sound reasons for having a local presence to assess the current prospects in inflation and devaluation; and insofar as credit plays a very important role in export sales, the possibility of local credit rating checks can usefully be delegated to the sales company. Even the most conscientious agent can slip up on this issue unless he has del credere status and responsibilities. After all, he stands to lose his commission only if a default occurs: he suffers no positive loss of assets, as does his principal.

NON-TARIFF BARRIERS TO TRADE

The tendency in the postwar world has been for tariff barriers to be reduced, partly as a consequence of their indiscriminate effects, partly as a result of mutual tariff reduction negotiations through GATT, the General Agreement on Tariffs & Trade.[13] At the same time, however, the importance of non-tariff barriers has grown; and their role in making an enterprise consider going international is at least as great as the tariff issue.

Firstly, there are the administrative procedures which can be classified broadly as import quotas and import licence procedures. Import quotas are more precise in their operation than tariffs. If a government wishes to protect a home market it can do so by precisely limiting the quantity of imports through quotas which cannot readily be evaded. Far more extreme in their effects are import licensing arrangements whereby national governments have to approve individual import orders and can therefore confine imports to absolute necessities. An American or European enterprise considering selling in the Indian market for example will find tariff duties virtually irrelevant. What matters is the import licence, and this system is increasingly applied by all underdeveloped nations and is likely to be far more important than a hit or miss tariff.

The implications for the international enterprise are twofold. It cannot export to such markets on a large scale, and immediately therefore has to consider alternatives such as local manufacture. And even if it is willing to contemplate local manufacture it still has the problem of getting import licences for capital equipment or imported raw materials. Generally speaking, it is no use merely relying on an argument that the national economy will benefit. Some positive and measurable benefit such as a guaranteed rate of export may be needed.

A second problem is bureaucracy which, deliberately or not, can prove more formidable than any tariff. If procedures are complicated, customs classification difficult, and the local officials either inefficient or unco-operative, delays can be frustrating. This is a situation which is not merely confined to the underdeveloped world.

Rightly or wrongly American officialdom has been accused in the past by potential suppliers of running a bureaucratic machine that defies all but the more persistent. Within the European Economic Community, the French domestic market seems to be less attractive to the other members because of documentation problems. When one gets to the less developed parts of the world there are areas where only bribery can accelerate documentation. Not all of these problems are solved by local production, but their existence does make markets for imports much less attractive than may at first appear.

Technical Specifications, Supply Regulations, etc.

There are obvious differences in technical specifications between one developed country and another and the more complex industry becomes, the more importance they assume. Some are obvious— different voltages, socket shapes, metric standards, etc. Some are less obvious—the interpretation of safety or hygiene standards, measures to control the spread of plant disease, etc.

The obvious measures require compromise or concession by one party or another. Britain and Ireland are progressively adopting metric standards. The whole EEC organization is attempting to iron out the differences in the mundane measurements from one country to another, and it is likely that other European countries will find it necessary to marry up their own specifications with any adopted by the EEC. If, in a few years, the U.S.A. is the only major industrial nation adhering to pounds, miles, gallons and the like, then almost inevitably it too will have to conform, a process which will be easier for the U.S. multinationals than purely domestically oriented concerns. In a sense, therefore, the obvious technical differences are transient. The logic of industry will impose compatability of standards just as, for example, IBM dominance in the computer industry has already imposed compatability over a wide range of electronics and data processing.

The less obvious differences present a bigger problem in that they are more overtly political. The U.S. food and drugs legislation has the reputation of being among the most stringent in the world. But so far as a non-American pharmaceutical enterprise trying to get into the U.S. market is concerned, any long delay in getting clearance for a product which has got clearance and widespread acceptability elsewhere is liable to be seen as a device to keep foreign competition out. The same argument has been advanced by European small vehicle manufacturers, who have found difficulty in meeting new and more stringent anti-pollution or safety standards which are surmounted easily by U.S. manufacturers. Finally there are a number of industries, where European suppliers simply do not compete any more in U.S. markets because they are convinced that safety standards will be used as a device for excluding competition. They will instead sell licence rights to U.S. companies or possibly enter into joint venture arrangements.

It is not proposed to analyse here whether these charges have any substance to them. The point is that such beliefs are fairly widely held outside the U.S.A.: and, of course, the U.S.A. tends to attract rather more publicity than, for example, similar complaints about say France or Japan. Such considerations then may make a manufacturer who is hesitating about exporting to a market, or manufacturing on the spot, decide for the latter course, for it is apparently a good deal easier to cope with such restrictions from inside a market than outside; and it has to be recognized that there is an increasing temptation for governments under pressure from home-producers to attempt to extend protection indirectly by the use of regulations on quality, safety, etc. The only long-term answer for the international enterprise may be to become one of the local producers.

Political embargoes are another important restriction. Their importance rises and falls with the temperature of the cold war or any more local conflict. At the height of the cold war the NATO allies imposed a fairly severe restriction on the type of product which could be sold to the Communist countries. Each individual NATO member however had its own standards, with the U.S.A. most rigid, Britain and France somewhere in the middle, and West Germany, especially in relation to sales to East Germany, most liberal in its interpretation. One result was that it was easier for the Western European businessman to conduct operations in the Communist Bloc than in the U.S.A. The embargo of communist Cuba was treated much more severely by the U.S.A. than by any other Western nation.

When the cold war thawed the situation became even more complex. There were 'good' Communists, e.g. the Russians, and 'bad', e.g. the North Vietnamese, and the categories did not even remain constant: some could be sold a wide range of manufactured products, others nothing.

Such political embargoes do not apply only to the Communist world. Rhodesia is officially under embargo of all nation states conforming to UN Resolutions on the subject. The Arabs have attempted, with varying degrees of success, to impose embargoes on companies trading with Israel, and virtually every minor war in the underdeveloped world produces some sort of embargo.

A complication about political embargoes is their variability from one country to another. This fact is both an opportunity and a source of friction for the enterprise operating on an international basis. If the parent country imposes an embargo, it may be possible, if the enterprise chooses to flout the intention, to supply from a subsidiary. It would appear that many subsidiaries of American and Western European companies have been willing to avoid embargoes imposed by parent governments. Here, as in so much else, the international enterprise may have room to manoeuvre. If the embargoes are trade barriers in one nation they are not necessarily trade barriers for the same enterprise elsewhere.

In conclusion, the problem of non-tariff barriers is that they may be operated to achieve trade effects while having ostensibly at least a non-trade motive. The very success of GATT has been to reduce the effectiveness of tariffs, but not the ability of governments to achieve the same effects in other ways. The international enterprise therefore adds a new dimension to the issue.

LEGAL ISSUES

Finally, in this brief assessment, the problem of conflicting legal systems must be mentioned. It may be possible in contracts to allow for arbitration in case of a dispute.[14] But arbitration requires both parties to agree to its taking place, and in the absence of this, or downright default in paying, it may become necessary to take legal action in a foreign court. Where the enterprise has no direct local representation, and no acquaintance with local legal conditions, its case may go by default. Indeed there may be occasions when an unscrupulous customer neglects to meet his obligations in the expectation that rather than incur the trouble and expense of a court case in an alien society, the exporter will write off the loss. A sales subsidiary is not a guarantee against this tactic but a buyer may hesitate to default when a local subsidiary is available to take prompt legal action.

MOVING ON, OR GETTING OUT OF A MARKET

So far this chapter has considered several methods of using trade channels to penetrate a market, with different degrees of control for the exporter over price, advertising and product policy. But all have perhaps one element in common: these channels provide a relatively inexpensive method of getting out of a market. A decision to withdraw from a particular market will prove to be little more expensive than a similar withdrawal in the home market.

It is as well to be realistic about this situation. Probably about

80 per cent of all new products marketed fail to make a commercial success. The situation is unlikely to be so discouraging in the export market of an enterprise which has the potential of becoming international. Here the enterprise's exports tend either to be industrial goods with a high success rate or consumer goods which have already succeeded in the home market. However, failures do occur and it is worth considering how the losses may be limited or eliminated altogether if, in spite of all the forward planning, the success of the export policy is not sufficient to justify that policy.

One must have some objective criterion of when an export drive is proving unsuccessful. What is needed to assess success or failure, is some form of forward planning, covering perhaps several years which will make some realistic assessment of when a profit can be expected. Clearly a company cannot assume that exporting on a sustained basis will be profitable from the outset. It will be able to assess and accept losses over perhaps a year or two without panicking. Conversely, it would be foolish to accept losses year after year, in the hopes of a sudden improvement, unless the forward planning exercises suggest that this is likely.

A foreign trade channel is only one link on a distribution chain which starts at the factory and ends with the overseas consumer, and that chain is only as strong as its weakest link. The fact that a distribution channel is not functioning as well as it should, may indicate that the export is not suitable, or that the channel employed is not satisfactory. But equally it may well indicate that the fault lies elsewhere—further along the distribution chain in the foreign country perhaps, or much nearer home.

If the difficulty arises in the foreign market, at the ultimate consumer end, there may be little that can be done. The commodities may be unsuitable or misused. But in other instances these difficulties may be corrected by a slight product change, different packaging, advertising, or instructions, and failing to spot the difference in conditions may be only partly the fault of the chosen distribution channel.

This sort of failure is bad enough; what is a good deal worse is the situation where the failure in distribution channels has arisen further back in the chain, at a point which is clearly the responsibility of the exporter himself. The most efficient agent in the world cannot compensate for unfilled delivery dates or wrong specifications and it behoves a manufacturer who is dissatisfied with the performance of a particular export channel to consider whether in fact the fault may not originate elsewhere in the chain and particularly in those links which are directly under his own control. This is particularly true so far as delivery dates are concerned.

It is unfortunately true that in some countries, industry has become conditioned to the idea that delivery dates, in the absence of penalty clauses, are merely desirable targets and not absolutes. This sort of attitude does not go down well in many parts of the world, and manufacturers who fail to meet delivery dates for foreign customers, or fail to supply adequate servicing facilities in time, are still surprised to find the customer turns elsewhere, blaming the channels of distribution rather than their own attitude for the loss of custom.

At the risk of overstating the obvious, most successful exporters never do go international, and are quite satisfied with an exporting role. The progression from exporting to foreign manufacture is by no means inevitable. But there are undoubtedly large numbers of enterprises in most developed countries, which could have gone international, very profitably, but which because of their very success in exporting by orthodox means, have cut out that possibility without consideration.

LICENSING

The right hand flank of Figure 1 dealt with an alternative both to exporting and going international in the conventional sense. This is the licensing out of patents, general know-how, and trade marks to local enterprises in foreign markets. In theory this method avoids the necessity to become committed to expenditure of money or effort abroad, but the practice can be different.

LICENSING BY NECESSITY

There are occasions when there is no real alternative to licensing because exporting or local manufacturing subsidiaries are not viable alternatives. Three types of market, and one type of product illustrates the situation.

Communist countries which are chronically short of foreign exchange and which for ideological reasons would reject the idea of wholly-owned foreign subsidiaries may be willing to deal on the basis of licensing arrangements which in effect gives an already tested product. A variety of West European motorcar designs are now available in Eastern Europe under new names: the Polish version of a Fiat model is available, a Romanian version of a Renault model. The origin of such products is obvious to any Western visitor. With other less identifiable products, the original designers may be under a practical obligation to settle for licensing on the grounds that if a licence were not granted it would be very difficult to prevent pirating of successful designs.

Something of the same situation arises in the underdeveloped world, although the options may be less stark. Even where Socialism is the official doctrine it may still be possible to set up a local subsidiary. Where import licences are being refused therefore, licensing is an answer, but not the only answer. Generally, however, such markets are relatively limited both in size and potential. Unless therefore a foreign enterprise anticipates being able to manufacture locally, and export, it may have to settle for licensing. At the very worst it may be the most practical solution where political and economic instability makes direct investment very risky.

Among developed western countries it is probably only in Japan that licensing might appear to be a virtual necessity for reasons that have already been discussed. The situation is easing somewhat owing to adverse publicity on Japanese methods, but in some ways importing is preferred to foreign ownership of Japanese manufacturing capacity and licensing remains a favoured solution.

Strategic Products

Apart from the types of markets outlined above there are certain types of products which any government would prefer to have manufactured in its own territories rather than bought abroad. The most wide ranging of these sensitive areas is in military equipment, aircraft, electronics, ammunition and the like. Not every nation can manufacture locally: very few can design and produce sophisticated equipment. But even where a country has to use foreign designs it may, given the choice, prefer to insist on local production under licence.

It is not only the less developed countries which insist on this. When U.S. military aircraft use Rolls Royce engines, they will be manufactured in the U.S.A., not in Britain. So too with electronic equipment. There is of course a twofold argument for such a policy. Firstly, no nation wants to be dependent on another, even an ally, for vital components in a crisis. Secondly, licensing arrangements give a greater degree of security about the type and amount of equipment being produced.

LICENSING BY CHOICE

A.   The Licensor

The idea of licensing has particular attractions for an enterprise which is doing well in the domestic market, particularly if its strength is in Research and Development and production, rather than finance and marketing. It may simply lack the ability or desire to exploit new and unfamiliar markets while being aware that, if it does nothing, its patent rights will simply erode away elsewhere.

Licensing used to be relatively popular among American enterprises who did not choose to look beyond their vast domestic market. At the other extreme it was also popular with manufacturers in small but industrially advanced countries like Switzerland, Holland or Sweden. In the latter case the motivation was often that the foreign markets, while large, were generally protected by tariffs: a small domestic market did not enable mass production techniques to lower unit costs so as to penetrate these markets by exporting.

The situation in both cases has changed. In the case of American enterprises it has changed because even the most inward looking manufacturer has become aware of the potential markets outside North America; in the case of the smaller countries because free trade or common market arrangements have made the larger markets accessible. Still, the flow of licensing from these sources into the medium sized European countries, and Japan, is considerable. The Japanese success has in no small degree depended on its having got so much U.S. technology on a licensing basis, as well as the remarkable efficiency of their 'scanning' practice. Any worthwhile development anywhere in the world is very rapidly identified and assessed from a licensing point of view apparently as a matter of course.

Given the choice, when does an enterprise consider licensing a product instead of exporting or manufacturing locally? Firstly, when the enterprise can be reasonably certain that it will be possible to continue to innovate, and by developing the product, keep the licensee interested. A major problem about using licensing as a long-term substitute for exporting or local manufacture is that the relative balance of power between licensor and licensee may change in favour of the latter. A licensor may grant the licence for say fifteen years, intending at the end of the period to renew on the same terms, only to find that fifteen years of producing and absorbing the technology has put the licensee into a very strong position if needs be to do without the licensor's authority in his own market. In this situation the licensee may be able to inhibit anyone else, including the licensor, from gaining a foothold. If, on the other hand, the licensor can anticipate constant innovation he may retain a bargaining edge since the licensee may decide not to attempt to innovate himself but to seek new and improved products from the same source. The vital issue is an awareness by the licensor enterprise that, by giving out a licence instead of exporting or manufacturing locally, an enterprise may be signalling its own weakness in international marketing.

B.   Licensing as an Entrée into a New Market

Sometimes licensing may appeal to the licensor as a first stage in developing an overseas market, i.e. by allowing a local enterprise to develop the market, and then either buy over the enterprise or simply decline to renew the licence.

The problem about the first case is that if the licence has value, it is going to increase the price which has ultimately to be paid to buy over the enterprise—an elaborate way of paying twice over. In the second case it may not be so easy to stop the licensee producing: if the local enterprise has control of trade marks as well as consumer loyalty the results can be unpromising for the erstwhile licensor.

If, therefore, an enterprise really intends to let the licensee open up the market and then take over it must be clear on its objectives from the outset. One precaution may be to take an equity holding in the licensee's enterprise also from the outset. But this of course means that the distinction between a licensing arrangement and a joint venture becomes very marginal.

It is probable that as domestic enterprises with a record of innovation become increasingly aware of the opportunities now becoming available on a world-wide basis, that licensing will become less frequent in its simplest form, and that the joint venture system will be increasingly insisted upon as a quid pro quo by the licensor. In that sense the joint venture is a sophisticated form of licensing— an illustration of the practical difficulties of drawing a clear distinction between one channel and another.

C.   The Licensee

A key factor in licensing from the recipient's point of view is that he may get rather more out of the arrangement than the simple right to produce in a certain market. The purchase of licensing rights can bring in technical expertise. Sometimes this will in effect be a free gift, as the licensor, anxious to see royalties materialize, gives more assistance than he originally intended. Sometimes this help will be paid for, but even so, it tends to extend beyond the mere solution of the particular production problem. The less technological expertise the licensee has at the beginning, the more he may have gained by the end of the licensing agreement.

RECIPROCAL LICENSING

One method of achieving a measure of equity between the two

parties to a licensing agreement may be possible when both enterprises have technology or trade marks of value, simply by a direct exchange of licensing rights or by including these as part of the deal. This may be the most satisfactory method of dealing in the Japanese situation where licensing may be almost forced upon a company by that government's attitude towards more direct investment. The flow of technology between Japan and Western nations is by no means one sided and a Western company might find a more satisfactory return than simply royalties. In theory too the same argument could be applied to licensing with Communist countries. After all, barter and bilateral deals are a commonplace in commercial deals with these countries. The limiting factor here, however, may be the almost obsessional desire for secrecy. It is difficult to find out what technological processes are worth licensing in Communist countries, because 'scanning' for promising new product ideas is much more difficult.

LICENSING AND ASSEMBLY

The point has been made earlier that licensing blends rather imperceptibly into a joint venture arrangement, if this is the only way the licensor can secure a permanent return on his technology. In the same way licensing can blend into an assembly plant operation. Two examples may illustrate the point. In the mid 1970's Turkey decided to enter the aircraft industry—a somewhat unusual ambition for a nation with a comparatively primitive industry, but understandable in terms of her wish for a degree of military independence. Her aircraft industry however depended initially on licensing entire designs from U.S. and British manufacturers. Initially all parts could be shipped on and assembled locally, but as and when Turkish industry could produce aircraft parts locally, they would be produced under licence. The distinction between the two methods, licensing and assembly thus becomes blurred.

Another example of the trend was to be seen in the efforts of international motorcar corporations to produce very simple unsophisticated models for assembly, or local manufacture in relatively underdeveloped economies. The possible combinations then included a) local assembly in a completely owned subsidiary b) sale of components for assembly by a national (possibly publicly owned) company in a foreign market c) part assembly part local manufacture under licence by another company or joint venture. Licensing in this situation can be one of a range of options, and the distinction between it and assembly can be very fine.[15]

Conclusions

In spite of its dangers, licensing has its attractions to the licensor as a substitute for more direct action in the international field. The arrangements will certainly protect any markets which are to be retained for the licensor, and if he can avoid too much involvement in solving the production problems of the licensee, any royalties which accrue are pure profit, in that no additional expenditure will be involved. Clearly, however, this implies care in definition of territories, not only to protect the licensor's own market but any territories where it wishes to make other provision. It is a good policy to follow where there is risk, political or financial, in exporting or direct investment.

Nevertheless when all is said and done, for the aspiring international enterprise, simple licensing against royalty payments tends to be a second best solution. Any enterprise contemplating going international has to consider very carefully before accepting what may seem to be a very attractive offer for licensing, in any area where alternative policies may be contemplated: and an enterprise operating a licence even confined to its own territory, may in time become a rival in a third market when patents or licences expire.

REASONS FOR GOING INTERNATIONAL

The long term motivation of a decision to become an international enterprise have been discussed in terms of increased freedom of manoeuvre. Generally, however, there is a specific incident or situation which will precipitate the decision: it is only afterwards the factor of freedom of manoeuvre becomes important.

The specific incidents can be looked at under two main headings a) reactions to a particular situation, which is developing unfavourably b) a more positive initiative from the enterprise. In some instances the distinction is rather fine but there is validity in it, particularly when the first heading implies a measure of hasty decision, which might not have been made if more consideration had been given.

REACTIONS TO A SITUATION

Where a relatively hasty reaction has been made a cautionary note will be injected into the discussion. The point has already been made that businessmen (and anyone else) may subconsciously adjust memories of any motives for a course of action, in the light of what follows. The recollected version is likely to be rather more rational (and far-sighted) than the ad hoc decision at the time. In a large number of cases a decision to go international at a particular time may have been an inappropriate response to a perceived situation, which turned out to be fortunate for other reasons. Large numbers of U.S. corporations went into Europe in the immediate post-war period to absorb surplus capacity at home, and then changed their strategy in the light of very transient currency problems. Others seem to have done so in imitation of what was something of a fashion. Most then achieved a roaring success in Europe for quite different reasons. But the longer ago the decisions were made the less clear-cut do the original motives appear.

Many executives would argue that it was the result, not the reasoning, which matters. There is a large element of truth in this, but it is as well to realize that the original decisions tend to get obscured as a situation develops.

Government Action in the Host Country

The major factor producing the 'going international' reaction is undoubtedly adverse policies, on tariffs, import controls, or currency regulations. There may be a fine calculation whether to pull out of a market or go for further commitment in this situation. At the very least, however, severe restrictions may encourage assembly operations as a means of reducing import costs.

Other factors are difficulties and complaints from customers about problems in delivery, installation and maintenance, where a conventional agent or distributor may be proving inadequate. Initially the answer may seem to be a sales company to which can be attached technical staff to handle maintenance. Often however such an organization can develop interests and responses of its own—an impatience, for example, with delays in obtaining parts from the home production lines, and an ambition to provide more and more services on the spot from local resources. So the situation arises that a decision designed to keep production lines at home busy, can eventually result in assembly, maintenance, and even production in another country, as the original motivation becomes obscured in developing a successful foreign operation.

Protecting Patents

It is in theory a simple matter to get patent protection throughout the world. It is in practice a good deal more difficult to enforce this in a situation where the enterprise has to go to a foreign court and argue that a local company, which is creating employment

introducing new technology and saving scarce foreign exchange.
is infringing someone else's interests and pirating their patents.
A local presence and some form of local production is the only
argument that courts or local enterprises will respect.

Actions of Rivals

Most countries prefer local production to imports. In the developed
countries, overt action against importers and in favour of new
local production is politically difficult, particularly if the country
is a signatory of a GATT agreement. In the less developed regions
of the world, any enterprise whether local or foreign, which is
prepared to manufacture locally is likely to be able to get positive
government support, in the form of restrictions in imports, by
tariff, quota, or licence. In this sort of situation, all foreign suppliers
are under pressure to produce locally. While no one wants to
be first to go to the risk and expense of local production, if one
enterprise begins local production the others may have to follow.

It may seem surprising at first glance to suggest that it is better
to be second, rather than first, into local production, particularly
since the local government and customers are probably exercising
pressure. The point is, however, not merely is it expensive and
risky to move away from a successful marketing strategy by export,
to local production: but, just as important, customer goodwill can
be lost if, as almost certainly happens, local production behind
new tariff walls means a much more expensive product, possibly,
too, of lower quality and with less variety. The second incomer
may avoid the odium of being the enterprise which pushed the
price up, and variety and quality down.

Reactions to National Legislation

The dominant nation in postwar internationalization of industry
has been the U.S.A.: the next candidate is probably Japan, for
the 1970's and 1980's. To what extent have there been specific
national reasons, apart from economic success?

In the case of the U.S.A. one answer at least is fairly clear.
It is the all pervasive issue of anti-trust legislation. Among advanced
countries the U.S.A. has been almost unique in its determination
to act against monopoly conditions or any activity by industry
which could be interpreted as acting in restraint of trade. In such
a situation the point may soon come for an expanding corporation
that its share of the market reaches a point which puts it potentially
under scrutiny. In the circumstances there was much to be said
for expanding any further outside the U.S.A.

The immediate effects, therefore, of U.S. legislation has been to encourage foreign ventures by the larger and more successful corporations. The longer term effects have been to increase the possibility of a conflict of interest, not merely between the American government and the new international enterprise, but also between the American government and the host governments of the enterprise. Attempts to apply U.S. legislation have been opposed by foreign courts, where U.S. courts have attempted to lay down rules of conduct to be applied outside U.S. territory.

So far as other nations have been concerned, the lack of anti-trust legislation has, if anything, inhibited foreign expansion. In the immediate postwar era, West Germany was influenced by American anti-trust concepts. The break up of I.G. Farben, the prewar chemical giant and the attempted break up of Krupps are examples. More recently, however, the prewar tolerance of cartelization has tended to return and enterprises do not feel the same pressure to avoid excessive success at home. There has been political pressure for Germany to invest elsewhere, but the scale has been limited, encouraged no doubt by memories of expropriations in two World Wars.

Elsewhere in the EEC, apart from Britain, foreign investment outside the Community has remained relatively modest, considering the economic power of the Community. In the early 1970's, however, there were signs of heavier investment in the U.S.A. by the Europeans (and the Japanese) at a time of temporary dollar weaknesses.

The Japanese motivation again has been different. Here shortage of labour and rising costs in Japan has encouraged what are essentially assembly operations elsewhere. Apart from these assembly operations much Japanese investment has been in *Category I* (page 19) extractive industries, particularly in the Pacific Area and Australia. The success of the policy has been marked but at the same time has attracted the hostility that such operations increasingly experience throughout the world. The Japanese are rapidly being cast in the role of exploiters in South East Asia, just as the Americans are type-cast for the role in Latin America and Europeans in Africa. More recently *Category II* (page 22) investment has appeared in the U.S.A. and Europe. In the former, Japanese corporations have been buying over existing U.S. companies, particularly in electronics: in Europe, they are building from scratch—aided by generous investment subsidies from European governments.

INITIATIVES BY THE ENTERPRISE

More positively, an enterprise may reach a stage in its national development when it decides to go international without there being any obvious crisis. Two or three generations ago, a number of international enterprises originated from small European nations at a relatively advanced state of development: Switzerland, Holland, and Sweden produced more than their share of such enterprises at this stage, as some of their domestic enterprises expanded to the point where there was no prospect of further domestic development. Either their dynamic management had to diversify into other local industry, a conglomerate development, or horizontally, by licensing out products or more positively producing abroad.

Surplus Equipment

A successful and prosperous enterprise is likely to be one which regularly innovates, not only in its products, but also in its production methods. The taxation systems in most developed countries encourages this by allowing the rapid amortization of new equipment, to the point where equipment can be written off for tax purposes and replaced long before its physical life is over. What can be done about relatively obsolescent equipment of this sort? If there is space in the plant it may be left where it can be used in an emergency. More often it is going to have to be disposed of—perhaps as second-hand machinery, perhaps as scrap. The difficulty about disposing of equipment with a scrap value only, is that it may fall into the hands of potential rivals, who, with much smaller capital overheads, can compete with relatively old equipment.

In many instances of course, such equipment is sold cheaply for export. This poses the threat of entry of a low cost producer in a traditional export market. Alternatively, an enterprise may usefully equip overseas subsidiaries on its own account. The major advantage, apart from the cheapness and the elegant solution of disposing of old plant is that the equipment may be better tailored for some foreign markets than the more up to date equipment which replaced it at home. A subsidiary market may be smaller, poorer and less developed than the home market, and for that reason is a technical generation or more behind. Obsolescent equipment producing obsolescent models is suicide in the advanced market. In the less developed, it may be the most appropriate, particularly when the market can be protected from outside competition. Indeed, it is possible to conceive of an enterprise operating several generations of machines steadily moving them down the technical scale of the subsidiaries. The policy may have to be discreet. Host governments generally want the most up-to-date technology, even if this is not the most appropriate, and if they are providing subsidies or tax holidays the enterprise may have to tread delicately in importing capital equipment whose valuation in its new location may be markedly different from its book value in the parent country.

As has been suggested, the same argument may apply to the products being marketed. Simplified, cheaper versions of an older design discarded at home, may succeed, both because they are more realistic for the effective demand, and also because their local production is protected by tariff walls.

Risk Spreading

A good deal of discussion on international business turns on the risk of foreign investment. But there are situations where the risk is greatest at home, of a hostile government, labour troubles, poor prospects. Foreign production may mean incurring risks, but it also means spreading them.

General Issues

International enterprises, or potential international enterprises have two characteristics which make them prized by host governments. They are relatively mobile, and being new to a country are not necessarily bound to one particular region. This ensures that they are potentially candidates for any regional incentives by host countries. The problem of relatively remote regions losing industry to the industrial heartland of an economy, and being drained of many of their most mobile workers is not an isolated phenomenon of any single industrial country. The regional incentives of the member nations of EEC and their regional fund represent readily tapped sources of finance for the Americans and increasingly the Japanese, as well as Common Market industry; and, given the choice of foreign investment or a constant population drain, countries like Spain and Portugal are becoming more and more ready to subsidize or support foreign enterprises.

THE INTERNATIONAL ENTERPRISE CONDITION— DEGREES OF COMMITMENT

In preceding sections the precursors to going international were discussed in terms of degrees of commitment. It was noted that the demarcation between the precursors and the international enterprise was blurred because it was sometimes difficult to decide at which point a degree of commitment went over the line (see Figure 1).

The same problem of degree of commitment exists in terms of the forms the foreign activity of the enterprise takes. There are a variety of forms, which for purposes of discussion will be grouped into four. As in much else in international business the divisions between the groups are by no means absolute.

The forms are: a) The Sales or Marketing Subsidiary
b) The Assembly Operation
c) Assembly with Partial Manufacture
d) The complete Manufacturing Subsidiary.

A. THE SALES OR MARKETING SUBSIDIARY

This, on the face of it, is merely a selling operation, converting purchases by foreign customers into domestic operations, by undertaking delivery, and if necessary accepting payment in the local currency. It is possible in some instances to have some form of foreign branch without full legal incorporation. The difference this makes, however, is legal rather than in principle. The advantages are conventionally summarized as CTT, i.e. currency, tariffs and taxation.

Currency covers the situation that where currency restrictions apply either at home or abroad, and the dual or multiple legal personality of the enterprise enables such controls to be circumvented by transferring payment or retaining currencies in the most convenient market. It is not unknown for subsidiary companies to have their own subsidiaries in third host countries because it is easier to move capital from the first host country to the second than it would be for the parent organization.

Tariffs also cover two situations. Firstly the possibility that, by allowing the markup for profits and costs of distribution in the foreign market, to be imposed by the subsidiary, the tariff duties will be reduced—with the provision that the valuation is accepted by the Customs authorities involved. This tariff advantage operates only in the case of an ad valorem tariff, i.e. one which is proportionate to the value of the product. A specific that is a flat rate tariff would not be affected. The other situation which is eased by the existence of a sales company is that advice on the description of imports to ensure the most favourable tariff rate is easier to come by.

Finally, *taxation* is an area where the sales subsidiary gives the advantage of a degree of choice in where profits are made, i.e. by the parent or by the subsidiary.

The three aspects may conflict of course: there may be a fine calculation on whether an advantageous tariff policy involves paying higher taxation. Equally, however, all aspects may point in the same direction. An ideal situation would involve exporting to a hard currency, low tax area with substantial tariffs—all of which would indicate that the subsidiary sales company would become a profit centre from the outset.

Possible Conflicts

The assumption is that a sales company exists to serve the interests of the home production line. It is possible however that a conflict of interest may arise because the sales company wants to extend its interests, e.g. it may argue that it should not only install equipment, but also service it, particularly in the case of an industrial product. It is not too uncommon for friction to arise if the subsidiary feels that there is a delay in filling any replacement orders: it may feel it would prefer to supply certain products and services itself, although the original intention was merely to funnel these through the subsidiary from the parent factory. Again a move intended to keep home production lines busy ends up in creating new production lines in a foreign market, a point already commented upon.

Is there a difference between a sales subsidiary and a marketing subsidiary? The answer is probably not, at least so far as most enterprises are concerned. The term 'marketing' is too often regarded as a more prestigious version of selling, regardless of the fact that marketing comprises a good deal more. There is a case for distinguishing between a sales subsidiary and a marketing subsidiary on the principle that the latter is a good deal more than merely an order-taker and deliverer; it has to be said that the distinction is rarely made in practice.

B. THE ASSEMBLY OPERATION

For a number of products an assembly operation in the foreign market is a necessity. Many large consumer goods (including cars), and most industrial equipment of any size may have to be sent abroad in a 'knocked down' form, to prevent damage and cut freight costs. A 'one off' order can be assembled as part of the contract but repeat orders require an assembly operation.

Apart from the need to ship in knocked down form, there is a case for sending products in component form, shipping the same components in bulk rather than have each crate contain all the components for one product. The more the cost of assembly the more room there is for choice in allocating costs in one country or another; indeed all the possible advantages inherent in having a sales subsidiary in terms of currency, tariff and taxes are increased because that much more of the total cost becomes mobile as between profit centres.

At this point the attitude of the host country becomes important. Clearly the latter may have an interest, both in reducing the foreign exchange component of the cost, and possibly introducing more job opportunities. Ideally, the host government may prefer some operation a good deal more extensive, but as a first step even an assembly operation is better than importing completed products.

Some markets are too poor or too small to attract large scale industry. It is difficult to envisage a full-scale car industry in countries such as, for example, Portugal, Malta, New Zealand or even the very rich Saudi Arabia. But each of them can reasonably be expected to support an assembly operation, and so limit the direct importation of complete vehicles. In a sense, they merely duplicate the situation in a country like Britain where a car plant essentially assembles components brought in, not necessarily manufactured within the main plant; the main difference being that in Britain most components will be manufactured domestically, in smaller countries they are imported.

Another type of assembly operation is of components for another market—largely for purposes of cheap assembly, e.g. electronic equipment, watches, precision machinery can be assembled by hand, where labour is cheap and the finished products sent back to the country of manufacture—i.e. a *Category III* type of enterprise operation.

C. ASSEMBLY WITH PARTIAL MANUFACTURE

Governments which insist on local assembly are generally looking for a more thorough commitment, namely local production. Initially however this may mean that only certain components will be produced locally.

In this situation the normal pattern will be that the government will issue import licences or make financial concessions against an agreement that a certain proportion of the components will be locally produced. There are obvious problems of valuation, but the principle is simple. And a motorcar manufacturer may feel it is worth while to gain a privileged place in a market by assembly plus local manufacture, either in his own factory or from local subcontractors. As can be expected, the imported components will be the more complex—in the case of cars, engines and gears perhaps, while the body, windows and interior fittings may be locally produced.

The tendency will be for the home-produced components to be upped in value as time passes, although this is not always the case. Spain, for example, insisted at one stage on 90 per cent local components for Ford cars, and appeared to be heading for 100 per cent. But when Ford offered to build a plant which would not only meet the needs of the local market but permit substantial exports, the Spanish government dropped the 90 per cent required to nearer 50 per cent. The principle of permitting an increase in imports to be compensated for by exports of the completed product has a fairly widespread application in international business.

It has been implied thus far that the international enterprise owns the assembly operation. It is possible, however, that this may be a joint venture or even a locally owned enterprise, possibly State-run. In this situation the assembly operation may be blending into a licensing operation. Alternatively the local enterprise may be marketing on the domestic market a product which is ostensibly designed locally, but may owe a good .deal of inspiration to the original product. The major conflict will arise only if this is subsequently re-exported.

An assembly-cum-manufacturing operation which is not wholly owned and controlled by the parent enterprise has obvious limitations compared with the straightforward subsidiary. It may, however, be the only option available.

D. THE COMPLETE MANUFACTURING SUBSIDIARY

The ultimate degree of commitment is subsidiary manufacturing in the foreign market. The manufacturing plant may be wholly owned by the international enterprise or jointly with a local partner or partners. The degree of ownership by the international enterprise may be a matter of comparing policy, local legislation or even conventional national practice—American corporations generally preferring total ownership, Europeans readier to accept local participation and Japanese enterprise possibly most ready to accept local partners.

The intention may be simply to replicate the same product or products as at home: to produce an alternative designed for local conditions—and this often means a less sophisticated version, perhaps one that has been discarded in the home market: or even to go in for a degree of international specialization whereby products to be marketed internationally are allocated as between subsidiaries.

The implication of the various degrees of commitments will be explored in more detail in subsequent chapters.

4. The Structure of International Business

INTRODUCTION

There is a variety of possible organizational structures which may be adopted by an international enterprise. Two factors which ought to determine the most appropriate structure are Corporate Strategy, and the attitude of governments, particularly the host governments whose territories will contain the end product of the structures. This section will consider some of the implications of corporate strategy. The national aspect will be considered in more detail in a later chapter.

In passing it should be remarked that the second sentence in this chapter contains the word 'ought'. The problem here as in so much of management writing, is the gap between descriptive summaries of what enterprises actually do, and the normative approach, i.e. summarizing what in an ideal world they should do: with, of course, the additional dimension already noted, that businessmen are liable to rationalize in hindsight what they did and then ascribe more considered motives.

So far as corporate strategy is concerned, there is at least a suspicion that nature now imitates art in that businesses are now begining to use techniques which have been written about or theorized upon, rather than actually described. Much of what is written in the following section is possibly more valid of an ideal approach rather than what actually happened a few years previously, when the major enterprises in the U.S.A. and elsewhere were going international.

CORPORATE STRATEGY AND STRUCTURE

The objective of corporate strategy might be paraphrased as ensuring that an enterprise has the opportunity of shaping its future instead of simply reacting to events. Although the concept of corporate strategy has almost universal approval it appears to have played surprisingly little role in the past in affecting developments in international enterprises, particularly where structure is concerned. As has been noted before many enterprises which have gone international in the postwar period do not appear to have done so on a planned strategy. They have seized opportunities to create new markets or have reacted to external circumstances, favourable or unfavourable. Often, in fact, they have gone international as an inappropriate response to a particular situation. They have come up with the right answer, but to the wrong problem.

The same process may still continue for enterprises, but in a more subtle way. Strategy should affect structure within the company: often however structure may determine strategy by decisions on distribution channels, etc. on lines already discussed which in effect determine the size of markets. What follows therefore is an outline of alternative structures, which may reflect methods of implementing an overall corporate strategy—but which equally well may be determining it.

1. ALTERNATIVE STRUCTURES IN INTERNATIONAL BUSINESS—ORGANIZATIONAL

There are a number of possible variants in organizational structure which for the sake of simplicity will be considered under seven headings, three relatively simple in concept, three more complex, and one highly complex.

A. THE INTERNATIONAL DIVISION

This division exists to handle exports for the production divisions of an enterprise, as well as to develop alternative methods of making these products available. In a relatively small enterprise the division may be part of the single company: in more large scale operations where the enterprise may consist of several companies, the international division may be a trading company with its own legal personality.

The general principle is to concentrate the exporting strengths of the organization into one group which will review the various product lines of the enterprise and seek out from among them those products which may sell well in foreign markets. In essence then the system starts out as basically a product-oriented system where existing products are being used for export: the system also implies that this is a mainly export operation, in that manufacture by subsidiaries in foreign markets represents a stage where the international division begins to lose control.

A major problem of this structure is the possibility of conflict between the international and product divisions, both about which will be a profit centre and the extent to which the international division will have a say on which markets are to be exploited, and whether or not products will be adapted substantially for export. What may happen is that some products or markets will be handled directly by product divisions and companies, while others—more marginal perhaps—are the preserve of the international division: the actual markets and distribution of export personnel again being a possible source of conflict. Thus, an American corporation might decide that its major products in the Canadian market will be handled directly by the product divisions and other products and markets by the international division; or a British company might choose to treat other markets of the European Community directly, while markets beyond the Community would be the responsibility of a trading department or company.

The international division structure is favoured mainly by American enterprises. The original reason was probably that such enterprises had very large domestic markets where new products could be developed and tried out before the foreign demand had developed for such products. What was needed therefore was a convenient channel through which these products could be made available abroad as and when the demand developed, without there being too much adaptation to individual markets. Smaller American enterprises for whom the international division was less necessary may nevertheless have adopted the structure which they saw being used by larger, and successful, enterprises.

B. THE GEOGRAPHICAL (POLITICAL) STRUCTURE

The most common first stage is to set up a grouping of subsidiaries based on a geographical or political unit. The subsidiaries may initially report to an international division in the parent country, but generally develop more direct links to corporate management.

The major problem about a simple geographically based structure with subsidiaries in individual national markets, is that while market knowledge at the host country level is likely to be excellent, product knowledge may not be so good. If the subsidiary is handling only its own manufactured product all may be well. But it is likely to be importing some of its products from the parent company or other subsidiaries and be less familiar with them. In that sense the geographical structure has the same weaknesses as an agent handling a whole range of products. The system cannot guarantee that the subsidiary will know all its products equally well, or be able to recognize the potentiality of a new product line developed elsewhere in the enterprise which it may have to assess for its own markets. If the subsidiary becomes large enough, the problem becomes less, because specialists and, if necessary, brand managers can be appointed for all the lines, and possibly several companies created within the one national frontier, instead of one. In the smaller company it may be necessary to reinforce the local personnel from time to time by visitors from the parent enterprise, and this can create problems of authority and lines of responsibility.

If there are several companies in the same territory it will probably be necessary to create a national headquarters, or even a regional headquarters for several countries. If such regional headquarters are intended merely to cut down the numbers of subsidiaries directly reporting to the parent enterprise, no change of principle is involved. Regional headquarters of this type can have a more complex role, which will be discussed under section (f).

The terms 'geographical' or 'political' have been used interchangeably till now: when there are a large number, the division may be into geographical proximities, i.e. Western Europe or Latin America. In other cases the grouping will have political or linguistic logic. Thus an American corporation may have a regional HQ in London, Brussels, Paris or Frankfurt covering Western Europe: or a London HQ covering the British Commonwealth markets, except Canada. A Paris or Belgian HQ might cover French-speaking countries, and so on.

C. THE PRODUCT-ORIENTED STRUCTURE

This operates as its name suggests on the opposite principle. Subsidiary companies handle particular product ranges and work directly with the product division of the parent enterprise. If the enterprise is large enough it may be operating a number of subsidiary companies in a single foreign territory, a situation which on the surface looks like a repeat of the multi-subsidiary geographically based structure. The important difference is that the links between product line specialist subsidiaries and the product divisions of the parent company are more important than any administrative link up within a national territory between widely differing subsidiaries. Indeed, if the enterprise is very large and conglomerate in nature, with unrelated lines of product, there may be virtually no national contact between subsidiaries in the same country.

In general, the potential advantages and disadvantages are the

obverse of those in the geographically based structure, better knowledge of new product development being balanced against less
familiarity with market conditions. If the enterprise is large enough
the disadvantages disappear.

The three types of structures described thus far are relatively
simple in principle. Once, however, the enterprise develops any size
or complexity the simplicity or purity of the structure begins to
be lost and more complex organizations appear.

D. THE GRID SYSTEM

This is an attempt to compromise between the geographical and
product oriented organizations, which ensures that whichever system
predominates, there are adequate cross-references at a functional
level. In practice this often means that in a geographically oriented
organization there will be adequate provision for production
specialists to visit the various subsidiaries to acquaint the executives
there of new developments and possibly persuade them to adopt
new products. The emphasis here is on information and persuasion,
not on passing orders down the line through another channel of
command. It is essential that the hierarchy of authority be undivided
so that the chief executive of the subsidiary knows clearly the
chain of command. In a grid system therefore either the geographical
or the product line organization dominates the grid and the other
is there in an informational capacity only. Even so, the problem
of conflict of authority over subsidiary companies can create
problems in that executives of the subsidiary can never be sure
that if they reject advice on new products in the case of the
geographically dominated grid or on new market opportunities in
the product oriented system, they may not be receiving a black
mark somewhere in the domestic hierarchy. Sometimes it can even
happen that a local producer with a good 'scanning' procedure
will spot useful products of the international enterprise available
in other markets. He may then seek to license from the parent
enterprise before the local subsidiary of the enterprise is ready
to market, or even before the latter has even evaluated the product.

E. THE MIXED STRUCTURE

As has been suggested earlier, strategy ought to determine structure.
If, however, the strategy is confused or has not been fully worked
out the structure may also be confused—an historical inheritance
of ad hoc decisions in the past on how to exploit particular
product or market opportunities at a moment in time. Sometimes

enterprises grow by acquisition or merger and may choose to absorb an existing structure for a subsidiary, rather than rearrange and so vivisect a functioning organism. The result may be an organizational tree containing elements of a geographical or product structure with no predominant principle.

Such confused organizations can continue and flourish for a long time. It may make sense to leave a structure alone for years after a merger simply because it works. Career interests are jeopardized by any more logical rearrangement, and as a result considerable internal resistance to change will be generated. Reorganization, if it comes, is a bloodletting operation, often as a result of poor performance or inadequate control being made all too manifest. Even after such a painful restructuring to produce a more logical and efficient chain of command, anomalies may have to be accepted, because local political considerations limit the amount of restructuring which is possible; or because a policy of acquisitions has produced product lines which are unrelated to the main business of the enterprise, and which are too enmeshed in existing plant to be sold off, and too profitable to be stopped.

F. THE REGIONAL HQ SYSTEM

The tendency has been noted for a very large geographically oriented unit to develop a regional HQ as an intermediary to cut down the number of subsidiaries with direct access to the parent enterprise. However, regional HQ's can have more subtle functions. Effectively, they downgrade the national autonomy of subsidiaries. This may be necessary if regions are to be dealt with as a unit, i.e. increasingly the European Economic Community may best be treated as a unit with subsidiary companies specializing by products over the whole market instead of each trying to produce a whole product range for each country. While such national specialization could be imposed by a very centralized parent organization it is probably a good deal easier at a regional level. The U.S. car companies are increasingly developing such a degree of interdependence for products and even components among various European plants. IBM too have tended to specialize production for the whole of Europe in the same way: Philips of Holland too are moving in this direction with casette recorders being produced in Austria and so on.

More subtly too, the regional HQ concept may limit the effect of national legislation, for example, to ensure that key appointments are held by nationals of the host country. The international enterprise can concentrate its own nationals in the regional HQ without necessarily incurring the same hostility as would arise if it attempted to retain the publicly prominent posts for its own nationals.

The system can be used effectively only where there is an obvious geographical and political unity, preferably backed up by free trade between host countries. Thus a European HQ for an American corporation makes sense for the EEC countries and those with free trade arrangements with EEC: it makes less sense if one tries to include European countries which have neither free trade arrangements nor associate member status. If a country like Spain is included it may be because there is no obvious alternative or because EEC membership is assumed to be only a matter of time. Less certainly, the system may be applied say to Latin America, where it seems logical but where there is less room for international specialization via free trade. The economic and political groups there are a good deal less developed than in Europe, and the regional HQ concept is rather more like the variant of the geographical based organization described in section (b), with perhaps advantages in enabling the nationals of the international enterprise to maintain a 'lower profile' in a nationalistic environment. [16]

G. MORE COMPLEX ORGANIZATIONAL STRUCTURES

At least two largely theoretical structures are also possible. One is the extreme functional specialization of subsidiaries reporting to various divisions of the parent enterprise according to their degree of development, i.e. production plants reporting to product divisions, marketing or sales subsidiaries to the marketing division, even financial divisions direct to the financial division. There are perhaps two major objections: first that the human instinct 'what we have we hold' might prevent the evolution of subsidiaries say from sales to production; secondly the situation might work to the benefit of the financial division which might be in a better position to determine which were the profit centres, and so dominate the organization at the expense of production or marketing executives.

The other situation is an adaptation of elaborate structures designed for the evasion of financial or other controls by national governments. If a national government decrees that only a certain proportion of equity capital may be held by the parent company, a series of pyramid building exercises may obscure the real situation but leave control firmly fixed in the HQ. Funds may be filtered through tax haven subsidiaries all in an attempt to evade national control.

The difficulty about such an elaborate system is that it is difficult to conceal from shareholders and sooner or later it comes to the notice of the national government whose intentions are being thwarted. Retaliatory legislation is then liable to reveal that the whole structure is a pack of cards which stands only as long as the victimized national government is prepared to tolerate the situation.

Future Developments

There are arguably two contradictory tendencies. The first is the rapid growth of telecommunications which lessens the degree of freedom of manoeuvre of the subsidiary. This may tend to lessen the classical distinction between the geographical and production oriented division by ensuring that an HQ executive can effectively be in several countries at once. The second is the increasing insistence by new nations, especially with non-Western cultures and ideologies that key positions are held by their own nationals, with the implication that effective control of the subsidiary is weaned away from the legal owners or their parent company executive board. Whether the quasi science fiction concept of an HQ executive establishing an effective presence halfway round the world and imposing the enterprise's overall strategy on even the most distant and culturally alien subsidiary, can staunch the drift towards national executives and national control, may be one of the key issues in the remaining years of the twentieth century.

2. ALTERNATIVE STRUCTURES IN INTERNATIONAL BUSINESS—FINANCIAL

The term financial is not perhaps the most precise but will serve as a convenient shorthand for a classification based on ownership rather than lines of command. The diagram opposite shows the alternatives.

A. LICENSING AS A POSSIBLE STRUCTURE

Licensing, as was suggested in Chapter 3, does not involve going international. It is possible to have a licensing arrangement that merely involves the selling of technical knowhow without any further advice. In most instances, however, where the technological expertise of the licensor is greater than that of the licensee he may find himself supplying personnel and advice. It has already been suggested that if he does this, he may find it expedient to have an equity interest in the licensee enterprise—a stage which brings a situation very like an orthodox joint venture.

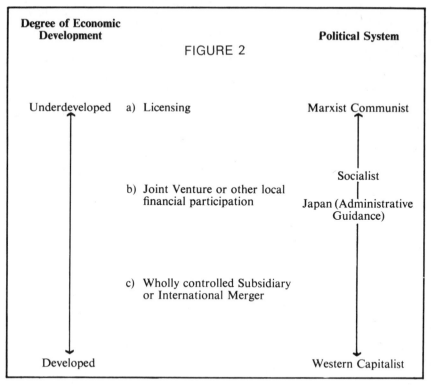

FIGURE 2

Degree of Economic Development		Political System

Underdeveloped   a) Licensing   Marxist Communist

Socialist

b) Joint Venture or other local financial participation   Japan (Administrative Guidance)

c) Wholly controlled Subsidiary or International Merger

Developed   Western Capitalist

N.B.—The stages in practice blend into each other.

In the case of Marxist Communist countries, particularly those chronically short of foreign exchange, the deal may bring payment in kind rather than currency, and this may involve further international transactions to convert this into some form of more acceptable payment.

B. JOINT VENTURES

There are different meanings attaching to the term 'joint venture'. What is being described here is the situation where one or more foreign partners link up with a domestic enterprise to develop a market. The foreign partners supply the technology and perhaps the finance, the domestic partner knowledge of the market and perhaps an entrée into government and commercial circles. Joint ventures in this context may be a rather sophisticated form of licensing with rather more control on developments by the technically advanced partner.[17]

A joint venture may be the method dictated by host country policy, or by the foreign enterprise's own policy. In many instances, particularly in the underdeveloped world, the only way of being permitted direct investment in the market may be in a joint venture with a local entrepreneur or even a state enterprise. The tendency is strongest among those nations which put most emphasis on their socialism, though practice varies widely. Until a few years ago it would have been possible to dismiss out of court the suggestion of joint ventures in Communist states. Now, however, Rumania permits a form of joint venture which may be imitated elsewhere in the Comecon world if successful. In the middle 1970's, however, the number of Western Rumanian joint ventures were to be numbered in single figures.

Generally speaking Western developed nations do not impose such conditions with the possible exception of Japan where the pressure to agree to this form may be considerable. At the other extreme to Japan is the U.S.A., where, if anything, public policy is rather hostile to joint ventures between U.S. and foreign enterprises on the grounds that such an arrangement produces one company instead of two competing ones, i.e. prima facie, joint ventures are in restraint of trade. The logic of this stance is that the U.S. authorities would favour wholly owned foreign subsidiaries, but preferably those which were created from scratch not by buying over established companies.

Even where joint venture status is not imposed by the host government, some international enterprises, as part of their corporate strategy, may prefer this form of local participation. In such a case, policy may be to hold a majority share, an equal, or possibly even, rarely, a minority share. If anything, the number of enterprises going international via joint ventures is increasing, particularly among small or medium sized enterprises because this structure requires less capital.

The international enterprise may hope ultimately to absorb the locally owned partner into its own international structure by buying out the local owners. The argument for such actions in an underdeveloped country is that the joint venture approach enables an enterprise to obtain a foothold at a time when it is expedient to tread delicately for fear of raising anti-foreign sentiment, but in the hope that as prosperity comes and xenophobia dies down, a more satisfactory arrangement, giving full control, will become possible. To what extent such reasoning was behind some of the decisions on joint ventures by international enterprises in recent years in the underdeveloped world, it is difficult to say. The situation however is at best a gamble, for the digestion process may go the other way with the local partner, supported by the host government, taking over completely.[18]

Other practical difficulties exist in terms of possible conflicts of interest between the international enterprise and its individual domestic partners. Basically, however, the conflict arises when the local partner who is familiar with the market has different policy objectives from the international partner. In many underdeveloped countries, the local partner may have more interest in furthering family interests, than overall efficiency. An attempt, therefore, may be made to limit the ambitions of the partnership to a size which keeps the local subsidiary under personal or family control—a situation which is calculated to create friction between the thrusting foreign partner and a more lackadaisical local one.

Other Aspects of the Joint Venture Approach

As in so much else in international business the joint venture may seem a convenient way into a new market but have long term implications which may not be foreseen at the time. The structure may determine the strategy not the strategy the structure.

There is some evidence that the joint venture is growing in importance relative to the wholly-owned subsidiary discussed later in the chapter. Indeed, some writers would claim that the joint venture is the logical next step *after*, not before, a wholly-owned subsidiary. Before considering these issues in any detail, however, it may be useful to consider why the joint venture is growing in importance.

1) Many national governments will insist strongly on local participation if a subsidiary is being set up. Sometimes indeed the partner will be a state owned corporation, not only in the odd Communist country which tolerates joint ventures, but in many underdeveloped countries with relatively left wing governments.

2) A second cause of increased joint venture participation arises from the issue of licensing. Earlier, it was suggested that joint ventures may be a sophisticated form of licensing. The evidence suggests that licensing when it involves considerable technology transfer instead of merely a licence to use a design almost certainly works more in favour of the licensee than the licensor. There appears to be a tendency therefore for the technologically advanced enterprises, when approached for licence rights by foreign companies, to counter with proposals for joint venture as being more profitable in the long term. It may be in the future that licensing will be a way of Western enterprises using Communist technology and vice versa.

3) Particularly in underdeveloped countries with relatively un-familiar cultural patterns it is difficult to start from scratch. It may make sense to look around for a local partner, perhaps someone who has already established himself in the distributor field, or has perhaps license rights in related fields. An unstated qualification for a local partner in some underdeveloped countries will be someone with a family or financial connection with the local establishment. But this is a two-edged weapon, in for example a political upheaval, or in the event of a disagreement between the partners which may result in the expulsion of the foreigner to the benefit of the local.

4) Finally, the joint venture has a particular attraction for the small enterprise with limited financial resources.

There is one area where politics and finance may overlap. The joint venture is particularly common in left wing underdeveloped societies where there is a drive for local participation, as well as restraints on profit repatriation. The legislation does not in practice hurt the local partner but it does inhibit the interests of the foreign partner very considerably. A typical reaction may be for the enterprise baulked on the repatriation of profits to attempt to avoid the consequences either by transfer pricing if it exports (ideally to another subsidiary) or by paying royalties instead of dividends on technology, knowhow, etc. Such an arrangement however does not suit the local partner.

The issue of royalties goes a long way beyond this. A joint venture may appear satisfactory at the time of the agreement but may not be quite so satisfactory later if the foreign partner spends a good deal of money introducing new products. How does one allocate R & D costs on the one hand and royalties on the other, when there are other interests involved?

There are other problems too. Basically, the host country, if it insists on joint ventures, is interested initially in supplying its own market and possibly earning foreign exchange. But a truly international enterprise is something more than merely a series of local production units, each serving its own domestic market and perhaps marginally exporting. Global marketing or anything remotely approaching this stage, implies specialization by product and market. Plant may produce a specialist range of products for several, perhaps all, of the enterprise's markets. This means that other subsidiaries will have to be instructed clearly that they shall not produce that range even for their own markets but will instead import from the appropriate plant, possibly at a disadvan-tageous transfer price, if this is in the overall interest of the enterprise. Sometimes it may be necessary to stop a subsidiary supplying even its own market if production is to be concentrated somewhere else. This is a difficult enough policy to enforce where the executives are locally recruited and see this as a blow to the interests of their own economy. Where there is a local partner any overall global strategy may be rendered impossible.

The situation therefore of a joint venture may be similar to the issues already discussed in terms of channels of distribution or licensing. Where a joint venture is accepted as a temporary solution to a problem of entry to a market, it may inhibit the evolution of the enterprise to true global market policies. At the risk of oversimplification, it could be summarized that the advantages of the joint venture approach tend to be immediate and temporary, the disadvantages long-term and permanent. Where joint venture status is a primary condition imposed by the host government, the prospects of the enterprise really operating globally, are effectively diminished.

C. THE WHOLLY-CONTROLLED SUBSIDIARY

The wholly-controlled foreign subsidiary is probably the most widely favoured structure for those international enterprises with the resources to make this possible. The main advantage is that this particular structure eliminates one source of conflict. The enterprise may choose to keep all its markets separate and supply each by its own subsidiary: or it may choose to switch product lines and markets, even perhaps attaining a degree of international specialization. IBM in its European operation is a prime example of this. But it is difficult to envisage such a policy being possible if there were any local interests represented at the subsidiary level by a local partner or local equity holding.

There are two possible ways of achieving wholly-owned subsidiaries, to buy over existing plant in the foreign market or to build from scratch.

D. BUYING OVER EXISTING PLANT

Sometimes this plant may have been part of a joint venture project, where all that is happening is that the local partner is being bought over or bought out. Sometimes the plant may have had a close connection with the purchaser through licensing or similar arrangement.

The buying over technique is most practical in a developed country simply because there is more likely to be suitable plant. In less developed countries there is growing hostility to the buying over of local enterprises, as a means of direct investment. The authorities want new productive capacity to be created not 'buying over', a procedure which increases foreign dominance of the economy.[19]

The most obvious advantage is that the international enterprise obtains not only a ready-made manufacturing unit, but also, hopefully, distribution channels and goodwill. In some instances, particularly the acquisition of a subsidiary in the consumer goods field, there will be a strong case for continuing to trade under the local name unless there are good and compelling reasons to change. The British market has for long been a favourite area for U.S. takeovers: most British housewives are probably unaware of the extent to which they are buying products of Nabisco or General Foods subsidiaries under their long established and well known names. The process is being duplicated in European countries as British enterprises like Cavenhams buy their way into French food processing enterprises. If, however, the international enterprise has a reputation in its own particular line, which is better known than any local one, then a change of name may make sense.

There are two qualifications which have to be made in assessing the merits or demerits of buying over. The first is to find a suitable subsidiary for the conditions which have to be met are to some extent contradictory. It is desirable to take over a well regarded enterprise, certainly not one whose reputation is at all suspect. On the other hand the type of firm which can be bought at an acceptable price may not always measure up to this requirement. The ideal takeover prospect may be very unwilling to surrender its independence and it could be unprofitable to risk local unpopularity by attempting to win control as a foreigner against the obvious wishes of existing management.

Quite apart too from the opinion of shareholders and top managers, the attitude of staff, whose local expertise is being sought as much as the plant, matters a good deal. Sometimes they may be pleased at the prospect of a takeover with increased opportunity. There may even be some prestige. But more often there are fears, justified or imaginary, that beset local staff at managerial level or lower, when for example the prospect looms for a non-American enterprise at the prospect of a U.S. takeover. The Americans have the reputation of being fast hirers and firers—and it is the latter attribute that makes most impression. Gaining control is not merely a matter of finding the right plant at the right price: it also involves assuaging staff fears at the prospect.

A second complication is one which also arises in any takeover operation whether internal or international. This is that the acquisition may bring with it opportunities or commitments in product lines which do not fit in with the existing product range. Not every prospective foreign subsidiary is likely to be exactly tailored to the needs of the potential buyer, who may have to give considerable thought on how to dispose of or develop other products and markets outside his own interests. The situation is the obverse of the issue raised later in the chapter in terms of the more underdeveloped nations where the range of ancillary operations and services may differ substantially from those in the home country.

Finally in a period of floating or potentially floating currencies contingency planning may be important. The fact that the value of the U.S. dollar fell by about 20 per cent between 1971 and 1973 made U.S. subsidiaries very attractive to European and Japanese enterprises. The same situation was repeated on a smaller scale in Britain a year or two later when the combination of a hard Deutschmark and weak Pound Sterling enabled German companies to acquire British plant at virtual giveaway prices. An enterprise which had vague plans to expand in a particular market might suddenly find a very favourable exchange rate situation developing which required quick decisions several years ahead of a planned programme.

E. STARTING FROM SCRATCH (A GREEN-FIELD OPERATION)

The most ambitious, risky, but potentially the most profitable method of going international is to start a subsidiary from scratch. Sometimes, of course, the situation is not quite so stark as the phrase suggests in that some form of distribution organization, a sales or marketing subsidiary may have been in existence. Nevertheless, the problems are considerable, not least in finding personnel to form a cadre of the future management.

The decision to start from scratch may be positive in the sense that a new product line has to be established and existing facilities are therefore irrelevant. Often, however, particularly in brand new industries or in underdeveloped countries, the decision may be negative in the sense that there is no real alternative, since the industry simply does not exist locally, or there is a legal prohibition on the acquisition of an existing domestic enterprise by foreign interests.

The situation is not so difficult in developed countries where both management and workers are available and where basic scientific knowledge and technical skills can be adapted from similar industries.

Where international enterprises have been particularly successful in building a fairly complex production unit from scratch, has been in those other developed countries, largely because the necessary skills can be taken for granted. Most craftsmen can readily adapt from one industry to another, even the semi-skilled machine operator can adapt to a new machine but the same skills and indeed the same ambience of technical sophistication cannot be taken for granted in less developed parts of the world.

In the underdeveloped world, therefore, problems are great because parallel skills are not readily available. Industries do not spring up fully fledged but develop gradually over the years often from international enterprises whose original presence was in the role of trader or extractive industry.

In general, however, the environment is likely to be encouraging. If a government is willing to permit a wholly-owned subsidiary, it will probably positively encourage it for the technology it brings in. It is not likely deliberately to be obstructive though sometimes its bureaucratic procedures are an obstacle.

What will determine the role of development is not so much government encouragement as a more basic policy decision: whether growth is going to be linked to the local market or whether the subsidiary is to have, almost from the outset, its own exporting role, either into the enterprise's own home market, or into other markets which will be allocated to it, even possibly having been developed by the parent or another subsidiary.

Finally there is the possibility, already alluded to of installing, virtually complete, a production line withdrawn from elsewhere on replacement. There are dangers, not least political dangers, in deliberately using second hand equipment of a semi obsolete design. But a complete assembly line-tested out elsewhere and in working order is an attractive proposition.

STRUCTURE AND THE IMPLICATIONS FOR CONTROL

It will be necessary to discuss business policy again in a later chapter. Two issues of control will however be outlined at this stage, for they have structural implications for the foreign subsidiary.

A. *Conflict of Interests and Suboptimization*

It is difficult for an international enterprise to pursue an overall policy which is optimal for all subsidiaries and for the enterprise as a whole. That statement could probably be made about a domestic enterprise with domestic subsidiaries, but it is particularly applicable in the international field. Variations in tariff levels, taxation, the strength or weakness of national currencies with differing rates of inflation, varying economic and political conditions, all exist for the enterprise and have to be taken account of. Briefly, the major problem is that these factors make it difficult to apply a consistent measure of performance to all subsidiaries.

In the current jargon it may be necessary to suboptimize policy, because the freedom of manoeuvre of the enterprise is restricted.

So far as the implications of movable profit centres on structure are concerned, any form of organization which does not carry full ownership and control by the parent enterprise limits the freedom of manoeuvre even further. It becomes impossible to treat the interests of the subsidiary as subordinate to the interests of the parent company where there is a local partner, local equity participation, or any other form of international merger.

B.   Centralization and Decentralization

The second issue relates to the issue of how much decentralization is to be permitted. At the risk of being accused of cynicism it is difficult to avoid the conclusion that there is a good deal of transient fashion in the decisions made in this area. Currently perhaps, decentralization is in vogue, particularly if this can be presented as a polycentric approach. Nevertheless both centralization and decentralization have their merits and drawbacks.

The case for centralization is that it makes a consistent and long-term corporate strategy more practical. The disadvantages are that it is sometimes unexpectedly difficult for the parent enterprise to react in a reasonable time to a changing situation. In part this may arise because the headquarters is trying to do too much detailed planning, in part because the amount of information which is passed back to HQ tends to overwhelm.

In the longer term there may be a strong case for decentralization particularly if no substantial changes in strategy are anticipated. The subsidiary knows its market and can react to it, deciding when it is appropriate to pass information of general interest back to headquarters. In the short-term, however, the case for decentralization may create problems. The subsidiary management is left more or less on its own, lacking possibly finance, certainly experience. It cannot decide for the parent enterprise whether more resources ought to be put into the operation, or whether the overall interests of the enterprise require resources to be used elsewhere.

These are issues to be enlarged upon at a later point, but they have to be considered in the context of the structure. Once again there is the problem of conflict between the interests of parent and subsidiary with the additional restraint arising where the subsidiary is not wholly-owned by the parent enterprise. Whatever may be the appropriate policies a jointly owned enterprise, under whichever shape it arises, puts a limit on policy action. If suboptimization and decentralization are acceptable then it matters little that the enterprise does not have complete freedom of action. But the policy ought to precede the structure, rather than be dictated by it.

5. *Production and Technology Problems*

MULTICENTRE PRODUCTION

Important product decisions may have to be made by the international enterprise which is manufacturing essentially the same products in different national plants. There are three possible approaches.

A. To manufacture identical products in different plants
B. To manufacture essentially the same product but to different quality standards
C. To manufacture significantly different varieties of products, e.g. older designs in some plants.

Approaches *A* and *B* imply that production methods are not significantly different from plant to plant. Approach *C* implies that relatively obsolescent methods are being used in some plants. Let us look at these approaches in more detail:

A. The identical product approach may be found in the market for industrial equipment although the pattern is by no means universal. In the durable consumer fields too, there have been significant moves towards standardization. Up to the middle 1960's the U.S. automobile corporations tended to permit their European subsidiaries to design and manufacture models essentially for their national domestic market. There was no particular technical reason for this multiplicity of models, e.g. the Vauxhall range in Britain, and the Opel Kadett range in Germany, or the Ford Consul in one market and the Taunus in the other. What determined the policy was presumably residual consumer loyalties to individual brand names.

   By the early 1970's, both in cars and commercial vehicles, the tendency was towards identical products. Ford of Europe led the way with the Capri on the private car side and the Transit range in the commercial side—vehicles which were being produced in Britain, Belgium and Germany to the same design with standard and interchangeable parts. Insofar as Western Europe represented substantially the same conditions in eight or more countries—conditions quite different for example from those in the U.S.A.—the move represented a logical step forward as consumer loyalties to individual national brand names eroded.

The pattern of identical products was already widespread in the processed food and drink industries where Kelloggs and other breakfast cereals had been largely standardized as were the various Colas, and household detergents and related lines.

B. An alternative approach, but one which was understandably played down by the international enterprise was that of the same product being produced to different quality standards. In many industries there has always been a tradition that export versions of products had to be rather better quality than the average domestic products. But in more general terms there has always been the possibility either that lower purchasing power in a particular market might mean that a lower cost structure had to be set; or, alternatively, that a market might exist which could and would pay for extra refinements over and above what might be regarded as the basic model.

1) The lower quality model. The quality may be lowered in several ways. The product may be a stripped-down version of the unit sold in advanced markets: it may lack refinements— a car without automatic gear change, more spartan interior furnishing, and so on. An industrial product may lack labour saving devices, or even safety devices. Technologically advanced economies, increasingly concerned with individual safety and community health, impose more and more safety standards, noise abatement conditions, pollution control measures, etc., all of which cost the manufacturer money. The tendency, therefore, where these refinements are not mandatory and can be left out easily, is to regard them as expensive luxuries.

2) The higher quality model is more unusual. One example, however, is the one quoted above, in reverse, so to speak, of European vehicle manufacturers having to incorporate safety standards for the U.S. market which are not required in the home market. While this can be done on export models, there is no doubt that decisions to assemble Swedish Volvo and German Volkswagen models in the U.S. market will give a greater degree of flexibility in raising standards, if this proves necessary.

Apart from modifications to meet higher standards, it may also happen that in a foreign market a product has a cachet absent at home, and therefore is capable of appealing to a different market segment. The Mini range produced by British

Leyland, was intended for the less wealthy motorist or the second car of a two-car family. It was, however, subsequently produced under licence by Innocenti of Milan. The Innocenti version was a much more luxurious model for a wealthier market segment than either the Mini in Britain or the Fiat equivalent in Italy. [20]

C. The significantly different product. Here again there are two possibilities.

1) The product may simply be of an obsolescent design which is being phased out in richer more technologically advanced markets in which R & D costs have been recovered. The advantages of this type of production in a less developed but well protected market have already been alluded to.

2) The product represents a different stage in the product life cycle. The conventional life cycle approach is now relatively well known, but it may be desirable to outline very briefly the concept before considering its application to international business.

THE INTERNATIONAL PRODUCT LIFE CYCLE

The international product life cycle has been developed along slightly different lines by two American writers, Vernon and Wells; their comments on the field are well worth study. At the risk of over-simplifying their concepts it is useful to summarize their arguments in the conventional four stage variety, with particular emphasis on the production implications. [21]

Stage I. This development stage occurs almost inevitably in an advanced country. Indeed it might be argued that all the significant technical breakthroughs tend to occur in a handful of the developed countries. It is these countries who can afford extensive expenditure on Research and Development. The whole culture tends to operate on the premise that any product can and will be improved. Innovation results from the combination of wealthy markets and intense competition.

It is not always easy to predict where the technological breakthrough will come, though it is probable that economies which first encounter a technological bottleneck are first to find the solution. This has been true since industrialization in the modern sense was originated by an eighteenth century technological breakthrough in Britain where that country was the first to reach a crisis of rapidly rising population, just as traditional sources of raw materials were petering out.

In passing, it is interesting to consider why the Communist world has been so slow at innovating in virtually every field except military hardware and space technology where motivations are rather different. Most Soviet equipment, whether capital or consumer, has tended to be derivative not original in concept, in many instances well made and sold very cheaply in foreign markets but lacking originality. In a later chapter it will be necessary to discuss the gap in technology which has persisted between the Soviets and the West. But, in part at least, it may derive from an economic system which does not encourage the individual production unit to steal a march on its neighbours by attempting to break new ground.

Stage II.   This stage involves the general acceptance of the new product in other developed nations. It corresponds with the period of general acceptance in the orthodox life cycle.

It is, as has been suggested, impossible to prevent a new product or technique being duplicated elsewhere even though patent protection has been sought. All that a patent does is give a period of grace for the innovator to exploit his idea before anyone else, or give him a reasonable opportunity of collecting royalties or other payments from those who apply his ideas. If other developed nations have the technological potential, they will produce through a subsidiary of the originator under licence, or simply by evading any patent protection.

A number of variations are now possible. The first models appearing in these new markets are export versions of the original and not perhaps the most appropriate for foreign markets, even when these are in developed countries. Additionally the different size of a market, and possibly the difference in factor costs (e.g. labour may be cheaper) may mean significant changes in production methods. Within a short time too it is likely that both the originating country and the adopting countries of the second stage will be competing strongly in third markets.

Stage III.   Stage III in the convention product life cycle 'saturation', is the period of general production spreading to what are conventionally regarded as the less developed countries. As well as Western type consumer goods and processed foods and drink, there are a number of industries where technological development has stabilized to the point that production in technologically less advanced countries can be considered. Relatively simple versions of cars, ships as well as household accessories are now being produced on a significant scale in these areas.

The means by which this transfer of technology can be accelerated have already been discussed: pressure from the governments concerned by means of tariffs, import licences, subsidies or tax holidays to encourage local production by international enterprises, or where this does not have the desired effect, at least local assembly or licensing of knowhow.

The implication of all the pressure which is brought to bear is that initially the local product cannot compete either in the local producer's own domestic market or in export markets with the products of the developed countries represented in Stages I and II. Nevertheless, the problem of developing these products depends in no small measure on the steady progression to the next stage, i.e. the export of models to the developed world. This is necessary for two reasons. Firstly the industry, if it is to absorb modern technology, has to have access to large markets. It is the scale of the market which determines production methods, and large markets are rarely to be found domestically in underdeveloped countries. Secondly, unless the product can be raised to a level of quality which makes it acceptable even in the competitive developed market what remains is, in effect, a subsidized and highly protected infant industry.

The chance of success of moving on to Stage IV is increased if the particular production units are subsidiaries of international enterprises which have ready access to the developed markets. An attempt to enter these markets will be resisted by vested interests, both manufacturers and trade unions. At least the former can be neutralized by ensuring that the product is fed into the market by an international enterprise with established distribution channels.

Stage IV. This stage closes the circle. The underdeveloped countries are now the main manufacturers and suppliers of a product whose technology development has slowed down. The originating nation may virtually have stopped production and have moved its resources into new technological developments which will in turn follow the pattern.

As in the case of the orthodox life cycle, certain assumptions or qualifications have to be made. The most important is that the life cycle of the product is neither too short for the technology to spread, nor too long for there to be much useful technology to pass on. A transient fashion at one extreme, traditional steel production at the other, are not appropriate for this kind of treatment. A fairly typical example, however, might be the development of a new plastic which is mass produced, then over-produced. Another example might be found in a wide range of radio and electric equipment, where the life cycle for a particular technology is twenty years or thereabouts. A third example might be the

motorcar where the entire life cycle in its present internal combustion form may prove to be about a century. Not the least
of the qualifications which have to be added is the danger of
using what is essentially a biological analogy, which like any other
analogy can be pushed too far.

The implication for the international enterprise of the international
life cycle is clear. Firstly, as has been suggested earlier, no matter
how technically advanced and innovative an enterprise is, it cannot
hope to maintain a monopoly of its own product concepts. It
can limit the leakage of its own concepts by co-operating with
the inevitable, either by licensing instead of waiting for its technology
to be pirated or evaded; or even more powerfully by introducing
the process through its own subsidiaries into new markets, as and
when the time is ripe, phasing down production at home and relying
on its foreign subsidiaries to supply its home markets with the
now technically stabilized stock products.

THE TRANSFER OF TECHNOLOGY

The previous sections introduced the concept of technology as
one of the major factors affecting the international enterprise. This
section will consider in more detail what is involved and how
far it is practical to transfer technology.

A major reason for the gap between rich nations and poor
is simply the gap in technology, the factor which largely determines
a nation's wealth. Virtually any nation therefore is anxious to
increase its economic and political strength by acquiring any relevant
technology which has developed anywhere in the world. For the
underdeveloped world acquisition of the appropriate technology
can literally mean the difference between starvation and prosperity.
The international enterprise is not the only channel through which
technology can be transferred. It is, however, one of the most
efficient.

Defining Technology

Like so many other widely approved concepts, technology is not
very closely defined by its advocates. Three possible definitions
are given below:

a) Technology consists of a patent or group of patents and
the relevant knowhow to use the patents. In this most precise
of definitions, it is something which can be specifically licensed.

b) More generally, and at a lower level it may simply be skills
possessed by craftsmen or tradesmen. These skills may not be

generally thought of as technology in a developed society, e.g. a plumber or electrician is not regarded as a technologist in the U.S.A. or Western Europe. But, in a more primitive society lacking widespread sanitation or electrical facilities, these trades represent a highly appropriate type of technology—far more appropriate indeed than for example the graduate engineer or systems analyst who would be more obvious candidates for the title of technologist in the developed society.

c) The most general definition of all sees technology as basic education, combined with an attitude of mind which favours innovation and accepts change both as inevitable and desirable. Western societies are technologically oriented in the sense that change and improvement, at least in the material needs of life, are constantly taking place. The so-called technological gap between nations may be less a measurable gap in output and means of output between one country and another; rather it may be, more profoundly, a different attitude towards the acceptability of change. The gap, therefore, is not so much a question of availability of technology as a willingess to, and capability of, using it.

What Technology do Nations Need?

The point has been made that it is not always appropriate to introduce the most up to date technology into a society even if the national government wishes it. Technology has to be at a level where it can be absorbed into a society without destroying the existing fabric of that society.

There is no particular need in a developed society for a selective process in deciding what technology to acquire in that these societies can absorb the most up to date technology from each other without running much risk of wrecking their infrastructure. If the national government chooses to filter the type of technology which is to be introduced, or decides *how* it is to be introduced, i.e. by licensing a joint venture or foreign subsidiary, it is doing so for very specific ends.

In underdeveloped societies the problem for the national authorities and for the enterprise are greater. The government may decide either not to intervene but let the existing society absorb the impact, or it may try to cushion it. The problem is that what is most prestigious is not always most appropriate. There are two extremes of failure: either the process is too advanced and fails because the infrastructure and markets simply do not exist; or worse, the technology succeeds but ruins more of the existing economy than it benefits.

THE ROLE OF THE INTERNATIONAL ENTERPRISE IN THE TRANSFER OF TECHNOLOGY

Why should a national government, particularly of left wing convictions, as is the case in most underdeveloped nations, choose the international enterprise as a means of introducing new technology? The main case for the enterprise is that it has to be practical. It will introduce methods which are profitable, and provided these profits are not at the overall expense of the society, this is as good a method as any of ensuring that the technology introduced will be appropriate. If the appropriate technology requires larger markets than are immediately available in the domestic territory it is for the enterprise to seek out larger markets, possibly those already supplied by it from other production sources. As a method of cross-fertilization, both of technology and market access, the international enterprise is possibly unique.

It would be naive, however, to assume that decisions on technology can simply be handed over to the enterprise. There are at least three major issues to be resolved:

a) what does the nation want in terms of technology?
b) what can the enterprise supply?
c) how is the enterprise paid?

A. What does the nation want in terms of technology? The question of whether the most up to date technology is most appropriate, has already been discussed. There is, arguably, a more profound question, namely what *kind* of technology in what industry? Some industries and their technology are now almost stable. At the risk of raising the wrath of motorcar engineers it may be said that this is the situation with road vehicles. There may be marginal changes, even in engine design, but it is reasonable to expect that for the next twenty years the vehicle will be wheeled, with an internal combustion engine. The vehicle of the 1990's will probably be recognizably a descendant of the vehicle of the 1970's. Perhaps by the end of the century wheels and the internal combustion engine will be outmoded, but even an automobile built to today's specification will not be entirely inappropriate. The Volkswagen 'Beetle' is already forty years old in concept, and still being produced.

Could the same thing be said of military aircraft, computers, nuclear power? On the evidence of the past two decades there is every reason to assume that these products are still accelerating their rate of development and may well be virtually unrecognizable in AD 2000. The significance of rapid acceleration of technology is simply expense. Only half a dozen nations can afford a complete range of technology for any one of the three products listed above, and the numbers are likely to drop in view of rising costs. No Western European nation could start in any one of these industries from scratch today. Many no doubt wish they had never got in, and if they are to survive in the industries at all, can do so only on a European basis.

What is the significance of this in terms of technology transfer, particularly for underdeveloped nations? Simply, that some types of technology, those with most prestige in most cases, are hideously expensive already and likely to become ruinously so. Some nations may acquire the technology of these industries only in a very limited sense; they may buy nuclear power stations, aircraft and computers and train personnel to use them. To imagine, however, that having bought the initial stake, these nations will then be able to raise the ante, so to speak, i.e. to push forward the frontiers of technology in that industry, is a pipedream. In this sense, technology transfer may be very expensive initially, and then merely confirm a permanent technological gap in Research and Development.

Decisions by national governments therefore to invite in international enterprises with certain types of technology in the belief that the latter, once imported, will become self-sustaining, is based on an over-optimistic assessment of what can be sustained. The example of a country like Iran, bartering oil and other products against French nuclear technology can be regarded only as a gamble. Other countries developing industries like aircraft and computers are likely to be frustrated. Either they will have to absorb soaring Research and Development costs to stay ahead and independent, or they will find their technology consists of little more than the ability to buy and operate advanced products from elsewhere. The dynamism and expense of modern technology present at least as potent barriers as any deliberate restriction of export of knowhow by the governments of advanced countries.

In recent years some developing nations have set up administrative machinery to screen foreign technology, and so ensure that what is brought in is most appropriate. Mexico's Foreign Investment Law of 1973 was brought in against a background of complaints that foreign investors were bringing in outdated technology and overpricing even that. The new legislation through a Foreign Technology Register attempted to screen all contracts for foreign technology. The problem about such legislation, however, is that it requires a fair degree of sophisticated knowledge of what is involved. Screening which could be adequately carried out in an economy like Mexico, which was poised for an industrial break-

through, could still be an impossible ideal for a really underdeveloped
economy.

B. What can the enterprise supply? The obvious answer
appears to be, as has been suggested in earlier sections, 'the appropriate technology'. The situation however is not merely a technological problem. In many underdeveloped countries of left wing
ideology there is a curious dichotomy operating in industry and
commerce. Traditional manufacturing and distribution may be a
carry-over from a colonial and certainly pre-industrial past, and
will be a free enterprise system operating at a primitive level, but
very efficiently at that level. Superimposed on this, however, may
be a planning authority responsible for the systematic development
of new industry, which is to be publicly owned or at least regulated
to the needs of a central plan. It is with this planning division
that enterprise may have to negotiate.

A curious characteristic of planning, whether in Western developed, Communist or underdeveloped societies, is the tendency to write
off the importance of marketing. It is simpler and bureaucratically
tidier to assume that once production is achieved, consumption will
give no problem. The underdeveloped world is littered with the ruins
of ambitious projects, often Soviet financed, which have simply run
down because the products were either unsuitable or unappreciated.
Time and time again the classic assumption is made, 'first we
produce, and then, automatically, we sell.'

The enterprise, being commercially based, has to make technology
work if it is to make a profit. It has to apply the marketing
concept, and the marketing concept with its emphasis that products
have to be consumed, as well as produced, is at least as important
as the technology itself.

C. How is the enterprise paid? The issues here are royalties
and profits, perhaps indeed monopoly profits, in an acceptable
currency. The distinction between royalties and profits is often
ill-defined, but the possibility of varying methods of securing the
returns is a valuable weapon in ensuring satisfactory profit repatriation—a point to be followed up in a later chapter.

The alternative is payment in kind, either in the form of raw
materials (if, for example, the technology is being applied to developing natural resources), or by a share of the manufactured
products, which can be sold by the international enterprise, either in
its domestic market or anywhere else it can secure payment in an
acceptable currency.

FINDING THE APPROPRIATE PRODUCTION TECHNIQUES

Two policies in production plant installation in subsidiaries have been noted. Firstly, the tendency in certain circumstances to use equipment which has been phased out elsewhere, possibly from the parent company plant. Secondly, a tendency to build plant which duplicates the techniques used in the most recently installed assembly line elsewhere: the latter often being demanded by the host government, or installed, almost without thought, by engineers who are finding solutions to problems which exist somewhere else.

What ought to determine the type of production facilities? Arguably three factors, the first two of which are interconnected:

A. The distribution of production factors. i.e. the relative costs in economic terms of capital, land and labour, particularly the latter. In most instances, if there is a perceptible difference in costs between the parent country and the host country, it is that in the host labour costs are cheaper relative to capital. In this situation it does not really make sense to install plant whose ratio of capital to labour reflects the costs of the last plant.

B. The level of technological development. It has been argued earlier that in some underdeveloped countries there is a case for an intermediate or 'appropriate' technology, which is very far from being the most modern, but which most easily fits into the existing society.

This conflict of the latest as opposed to the appropriate level of technology is at its most acute in the contrast between a sophisticated economy like the U.S.A. or Western Europe on the one hand, and relatively primitive societies in Africa or Asia on the other. But it may also create problems in developed societies. It pays an international enterprise to be five years ahead of its time though it could be dangerous to be twenty years ahead. The first two factors are different sides of the same coin. The third factor however is probably the key one in developed societies.

C. The size of the market. This in large part determines the level of technology. The effect of technological improvement is at its most striking in mass production. It is a truism to say that mass production requires mass markets. A factory layout which is appropriate for 200 million customers in the U.S.A. is hardly appropriate for 3 million customers in Ireland. In most industries, plants are not only more numerous in the U.S.A. than in individual

European countries; plants individually tend to be bigger, and the size of individual plants is a reflection of the production methods used.

The comparison between the U.S.A. and individual Western European countries is becoming less valid as the European Community alters market scale and so market technology. This is one reason why initially U.S. corporations showed more confidence than their European rivals in the 1960's, and then were matched by the latter.

The issues in the less developed world are more complex. Modern technology, and so most modern industries cannot take root in a single poor and underdeveloped nation state, except in some varieties of consumer goods, textiles, etc. The home market is simply derisively small in effective purchasing power. If the market for cars in the U.S.A. is literally two or three hundred times as large as the home market in an underdeveloped country, how relevant are U.S. production methods: indeed how relevant are any production methods for manufacturing cars?

The implications of this fact are that underdeveloped countries may need unrestricted access to richer markets than their own domestic ones if their industries are to develop; and they may need this access without necessarily giving equivalent access to their own domestic market. Attempts are being made mainly through the appropriate UN agencies to get national acceptance of the virtual transfer of whole industries, textiles, shoes, and such like to the underdeveloped world on this basis. The success of such moves through international political organizations however is limited because national governments, who might be ready to acquiesce, face bitter opposition domestically from national manufacturers and trade unions, who argue that cheap labour industries destroy jobs in the developed world. [22]

Such a transfer can be achieved, more discreetly perhaps, by the international enterprise which having secured its lucrative Western markets can feed in supplies from outside. If such a transfer of suppliers can be accomplished by international enterprises which are prepared to supply their existing home markets from the underdeveloped world, then a scale and technique of production resembling existing production techniques in the Western mass markets becomes possible. Such a move fits in well with the hopes of the host countries of earning foreign exchange as well as obtaining industrial development and jobs. But if large markets, much larger than the domestic market of the host country, cannot be found then production techniques are likely to be comparatively primitive in most industries, while some will remain unattainable.

This section started by considering relatively easily absorbed consumer goods which traditionally tend to start off industrialization. So far as more advanced products like cars are concerned, the 'take-off' point is more difficult to achieve. Three contrasting approaches are illustrated below.

In the early 1970's Peru was a relatively poor economy with a domestic market for cars of about 30,000 vehicles—a miniscule scale of market for any recognizable production pattern. There was, however, some hope of a larger market through Peru's membership of the Andean Pact with five other South American countries, representing a domestic market of some 150,000 vehicles.

At this time there were a number of assembly operations, comprising U.S., European and Japanese interests. General Motors, Ford, Chrysler, British Leyland, Volkswagen, Nissan (Datsun) and Toyota all assembled vehicles; the large number of assembly operations meant that all were marginal in the market. The Peruvian government took the highly risky decision to force out all assembly plants except one which in the event turned out to be Toyota. The intention then was to give Toyota the opportunity to move on from assembly for the Peruvian market to local production for the Andean Pact market; again hopefully bringing industry, employment and export earnings. There were obvious dangers not only domestic, but also external, i.e. in getting acceptance of Peruvian dominance in this market throughout the Andean Pact region.

At about the same time the government of Iran was seeking to create an automobile industry. Several assembly operations were established, of which the most important was at second remove a U.S. operation. Chrysler's British subsidiary (formerly Rootes) had a model produced by such an assembly operation under the local name of Peycan. The Iranian government was not apparently satisfied with this assembly operation and sought an arrangement once again with Toyota.

There were obvious reasons for Japan, desperately short of oil, to make a deal with Iran. There was immediately a market for about 60,000 vehicles and Toyota were apparently willing to produce locally about 50,000 vehicles. The deal ran into difficulty because the Iranian government wanted eventual production at ten times that number. Toyota was in fact being asked to produce on a scale which would require its plant to export very rapidly— presumably at the expense of home plants. A further delicate point, not apparently brought out into the open but probably highly relevant, was the fact that, thus far, locally produced vehicles were scarcely of the quality which would attract many foreign buyers.

Iranian government complaints about the existing Rootes Hillman
range were known, but the market price which could be commanded
by a British manufactured vehicle was unofficially about double
that for the identical locally produced Peycan.

There can be little doubt that the Iranian vehicle market was
likely in time to be a very lucrative one, and every prospect that
Iran would become not only an industrial power but an industrial
exporter. The immediate problem, however, was whether Iran had
pitched the price too high—and in the short run it probably had.

A third example concerns a more orthodox approach to the
problem. South Africa, a rich but small market, with limited export
prospects, simply allowed more and more assembly operations for
all comers. The bargaining counter was based on the producer
showing a readiness to move on from assembly to local production
and thereby getting generous treatment and local protection.

The above examples have all related to motor vehicles precisely
because this is the type of industry which is now a practical proposition for many relatively underdeveloped economies. Indeed
within the next decade there are likely to be assembly or production
facilities in about half the countries in the world. How many of
these however will ever get to a take off point where Western
mass production techniques become possible, is debatable. Vehicle
production may be the key to industrialization of some countries.
For the great majority it may prove to be an illusion.

The Problem of Ancillary Services

Earlier, reference was made to the situation which can occur either
in exporting or in local production where the general level of technological sophistication is significantly lower than in the home
market. So far as local production is concerned, such a situation
is generally found where labour is cheaper to hire than in the
home market but very much less productive.

The first problem in designing plant for such a situation may
be to convince the designers that the production problems which
are encountered in the parent plant are not necessarily going to
be duplicated; that it may be more sensible to design a less
sophisticated, less labour-saving production system than at home:
that it may be more appropriate to go back a technical generation
even if the machinery to be installed is not of that era.

Other problems, however, can arise on the issue of supplies
and ancillary services. These may be readily available in the home
market with good quality and acceptable delivery dates. The same
however cannot always be said of the situation *vis-a-vis* the new
plant. For example, a decision may have been made, on the insist-

ence perhaps of the host government, that local sources are to be used for supplies, materials and services. What happens if quality, delivery dates and the general availability of ancillary services, components, etc. prove unsatisfactory? The subsidiary may be compelled as a short-term and expensive measure to make up some of the deficiencies from traditional home sources—probably to the irritation of the host government. As a longer term solution the subsidiary may have to move into these fields itself, although this solution is by no means always the best.

The end result can be that the subsidiary is at the same time smaller and less sophisticated as a production unit than the parent company, but is far more widely spread in its production facilities, in that it has had to buy into or set up service facilities whose availability had been taken for granted. The extension into fresh fields of activity may be achieved with a measure of success, but this is the sort of problem which perhaps could have been looked at in the planning stage. More often the decisions have to be made in an ad hoc way in an air of crisis with the host government displeased at the enterprise's lack of enthusiasm for local industry's efforts, and the parent company suspecting that unnecessary expenditure and 'empire building' is taking place in the subsidiary.

It may be both politic and most profitable to reduce the span of foreign operations as rapidly as possible to conform with the pattern adopted by the enterprise elsewhere. This, however, will necessitate the enterprise adopting a very positive attitude of encouraging and, if necessary, giving advice to local suppliers. In effect then the enterprise brings in skills and knowhow for which it is only in part being compensated.

6. *Marketing Factors in International Business*

INTRODUCTION

In a very real sense all factors in international business are marketing factors, in that the whole point of the operation is to ensure that all markets are catered for as efficiently and profitably as possible. Nevertheless there are some factors which can be described very precisely within this definition, namely Market Research, and those other subjects which normally are regarded as part of the marketing mix. This chapter therefore deals with some of the problems of systematic information gathering, and the Product Policy, Pricing, Promotion and Distribution, and other issues affecting the operation.

Some of these problems appear exclusively in an export situation, i.e. where subsidiary markets are being supplied from the parent enterprise or from other subsidiaries. Some appear exclusively in local production by subsidiaries or any other intermediate variation, such as partial assembly; others appear in both.

Logically in this chapter one might consider in rather more detail problems of supplying the home market from foreign subsidiaries — an issue already touched upon in the previous chapter. Some of the problems however go beyond marketing as the term is used in this chapter, e.g. into financial policy, and the implication of transferring production from one country to another without changing the markets served will be dealt with again in later chapters.

MARKET RESEARCH

Market research is a phrase which covers a wide spectrum, from the elementary application of existing knowledge acquired by an enterprise as a by-product of its main sales operations to the most elaborate and sophisticated of statistical and motivational techniques. But in its most widely used sense, it is taken to mean some form of investigation or survey of a market carried out either by the enterprise itself or a professional agency to obtain more positive information than is produced by the normal sales and other figures arising from routine operations.

The most noticeable characteristic of postwar market research developments has been the application of a range of scientific techniques to what had hitherto been a rather ad hoc subject. In most developed countries professional standards have been created and the number of agencies available has expanded steadily. For about twenty years, agencies have operated on an international as well as a purely domestic basis. In some instances these have developed from the international advertising agencies, but even relatively small domestic agencies tend to develop overseas contacts and associate agencies in other parts of the world.

This section is written on the assumption that the international enterprise has its parent organization in a developed country and has therefore fairly sophisticated techniques readily available.

It is exceedingly difficult to generalize in a very meaningful way about the problems of conducting market research in foreign countries. However, given some of the more conventional categories in market research, e.g. between desk research and field research, or consumer market research and industrial market research, a few comments remain valid.

a) In Western developed societies the following generalizations apply. There will be reasonably accurate statistical information produced and published by government and trade associations: there will be a number of standard surveys and comparisons published by official organizations like OECD which includes most developed societies outside the Communist Bloc, or EEC publications. Even where the figures are not collated by such organizations there is likely to be useable information in the form of household surveys, censuses, trade returns which are reliable and readily available. The attitude to genuine enquiries whether addressed to individuals, companies or government departments may not always be wholehearted co-operation, but a reasonable degree of success may be achieved. And not least there are likely to be market research agencies available to carry out ad hoc studies.

Statements about market research surveys in different societies, and their degree of success, have to be dogmatic since they are not easily validated or disproved. It may be said however that North America tends to be an area of relatively ready co-operation, Northern Europe rather less so, and Southern Europe more suspicious, and Japan highly suspicious. Industrial market research particularly in respect of published sources is relatively easy.

b) So far as the situation in underdeveloped societies is concerned anything written above about published information in respect of developed societies has to be qualified if not reversed. One of the more subtle dangers indeed is that national pride requires even the most primitive nation to publish a mass of economic statistics, which in print look as plausible as those of developed societies, but are in practice a good deal less reliable. It is not appropriate to discuss the difficulties in collecting statistics here. In brief, however, the point has to be made that most official statistics are the by-products of other activities, e.g. tax collection, and if the administrative machinery to do the job is primitive, the by-product information is correspondingly suspect.

Consumer Market Research

A sophisticated market research project in the consumer field at home requires the taking of a selected sample of a fair size from the whole 'universe' or population of potential buyers, and the examination of this sample in some detail: this is the principle. The practice will involve a good deal of work in defining exactly the subject matter to be investigated, preparing a questionnaire to be used in interviewing by the researchers or to be mailed out to the sample; perhaps testing the questionnaire by a pilot survey, refining the questions in the light of any difficulties thrown up, carrying out the survey, tabulating the results in a meaningful way and preparing a report and possible recommendations—all elaborate, highly technical and consequently expensive proceedings, particularly when the market to be researched is a foreign one.

The expertise lies in the selection of the sample and the process of extracting information from those being interviewed. In the use of such sampling techniques what matters most is often not the proportion the sample is of the whole, but the size of the sample. Putting the point another way, we may consider the population of the U.S.A. to be about 200 millions, Britain 50 millions, and New Zealand about 3 millions. A market research sample of 500 interviews would give nearly as accurate results for the U.S.A. as would a similar sized sample in Britain or New Zealand. Ignoring for the moment differences in costs between the three countries, this means that proportionately per head of the population, a survey would be four times as expensive in Britain as in the U.S.A., and about seventy times as expensive in New Zealand, with the accuracy in the last country not all that greater than in the first two. This example is of course grossly oversimplified but it does illustrate some of the financial issues.

What are the implications of this, for any plan by an international enterprise, to conduct a sophisticated survey of possible consumers in a foreign market where it is contemplated moving over from supplying by imports to local production? Four conditions can be defined.

A. Conditions similar—familiarity with product. The first group are those countries where conditions, tastes, and standards of living are akin to the conditions in the parent enterprise's home market, or in other markets where the enterprise already has subsidiaries operating, and about which it already knows a good deal; or where the enterprise's products are already imported on such a scale that their use is commonplace, and not confined to a small section of the community. For an American enterprise such a market might be English-speaking Canada; for a British enterprise, the Republic of Ireland, Australia or New Zealand; for a French enterprise, Belgium or French-speaking Switzerland, and so on. The point which is relevant here is that the size of the population is relatively small or widely dispersed compared with the enterprise's domestic market, and the expense of sophisticated market research could prove relatively high, although eminently practical.

B. Conditions similar—non-familiarity with product. The second group consists of other developed nations where a standard of living and technology approximating to the domestic market exists, where consumer goods from the home country of the enterprise are comparatively rare, but with perhaps a distinctive market segment which tends to be more willing to buy than the great majority of consumers. Here the prospects of carrying out an orthodox consumer market research project would be small. One might, for example, instance the prospects of carrying out an extensive market research project on the quality of small engined European cars which appeal to or repel buyers in the United States, e.g. the British Mini, the Renault, or Fiat models of 1000 cc engine capacity or less. At any one time it is doubtful whether more than a few per cent at most of all American drivers would have experience of small European vehicles, apart from the ubiquitous Volkswagen.

Thus, a sample hundred might bring in only a handful of useful replies. It would be a good deal more relevant to conduct the survey amongst those Americans for whom a small foreign vehicle was not a 'way out' purchase, e.g. those who had already bought foreign vehicles and might therefore be better prospects. Whether or not the segment of the market which bought or was likely to buy European in reasonable quantities, could be easily identified is another question. The point is that where the potential customers were so small a minority in the whole population and could be readily identified, then the returns on a sophisticated market research project might be small, even in a very large population. In passing, it is worth noting that, if instead of the European models quoted above, one had been dealing with, say, a Simca vehicle, the problem would be that much easier because of the fact that Simca is a subsidiary of the Chrysler Corporation.

C. Conditions dissimilar—familiarity with product.   This group consists of a large number of underdeveloped countries where the market for products is relatively small. Because of the absence of accurate official statistics which can be taken for granted in a developed country, the identification of prospective customers can be very difficult. Agents or distributors can identify present customers but would find it difficult to quantify future demand.

D. Conditions dissimilar—non-familiarity with products.   This situation is almost impossible to treat by orthodox market research methods without incurring inordinate expense for uncertain results.

How much Sophisticated Market Research is Possible?

Consumer market research as has been suggested more often than not turns on the ability of the researcher to select a representative sample of respondents and sound out their opinions. It is not proposed to discuss in detail the problems even in a developed society of obtaining a representative group of any section of society. The problem is compounded in a foreign market, not least an underdeveloped society, where the international enterprise is conducting its enquiries at long range and at second or third hand.

A major problem in an underdeveloped country, is the issue of answering questions. In a developed economy, the man or woman approached is co-operative, provided that he or she can be persuaded that a market research approach is not a selling gimmick. The average person, tactfully approached for an opinion, is, more often than not, flattered, provided that he is not being too inconvenienced. In an underdeveloped part of the world however, reaction to questions of this sort can be downright hostility, particularly in a male dominated society where attempts to get opinions from females can arouse resentment among husbands or fathers.

These difficulties in foreign markets, particularly in less developed countries, add up to the fact that while sophisticated market research is not impossible, it can prove incomparably more complex and expensive than in the domestic market. The enterprise may have to settle for information which is a good deal less sophisticated or even accurate than might legitimately be expected from the domestic market. An international enterprise considering a move into an underdeveloped country takes a greater risk in conditions of greater uncertainty than it would if the move were into a developed society.

Industrial Market Research

Most of the problems which face the international enterprise in consumer market research are also applicable to research problems in industrial goods, but there are some which are particular to the industrial goods market.

The advantages might be summarized as a greater degree of technical knowledge, sophistication and, hopefully, rationality in choice. This applies whether the market is in a developed or under-developed market. There are relatively few substantial differences between foreign and domestic market research in the industrial fields.

It is far more likely that a person interviewed in his capacity as a technician will be able to give a more reasoned and possibly less emotive reply in the field in which he is an expert, than he might be expected to give as a consumer in another field. An advantage which follows is that research might be carried out on the market prospects of what might still be a concept rather than a physical commodity. Opinions on the functions and price range of a new concept, either in the domestic or foreign field, could be obtained, for the expert would be able to conceive, in abstract, the new product. To carry out any meaningful research in the consumer field into an 'imaginary' object, in a foreign market would be a good deal more difficult.

If industrial market research affords the theoretical advantage of a more sophisticated sample, the disadvantages are at least as marked. If one lists the conditions which can prevail in the consumer field, a vast, relatively homogeneous population from which a random sample of considerable size can be drawn, and to which various statistical tests can be applied, the conditions are reversed in most industrial market research problems. There is not likely to be a large homogeneous population but rather a relatively small number of potential customers, more often than not of varying size and importance, so that three or four might represent the majority of market demand, with a considerable number of smaller customers—the tail of the market, so to speak. In this sort of situation any statistically random selection is of limited application. Common sense dictates that all the large cus-tomers are interviewed, and any sampling is confined to the smaller customers, a method which effectively prevents any sophisticated techniques being applied to process the results.

A less obvious difficulty may arise in identifying the individual who actually makes a buying decision, and whose opinion is the one to be sought. The problem is complex in the home market where the researcher may be familiar with the company set-up: it is far more complex in a foreign market.

The engineer or works manager who can appreciate and be persuaded on the technical merits of a product may have a very limited say on the issue of eventually buying. The person who makes the decision may not even be high in the hierarchy, and may be unwilling to change from an existing supplier to a new and foreign one, on the grounds that he will not be blamed for doing what he has always done, but would be blamed if the new supplier or new product proved unsatisfactory. In some parts of the world too, an attempt to assess the strengths and weaknesses of a product might be frustrated by a degree of polite acquiescence in the merits and a refusal to criticize—a practice which might give rise to a quite misleading assessment of the prospects of success-ful marketing of the product in the future.

Other aspects of industrial market research present peculiar problems in the foreign market. At the crudest level the extent to which bribery and reciprocal deals affect a situation. At a more subtle level, we are dealing with motivation and valuations which may be quite different from one country to another.

Finally, the degree of willingness of enterprises and governments to co-operate in research varies enormously. Even between the relative openness of American corporations, the relative caution of British companies, and the virtual mania for secrecy in France, Switzerland or Italy, there is a vast gap. When it comes to other cultures the gap is even wider, but its implications are often lost in a facile assumption that foreign businessmen and officials will readily give any information needed regardless of suspicion, national pride or downright dislike of foreign enquiries.

The other aspects of this which have to be considered are partly cultural, partly national pride and conventional behaviour. It might, for example, be desirable to find out a good deal about the ability of personnel in an underdeveloped country to operate and maintain sophisticated equipment, or to find out what growth in a market could be expected if a government planned project were to come to fruition. There is a tendency for national or company represen-tatives, in the presence of a foreign enquiry, to cover up national deficiencies, to deny difficulties, inefficiencies or breakdowns. It is a confident man, or a confident community, which can own up to failures. Sanguine market estimates, in this situation of 'covering up', may be misleading.

The other aspect of this problem is also cultural, namely the tendency to give a polite reply. In some economies market research enquiries about reputation or quality of a certain foreign-produced or designed product, will get a forthright reply, in others not. In, for example, the American context, an unfavourable reply will be given if that is the opinion felt. In another context, say Japan, businessmen may give a polite reply, praise a product which they may think is poor. Again, the classic problem of industrial market research is not the non-response, but the *inaccurate* response, because it is very difficult to judge whether a reply is to be taken at its face value.

Finally, there is the problem of simple comprehension. An international enterprise presumably wishes comparable information from one country to another. In some languages it is very difficult to render appropriately into the language the concepts which are to be measured, and the translations achieved are very approximate.

Market Research in Communist Countries

The Communist world is an entirely different proposition for conventional market research. Official statistics are contentious and are often simply presented as percentage variations on a base year. Virtually none of the routine statistical series produced in western societies are available, although broad indications of the areas of expansion may be deduced from national plan publications.

Field research either in consumer or industrial market research situations is very limited; a few years ago it would have been impossible anywhere in the Communist world. Now, however, several states in Eastern Europe have permitted the appearance of market research organizations whose methods are very similar to those applied in the West. An international enterprise might be able to use one of these but the ideal of field research by Western market research agencies or individuals can come very close to espionage in Communist eyes.

The overall problem however is a political one. Even if it can be established that there is a market for a particular product, the market will remain closed unless or until the state chooses to open it. It takes very little scientific enquiry to appreciate that there is an enormous demand for Western consumer goods almost anywhere in the Communist world. Even so, the market remains virtually a closed one. Until very recently it would have seemed pointless even to suggest that an international enterprise might have some interest in pursuing market research enquiries in such an unpromising market. Considering, however, how the original Communist denunciations of marketing and advertising concepts have been muted over the years, it is possible that market research may become more and more a realistic proposition in Eastern Europe. So far as China is concerned, the problem is likely to have to await the next century.

PRODUCT POLICY AS AN ASPECT OF MARKETING

The concept of an international product life cycle as developed in the previous chapter describes a gradual shift of emphasis from the developed to the less developed economies in the longer term. In the short-term however—and it is in short-term issues that businessmen are generally involved—there is likely to be a situation where an enterprise has production facilities and market opportunities in several markets for the same range of products.

In this situation, so far as industrial goods are concerned, market conditions may be virtually identical everywhere in the sense that a component for a machine tool or industrial process will be the same wherever in the world the process is in operation. But other industrial and most consumer products, which have originated in response to conditions in one particular market, may not be entirely appropriate elsewhere. For example, a British Mini car could operate on an American intercity freeway: conversely a very large American automobile could operate in the semi mediaeval conditions of some old British towns; but in neither situation could it be said that the product was ideal for the market.

Given that the general characteristics of the product have already been determined by home market, or one of the subsidiary markets, to what extent can an international enterprise match the product to other markets which it wishes to supply either by local production or by import from elsewhere?

There are two extreme approaches:

a) The ideal is to redesign the product to the extent required to match the new market: if necessary to the extent of creating a new product. The product is then perfectly appropriate to the market, or to segments of it, and little promotional expense need be incurred in selling. There is however at least one substantial limitation to this approach: the product development costs, over and above the original costs, may be prohibitive—unless, and exceptionally, the ideal version of the product is a phased out version already developed for the more advanced market.

b) The other extreme is to take the product as it stands and adapt the market to it. This process involves considerable promotional expenditure, advertising, etc., but has the compensatory factor that little or no additional expense is incurred in product adaptation.

In practice, neither product policy can be followed without qualification and some sort of compromise has to be sought. Nevertheless it is a useful exercise to consider in abstract the two extremes and decide on a coherent compromise, by a process of analysis of the situation in each individual market, rather than by a non-rational 'feel' of the situation. The first of the extremes represents the ideal market orientation, with every product tailored exactly to every market. A more realistic situation is probably somewhere in between, but rather nearer the second approach than the first, at least in an early stage of market penetration. Later, when the market is better known or its potential is seen to warrant another approach, then a market orientation approach becomes more realistic. But the average enterprise, with several lines of products and several markets with differing characteristics, may be fortunate if it can adapt an existing product for a new market without incurring substantial expense.

Given the initial decision on the extent to which the product will be adapted to the new market, what sort of problems are likely to present themselves? Some of these have been touched upon from technological distinctions, such as differences in measurements between national markets, two general problems require some thought.

The first of these arises when some degree of adaptation is necessary involving a change in quality of product. The point has been briefly touched upon in terms of production problems and there are also marketing implications. In most cases the decision which has to be taken is whether or not to lower the quality of the product to suit market conditions.

There are basically two situations in which a decision to lower quality might be considered, that of a more developed market and that of a less developed market.

So far as the richer economies are concerned, the argument on the question of quality can follow two somewhat contradictory lines. In a rich community people are readier to pay the higher price for the cachet of quality. This may account for the prestige of the 'imported' label, i.e. meaning possibly higher quality but certainly higher prices. The U.S. market shows this characteristic so far as many non-American enterprises are concerned. On the other hand, if the relative profession of wealth is expressed in a tendency to discard goods long before their physical life has ended—premature obsolescence, from the point of view of the moralist, planned obsolescence, from the point of view of the producer—then a different product strategy may be required. If a machine is liable to be discarded after five years, is there any point in building in quality standards which will ensure a life of fifty? There is no easy answer: an adjustment of quality may in practice show up, not as a realistic assessment of life expectancy, so much as in shoddiness.

In a poor community the reverse problem exists, namely how to build in as much quality as possible, without the expenses which would be acceptable at home but are out of reach in the new market. The compromise may be a significant lowering of standards, with the new problem of deciding whether to market the lower quality goods under the same brand name which has built up another type of reputation elsewhere.

The implications of such policy decisions are profound, and it is far easier to identify the issues than propose ideal solutions. But it is essential that the issues should be recognized, so that whatever decisions are taken are recognized as decisions, and not blurred over.

State Regulations

Government regulation on quality and safety standards, already discussed, is of growing importance in product policy for the international enterprise. The basic problem is that these standards vary from country to country and it may not be easy to meet stringent requirements for one market without accepting them and the expense in another market. A striking example mentioned earlier have been the recent regulations on safety and pollution standards for American automobiles which have created considerable problems for foreign manufacturers or for U.S. plants in Europe rather more than for the domestic producers. A non-American manufacturer is being required to rejig for perhaps ten per cent of his sales and has difficulty in isolating the increased costs from the remainder of sales. The U.S. plant is rejigging for 99 per cent of sales, and knows that rival producers are incurring the same costs. The larger markets impose unilaterally such standards, the more they compel the international enterprise to produce within the market, or at least gear production facilities elsewhere almost exclusively to that one market.

COSTS AND PRICING IN DIFFERENT MARKETS

The problem of allocating costs particularly overhead costs in a capital intensive multiproduct firm are not confined to the international enterprise; nor is the problem of determining the optimum price strategy. But the international enterprise faces these problems in many markets and it cannot be taken for granted that solutions arrived at for the domestic market are always best for each foreign subsidiary's market.

The situation is complicated by the fact that entirely novel factors enter into the situation, many of which have little or nothing to do with marketing issues. These factors can be lumped for simplicity into three groups, Financial, Political, and Marketing. The division however is by no means watertight.

A. Financial. The major problem here may be summarized as how large a contribution is the subsidiary expected to make to the historical costs of developing products, only tardily coming into stream in the subsidiary; or what contribution is to be made towards current R & D costs which may be expected to yield marketable products, initially for the parent company but eventually for the subsidiary. This might at first glance look like an accounting convention but it has implications for taxation and the valuation of assets in the event of nationalization. The political overtones are particularly pronounced if overhead costs are decreed to include substantial royalties or R & D costs. Some enterprises may choose to write off all costs against the parent—in effect subsidizing the subsidiary by technical knowhow; others may try to cost this out pro rata among all production costs. Most controversial, some will vary their policy from market to market, according to the political situation, tax considerations, and financial restraints on profits remittances by the host government.

B. Political. Government intervention usually has the effect of forcing prices down. The various income policies introduced in the early 1970's, first by the U.S. government and then imitated by the British and other European countries, are examples. Incomes policies are intended to be temporary but in the underdeveloped world, particularly where left wing governments are not overly tender of the interests of foreign investors, they tend to be a permanent feature of life. Their importance in the price structure is that in the long term they could compel rethinking on the cost structure to load 'permissible' factors into the system, e.g. royalties and R & D charges instead of straight profits.

Arguably neither the financial nor political factors have any place in a discussion on marketing strategy for the international enterprise. They are, however, given, and unmoveable constraints which must affect price strategy in particular, and marketing strategy as a whole.

C. Marketing.   The more purely marketing factors might be summarized as: 1) the general price level and living standards in the
market, which obviously determine how important price will be as a
factor in the marketing mix; 2) the subsidiary's position in the
market: is it a price leader or follower? Does it have a dominant,
significant or marginal share of the market? 3) the market segment
which the enterprise serves in this particular market—which may
not be the same as in other markets.

All of these can be encompassed, if desired, as stages in the
product life cycle, both in international and domestic terms. In
international terms, the issue of the stage of development has already
been discussed. In domestic terms, the conventional four stages of
Innovation, Rapid Growth, Maturity and Decline represent different
market segments and different price strategies. It is important to
realize that while there may be a product life cycle for each market,
these do not all start in the same period or last for the same time. In
other words, while the market may be about to flatten out or decline
in one country, another market may have just reached a phase of
rapid growth and a different price strategy is appropriate.

Given these constraints, what are the possible pricing strategies?

A. Cost-plus Pricing

The problem of operating in an area of uncertainty poses some difficulty, and many enterprises seek a solution, not necessarily at a
point which they can be sure maximizes profit, but one which
can be justified on some form of logic. At one extreme, there
is the 'cost-plus' approach, i.e. a summation of all the costs involved
in production, plus a 'reasonable' profit margin; at the other, acceptance of a price already prevailing in the market, and possibly
of price leadership. However, both of these approaches have serious
deficiencies.

The traditional criticism of any cost-plus approach to pricing
is that it takes no account of demand factors or competition. While
cost-plus can be used satisfactorily in the home market either of the
parent enterprise or of one of its foreign subsidiaries, its success
depends on the proposition that competitors in the market face
largely the same technical and cost problems. In a sense it is
not too dangerous to pay little attention to domestic competition
since the competitors' problems and advantages are not all that
different from one's own. A cost-plus approach in a foreign market,
where the competition may be coming from a firm of a different
size, using a greater or less amount of capital equipment in relation
to its staff, and paying substantially different wage and other charges,
may be more risky.

A further traditional criticism of cost-plus, the arbitrary allocation of overhead costs, has added relevance where the costing policy in the subsidiaries differs from that in the parent company, because of the loading on of acceptable overheads, e.g. royalties, already discussed.

Cost-plus based pricing, based as it is on the ideal of a 'reasonable' profit margin, carries over to pricing the lingering, but not always logical, assumption that there is a close and direct relationship between cost and price; that cost determines price. In fact the only valid relationship which exists between the two is that, in the long run, cost sets a lower limit on price.

B. Accepting the Prevailing Price

Faced with the problem of fixing price, some international enterprises accept the price which already exists on the market, altered only when a price leader decrees. Provided the prevailing price exceeds cost, no further pricing decisions need be taken. There are a number of obvious objections to this. The idea that market conditions determine the price, and that the firms have no effective control, is not realistic unless there exists something approaching the theoretical conditions of perfect competition—large numbers of firms, producing identical products, in a situation where the actions of any one firm have no appreciable effect on the market—a rare situation in the modern world. A second objection is that of acceptance of price leadership by established producers. While an incoming enterprise may accept this situation on occasion, price leadership can all too easily become technical leadership, and too passive acceptance of this state of affairs, merely to avoid difficult pricing decisions, may lead to a dangerous situation of atrophy.

The greatest objection is the more subtle assumption that price is the most important or indeed the only factor which matters in the marketing strategy. It is almost as dangerous a fallacy to assume that price determines everything else, including cost, as it is to assume that cost determines everything else including price. The immediate danger of the exclusive price approach is that, if an enterprise finds at the outset that its projected price is likely to be higher than its competitors, because of the lower limits set in practice by cost, it will either not enter the competitive market, or will enter it half convinced that it is going to lose out. For a relatively high-cost producer this could be a disastrous approach. Price is, of course, of tremendous importance but it is only one element in the entire marketing mix. The more the manufacturer can convince possible customers of the uniqueness of his product the more control he has over possible prices. He can achieve this either by a distinctive superiority in some technical respect, or by heavy promotional expenses, and the more successful he is in emphasizing the differentiation, the less he need regard price as being the determinant of everything else.

C. Other Pricing Strategies for the Subsidiary

There are a number of pricing strategies, from fixing highest possible price (for short-term gain) to a longer term 'pre-emptive' pricing, which sacrifices immediate gain for the possibility of keeping the price so low as to discourage the entry of a potential rival, and so maintain a virtual monopoly (although without monopoly prices) for as long as possible. For any of these to be rigorously pursued, it is of course desirable that the ultimate price be laid down as part of the pricing policy. It is pointless to attempt a pre-emptive pricing strategy if the ultimate distributor takes advantage of the situation to get a really outstanding mark-up. Control of the ultimate price not only gives greater control of pricing strategy, but makes the whole mark-up structure at each stage of the distribution chain more easy to regulate. Clearly, one of the prime factors in this situation is the particular method of distribution employed, and the further along the distribution channel control (and ownership) of the goods have been maintained, the easier it will be to impose the appropriate pricing strategy.

Price Maintenance

Whenever a company, and particularly a subsidiary of an international enterprise, attempts to lay down a pricing strategy involving price fixing at the consumer's end, it has to consider what sanctions may be invoked in the event of the ultimate retailer following a line at variance with company policy. It may not be possible to cut off supplies. The attitude of governments towards retail price maintenance 'recommended prices', etc. varies from outright rejection, to total enforcement, and it is essential to be clear on the official attitude before attempting to enforce a price. Even where there are no legal guidelines, the fact that the subsidiary is foreign-owned can have a significant effect on government reactions to attempts to fix prices.

In attempting to fix the price, not all of the relevant factors are within the control of the enterprise or its subsidiary. The greater the degree of uniqueness the firm can establish, the greater the degree of flexibility in pricing which will be achieved. And flexibility can be very important, because it is the only real defence against a relatively dynamic market. No matter how logical a cost and pricing system the company may have achieved, any system which proves to be too rigid to allow of rapid adjustment to changes in the market, to the increasing or decreasing of discounts when unexpected opportunities arise, is likely to lead to trouble. Ideally, having worked out a pricing policy, the firm may hope to keep the price unchanged for years, but unless the potentiality to react quickly is there the situation is more hazardous than it need be. And not the least of the problems in pricing over a few years arises from the problem of inflation, virtually omnipresent in the world today but proceeding at different rates in different countries. Even where there are no obvious signs of change in the value of money through changes in exchange rates, it is important for the parent enterprise to know how costs and prices are changing relatively in all the areas in which it is producing and marketing.

The Product Range of the Subsidiary

If an enterprise intends to produce or sell a range of products through its subsidiary, then an early decision has to be made on the relationship, if any, of the price of one product to another. There may be no connection, in the sense that every product might be priced independently, based on its production costs either within the market or elsewhere. Alternatively some method of establishing a joint pricing policy might be established. One product might be priced rather lower than what had been estimated to be the point of maximum profit, if it was intended to use it as a 'leader' to introduce the range of products; or possibly some variation of the policy discussed earlier: of basing long term profitability on the pricing of replacement parts as much as on the original equipment. Again, it might be found expedient to fix a price which is excessive in terms of cost or expected profit, for prestige purposes, on the argument that the general image of a high-price high-quality range should not be dented by one glaring exception. In such a situation, a product, which had to be priced either very much above or below the plausible price created by the rest of the range, might be more usefully sold without the trademark or other identification.

Transfer Pricing

An issue which has been left unexplored is that of transfer pricing, i.e. the price set for transactions involving the nominal sale of goods and services between the parent enterprise and a subsidiary or between subsidiaries. Arguably, transfer pricing is the most important aspect of all. It is not however basically an issue of marketing, but rather of financial or political strategy and will be dealt with later in the appropriate context.

The Pricing of Servicing

There are two approaches to the pricing of servicing:

a) To regard the sale of the product as being the main revenue raiser, with servicing being supplied near or even below cost to maintain customer goodwill.

b) to regard servicing as a continuing source of profit throughout the working life of the product.

Often the optimum policy is somewhere in between the two extremes. But whatever policy is decided upon, the question of the scale and pricing of servicing is likely to have repercussions on product policy elsewhere. Sometimes too the decision will have to take account of import licence regulations of national governments, which, to conserve foreign exchange, or to encourage local industry, may stop the import of complete units, vehicles, machine tools, etc. But even when the product can no longer be sold in the market from a foreign plant, replacement parts will still be allowed in, and other servicing costs permitted from abroad— another illustration of the interrelationship which may exist between financial, political and marketing strategies.

ADVERTISING ON AN INTERNATIONAL BASIS

The problems of advertising and promotion on an international basis are very largely extensions of the types of problems which have to be faced in the home market. The danger is to take for granted that what is good policy at home is invariably good policy abroad. Of all the activities in an enterprise, expenditure on advertising, the media and the message are most difficult to decide on a rational basis. Advertising is rarely a complete waste of money: obviously it can be highly effective in promoting sales. But in spite of all attempts to develop a coherent principle of optimizing advertising expenditure, it remains in many respects a hit or miss affair. And the further an international enterprise moves away from well explored and traditional markets into new territories, the more hit or miss it is likely to be.

Advertising Policy

A major problem for the enterprise which intends to spend a fair amount on international advertising is to decide whether it will keep overall control if its advertising policy, i.e. whether to have a general advertising policy throughout the world or whether to regard each market as separate and requiring a different advertising approach. The decision made on this is likely to affect profoundly the methods of control which are then applied to the advertising function.

An overall advertising strategy is particularly appropriate where a distinctive reputation, symbolized by a trade mark or perhaps a slogan which translates well into several languages, has been achieved. This overall symbol or slogan is more important than any variations to meet local nuances. Such a standard policy on advertising, however, may limit the extent to which the overall marketing mix has been successfully adapted to local conditions.

A small company, with no world-wide public image to be projected and protected, and whose international ambitions are limited to a satisfactory distribution of products exported from its home plant, can take a more ad hoc approach. For the enterprise which foresees substantial international expansion with multicentre production, an ill-considered or non-considered decision on advertising, at an early stage, can have lingering ill effects.

A considered decision on advertising policy leads to a decision on the degree of devolution which can be accepted. There are three possible approaches:

a) a completely centralized advertising policy.
b) one involving a measure of prior consultancy with local distributors or agents, or
c) a completely decentralized system in which the decisions are left to local subsidiaries, distributors, or agents.

a) A centralized advertising policy implies that basically the same advertising approach will be used throughout the world, the same materials and slogans with very exact translations where necessary. Apart from the advantages of economy it can be argued that where there is no local manufacturing or marketing subsidiary, any goodwill and customer loyalty built up will be identified with the product, not with the distributor or agent. The balance of power between manufacturer and the local distribution channel is tipped strongly in favour of the former. If necessary, he can change distributors or even change his entire distribution methods without too much risk of losing consumer loyalty. The disadvantage of centralized advertising of this nature may be summarized as a danger of relative inflexibility. Overall policy may become an alibi for inattention to detail in any particular market; and reaction to a change in a local market, i.e. a new competitor, legislation, etc. may be slow and confused.

b) The second approach of prior consultation with local distributors may be most appropriate where the manufacturer has a relatively small direct investment in the market and where the local knowledge may be rather limited. In this situation a mutually agreed advertising policy may also involve the distributor or agent meeting part of the cost, say fifty per cent of direct advertising. The obvious advantage is that the distributor/agent not only supplies the intimate knowledge of how and where to advertise most effectively, he has a direct financial commitment and will possibly devote more attention to the problem.

c) The third approach, total devolution of control is based on a concept of extreme market orientation. Here the local subsidiary, if there is one, makes its own decision on how much or where to advertise. The distributor/agent is given an allowance for promotional purposes which he will spend in the manner he judges will best work in his particular market. The advantages are obvious. A considerable amount of detailed planning requiring highly specialized staff is eliminated from the HQ staff. The disadvantages however are also obvious. If there is a subsidiary it may not be large enough to have its own experts in the field. If a distributor/agent is being used it is desirable to ensure that he is capable of assessing the best advertising methods and whether he can determine the optimum advertising budget. He may have an excellent selling record, but does this make him a good judge of advertising methods? May he not use the advertising and promotion appropriation to promote his own image, rather than that of the manufacturer or the product? He can, of course, be required to give an account of how his budget has been allocated. Misdirected promotional activities may be deliberate on his part or they may reflect a genuine difference of opinion on what constitutes legitimate promotion. Guidelines on definition of media to be used and proof of expenditure can be required, but, particularly in an alien culture, it is not always easy to evaluate what is done in a decentralized system.

MARKETING STRATEGY—THE CONFUSION OF AIMS

The point has already been made on more than one occasion that the move to go international often arises from a confusion of motives and responses to particular ad hoc crises. Some of this confusion is most evident in overall market strategy, not least on the issue of market orientation.

In recent years the concept of market orientation, i.e. what is loosely described as producing what the market wants, rather than what the enterprise can best produce, has been sold, probably oversold, to business. 'Going international' is even presented as an extreme of market orientation.

Market orientation implies adaptation of products to every individual market; but at what stage does adapting a product to numerous international markets become the evolution of numerous new products, each one having a segment on a national market? Excessive market orientation in this situation may mean loss of any coherent policy on product range, loss of overall control by the parent company and, incidentally, also a loss of all the technical advantages of size, large scale production and international specialization. If this excess of market orientation is allied to cultural or legal barriers which limit effective control, the enterprise may be virtually anarchic, able to adapt rapidly at the local level to changes in the market but with no overall strategy.

Arguably, if the international enterprise is to retain its unique advantage it cannot accept market orientation in an extreme form. It has a tendency to force standardization of product, to develop new products initially as national brands possibly in the parent market, but eventually with international launches without too much attention to national detail.

While control problems might appear to limit the adaptation of a market orientation strategy there are certain advantages in the situation. The major advantage is that a newcomer entering into a market has no stake, financial or emotional in the existing market pattern, in terms of price, promotion or distribution. The new company may choose to imitate the old established ones. On the other hand, the new company has nothing to lose if the existing market conventions are broken down. It is thus the newcomer from abroad who is often the catalyst of change. Air Products Inc. started in Europe and forced its way into what had amounted to a tacit division of the market for industrial gases between a single national company in Great Britain, France or Germany. The Japanese have repeated the process with ball bearings. Breaking conventions sometimes pays handsomely and market orientation is rapidly becoming a convention—or even a cliché.

7. The Human Factor in International Business

Any enterprise in the last resort is people and their relationship with each other. This chapter deals with two groups of people: the executives, whether line or staff personnel, and the shop floor workers.

The Executive—a National or International Career?

It is an accepted truth that international enterprises will rely as heavily as possible on local recruitment of executive personnel for their subsidiaries, although one or two key posts may be held by the parent country nationals. Even if in the early stages foreign executives have to be used to set up a subsidiary, they are normally expected to train replacements and withdraw fairly rapidly. Local recruitment of executives has three clear advantages. The executives are likely to be less expensive; there will be fewer problems of attracting high calibre personnel, particularly if the subsidiary is located in a country or culture which is remote from that of the parent enterprise and headquarters staff; and finally it removes one source of friction with the local community and hopefully too, with the workforce, if the bosses are not obviously alien.

Most executive careers in an international enterprise are national careers. In this sense, the international executive is a very rare bird.

THE INTERNATIONAL MOVEMENT OF EXECUTIVES

There are three types of executive transfer which affect the international enterprise, namely executives from the parent enterprise being sent to the subsidiary, movements in the reverse direction, and transfer of nationals from one host country to man posts in another host country.

HOME COUNTRY TO HOST COUNTRY

A senior executive may be sent out to set up a subsidiary company, see it through its first year or two and choose and train a national as his successor. Sometimes the man sent out will be nearing retirement with the implication that no further promotion is to be expected at home. Sometimes indeed he may have formally retired and has been recalled on a consultancy basis. If, on the other hand, he is in mid-career such a move may be a critical one, either a stepping stone to a top post at home when he returns, or a blind alley.

The second possibility is that someone is being sent out to give technical advice because his knowledge and skills are not generally available locally. Again he may have to train his own successor. Such a posting obviously creates problems when the technical man returns—generally, however, he is a line man rather than in the general management hierarchy.

The third possibility is the relatively junior executive who is sent out to fill what amounts to an upgraded post in the overseas subsidiary. In some ways the career problems of this man are the most difficult of all. In theory if he does a good job he will spend two, three, or four years there, and come back to a higher post. In practice, if the enterprise has not thought about the future, his career may suffer a setback. Out of sight is, too often, out of mind. When the executive comes back the organization may have made no provision and he has to be fitted in somewhere, almost certainly carrying less responsibility than in his foreign posting, and probably feeling disgruntled that a good job done in an unattractive area has brought no real recognition. Some executives who have gone through this stage claim that their careers suffered rather than benefited, because their stay-at-home contemporaries moved further ahead during their absence, being under the eye of senior management all the time.

Another aspect of the question is the calibre of the man sent out on posting to the subsidiary. If the personnel division is doing its job, then one of the most promising younger executives will have been sent off. If, on the other hand, a divisional chief is asked to nominate someone he may be tempted to keep his best subordinate and volunteer the person whom he feels he can best do without.

There is no easy answer to this situation. All one can say is that the parent enterprise has to protect its executives by ensuring that a suitable post will be available in a given time when the executive returns; and by making sure that the person concerned knows that when he returns, he is not just an embarrassing nuisance who has got to be found some job. At the same time, the enterprise has got to protect its own interests by making sure that if it wants a good man nominated for a foreign posting, it gets a good man and not a misfit.

Finally, there is the situation where a young executive may be given the opportunity of making his career in another country: sometimes in the case of an American enterprise he may have ethnic connections, i.e. a first or second generation American. In the case of British or European enterprises the posting may be to countries with an Imperial or Commonwealth connection. There are two qualifications which have to be made here. It is unlikely that an American or European will be able, even if he is willing, to make a career in most parts of Africa, Asia or even some parts of South America, because highly nationalist governments are going to insist on local executives. The days of the white man as executive in the non-white world are clearly numbered. They will be tolerated on a temporary basis, but a white caucasian in his twenties who imagines that, even if he wants to, he will spend perhaps forty years in an African or Asian country in the late twentieth and early twenty-first century is being naive. Americans in Europe or Europeans in North America or in the mainly white countries elsewhere are more acceptable. The days of the East India Companies or of Colonial-based enterprises relying on expatriates have gone irrevocably. And this may be as well. The young executive in an international enterprise who claims to be willing to travel generally means he is prepared to visit overseas plants, even with a reluctant wife and small family, and possibly to accept a temporary posting for a year or two. He does not often want to accept permanent exile. The permanent foreign posting for the young executive then is likely to be limited by racial or linguistic issues, and this situation is likely to prevail for the next two or three generations. There may be opportunities in this situation for minority racial groups in the parent country of the enterprise, e.g. for black Americans or Europeans to be used for such foreign postings by the enterprise to overcome what is literally a super- ficial problem. It would be a mistake, however, to suppose that the appropriate colour of a man's skin banishes all cultural problems. Black Americans in the U.S.A. are arguably longer established and more profoundly American in culture than any but the most rock-ribbed Yankee Wasp. British born blacks of recent West Indian origin are likely to follow the same pattern: whatever their dominant culture it is only remotely African. Nevertheless the possibility of American or European non-whites as emissaries of international enterprises in the so-called Third World certainly cannot be ignored as a factor in personnel selection for the remainder of the century.

Finally, although this would be firmly denied by the enterprises concerned, it is not unknown for a foreign subsidiary in pleasant and undemanding surroundings to be used as a receptacle for the well connected incompetent, who cannot be sacked but, equally, cannot be advanced.

HOST COUNTRY TO HOME COUNTRY

There are two variants on this type of transfer.

A promising young executive who has been recruited locally may be sent to the parent enterprise or one of its national subsidiaries for a year or two. It is useful training, not least in the ethos of the enterprise. Particularly if the subsidiary company is operating in a very different culture, the implication is that it is the values of the parent enterprise which will have to prevail, if only in a modified form. To put it at its bluntest, if a young man or woman has grown up in a society where nepotism and overt discrimination in favour of one's family and relations in business appointments is a virtue, or where bribery is regarded as the norm, if not exactly approved of, then the new recruit has got to be made aware of the mores which prevail in the parent enterprise. He may have to compromise between two cultures; or, worse, he may become an excessive convert to the new mores. But whether the results are quite what were intended, the young foreign executive has to know what culture and moral standards prevail in the parent enterprise so that he can judge what will or will not be acceptable.

The second type of transfer is on promotion to a permanent post in the host country. This is very much the exception, and is likely to remain so. The top home posts in the parent enterprise are tacitly retained for home nationals.[23] The exceptional foreigner who breaks through will probably have to change his nationality in the process. Even so, it still remains the case that cultural assimilability is an essential. Englishmen or Canadians can become sufficiently Americanized to reach the top posts in U.S. enterprises and Americans working for English or Canadian enterprises can have similar success. But for, say the black or brown-skinned African or Asian, the problem is much greater. Non-executive directoral appointments pose no problems of course, but for executive posts the situation is more difficult. Farsighted enterprises have to think out the implications of their acceptable image in the Third World, unless they are to avoid hostility or ultimate recourse to that most patronizing of all solutions, the statutory black or brown foreign-born executive prominently on display to visitors.

Fortunately, however, most executives want to make their careers in their own society. Although they will never run the whole global enterprise 99 per cent of executives will settle for success in their own country.

HOST TO HOST

This is perhaps the most difficult area in which to formalize transfers of executives. There are two types of executive who can be very suitable in solving problems of manning foreign subsidiaries or dealing with other foreign problems.

The first group speak the language of the subsidiary as their mother tongue but come from another country. It may be convenient for the enterprise to solve its executive problem by transferring such people from one host country to another. A U.S. enterprise might use an English executive instead of an American to take up a post in another English speaking state, or in a Commonwealth country. A French or Spanish born executive may be useful in other countries than France or Spain.

Finally, the tragedy of wars and political upheavals have created a wide dispersal of victims—very often numbering among them the elite of a society. In the wake of the Nazi era both American and English enterprises benefited enormously from the injection of European refugees, many of them Jewish. They played an invaluable role in building up a knowledge of the European market. The cold war refugees in their turn have made available to the same enterprises a fresh infusion of talent, which, as political passions have cooled, are proving invaluable in dealings with Eastern Europe.

LEGAL RESTRICTIONS AND NATIONALIST SENTIMENT

In general, both the legal sanctions and the nationalist pressures to force the employment of local personnel are strongest in the underdeveloped world, where work permits for aliens can be very difficult to obtain. Such aliens as are permitted to hold executive posts are there on a temporary basis until local executives can be trained up. The major problem here is that there can be an honest difference of opinion on when a local replacement is available. Where host government pressure is very strong the process may be far quicker than the enterprise believes is desirable. It pays an enterprise therefore to make it clear that it is genuinely trying to train up local executives as quickly as possible, not merely trying to delay what is, after all, inevitable.

THE LABOUR FORCE

General Considerations

A major consideration for the enterprise operating in foreign territory is the extent to which it will either conform to local practices in labour conditions or attempt to transfer its domestic practices elsewhere. A rule of thumb may be to conform to local practices in developed countries but to set its own pattern in underdeveloped countries.

In the *developed* countries, the necessary skills are available, work patterns and disciplines are understood, trade unions are probably strong. In very *underdeveloped* countries several of these factors may be missing. As well as a shortage of the technical skills required, the labour force, if not accustomed for example to factory discipline, may have to be introduced to the concepts of punctuality on arrival, and regular attendance. It is not unknown for workers with relatively low standards of living and expectations to work for as long as it takes to earn sufficient to stop working for a few days or weeks, and then return. An intolerably high level of absenteeism may thus be created, and it may be vital to instil what amounts to an industrial society work discipline into a pre-industrial work force.

The problem of *incentives* for the work force can cause problems both in developed and underdeveloped societies, as a trade off of more income vs. more leisure is created. Since many enterprises are capital intensive industries, they may be able to pay, on a comparatively generous scale, their relatively small labour force. One danger of this situation again is that the work force may settle effectively for a four-day week, particularly if taxation is high. Increased wages can merely worsen the situation. The situation is summed up in the reply of a miner who was being attacked for the high rate of absenteeism in his industry. When asked why he and his companions worked only four days a week, he retorted 'Because you don't pay us enough to work three days.'

Paternalism of a company is a relatively rare commodity in developed societies. Trade unions dislike its manifestation, blurring as it does any conflict of interest between management and labour, with the implication too of company unions. Some international enterprises practise this, although they will not use the term, with comparative success. IBM has successfully limited unionization in most of its foreign subsidiaries by this policy. Critics of Olivetti at its Ivrea HQ in Italy would argue that it is almost feudalistic in its sense of responsibility for the welfare of the labour force. Paternalism however may be a good deal more common and acceptable in the less developed countries, both because trade unions, the Western alternative, are weaker, and because the whole society turns on obligations and duties to an extended family. And an enterprise offering factory employment in such a society may be absorbed into the pattern if it chooses to do so. Whether in the long run it can maintain this pattern is another question, although the Japanese situation does suggest that a fair measure of paternalism on the one side and company loyalty on the other, can survive in a highly industrialized society.

Paternalism—the Japanese Variant

The extension of the Japanese international enterprise into Western developed societies is in its comparative infancy. Nevertheless, their philosophy in a green-field development situation is to attempt to create a Japanese ambience in management labour relations. Management attempts to make conditions so attractive that the labour force will be unwilling to unionize. Such a policy has been reasonably successful in small plants.

In larger plants the problem may be more difficult. In Japan trade unions tend to be what would be regarded in the West as Company Unions, whose officials see the interests of their members as largely identical with those of management. It has been reported that Japanese companies contemplating investment in Britain have approached the Trade Union Confederation there to see whether company unions would be acceptable, only to be rebuffed by the traditionalist TUC members who regard company unions as being the tools of management. It is quite probable that there is a genuine confusion of terminology; namely that what Japanese management would regard as being a company union approximates to an industrial as opposed to a craft union, and that what the Japanese would regard as eminently sensible would be a union representing the whole work force (as is the norm in say, West Germany). The British Trade Unions whose demarcation disputes are as often between unions as with management, are quite literally talking a different language, proclaiming explicitly the conflict between management and union and implicitly the conflict between union and union.

Where the Japanese enterprise is not involved in a green-field operation, but buys over existing companies, as is fairly common for example in California, the new owners conform to existing practices *vis-a-vis* trade unions.

Reactions to Current Issues

There are a number of issues likely to raise the hackles of any progressively minded executive in Western society. Some of the most obvious and current might be sex, racial, religious or colour discrimination. Even on pure expediency the executive is not going to let his corporation be exposed to criticism on any such grounds if he can avoid it. But in another part of the world, all or any of these situations can be found; women simply excluded from any responsibility in industry or commerce; Hindus and Muslims refusing to work together (one caste of Hindu refusing to share a room with another); separate wash rooms being demanded for each cult, religion or colour of skin, and so on; situations which would be regarded as outrageous in a developed Western society.

What does the enterprise do in this situation, when to accept such discrimination would cause an outcry at home, and to reject them would cause a riot among the labour force, or possibly even a compulsory closedown on the spot? The inglorious answer in most cases is to be inconspicuous: to accept the local standards and avoid drawing attention to double standards at home and abroad. It can then attempt discreetly to change the practices but only as far as it can do so without running into trouble and publicity for offending local susceptibilities. This is the sort of situation where any publicity, condemning the enterprise for knuckling under, or praising it for defying local practice, produces a 'can't win' situation.

An obvious example of how international enterprises can become involved in controversial issues, is apartheid in South Africa. The spotlight of publicity has made enterprises improve the lot of black workers, to the palpable irritation of the Verkrampt white politicians and white trade unions in South Africa. But no enterprise can have enjoyed being in the spotlight, and so publicly being seen to have adopted a personnel policy which could make life more difficult with the local power elite. Success in personnel problems in this sort of situation means keeping out of the newspapers.

RELATIONSHIPS WITH TRADE UNIONS

The key trade union problem for the international enterprise is whether unions are able to co-ordinate their activities internationally to deal with their employer. In international co-operation against the individual enterprise the trade unions have been left far behind by management. Their essential weakness in the international setting is that there is no overall controlling body, while there is such a unified control in the enterprise. Trade unions tend to react to moves by the enterprise rather than having much of an independent policy. This fact may enable the enterprise to follow a 'whip saw' policy, i.e. so to dispose its production plants internationally that even when a union dispute holds up production in one plant, it may be possible discreetly to make up the shortfall from other plants. In the longer term a 'whip saw' policy may mean simply cutting down investment in a plant where labour troubles are chronic rather than spasmodic and increasing investment elsewhere.

This is not to say that there is no co-operation between unions. It tends however to be sectional rather than for uniform objectives. Basically most moves for international solidarity among trade unions come from the unions in the parent country, which are also generally the unions representing the highest paid labour force.

Trade unions in the parent country of the enterprise have an interest in preventing the setting up of assembly or manufacturing operations abroad. This simply costs their members jobs at home, and, as they see the situation, enables the enterprise to substitute cheaper labour in foreign factories. The trade union phrase for the international enterprise is the 'runaway' company, a graphic illustration of the problem as seen from the labour point of view.

Logically, trade union opposition should start from the very outset, when plans are being discussed for the foreign subsidiary. In practice there is no very clear cut issue at this stage on which to rouse members because very rarely is there a clear cut cause and effect. Enterprises do not generally and publicly build a foreign plant to close down a domestic one. The effects are more long term in the shift of investment emphasis over the years. What is normally at stake are *potential* jobs, and it is with *actual* job losses that trade unions are concerned.

In a curious way the interests of the domestic trade unions and that of the national government of the parent company are almost identical. In the one case foreign currency is being lost, in the other, jobs.

One obvious response to the situation, once the subsidiary has been established, is to invoke trade union solidarity on an international basis. The unions which almost inevitably benefit, however, are those in the parent company. They, after all, have the established industry and the higher wages. They can therefore with perfect logic press for comparable wages and conditions in subsidiaries overseas, with a comfortable awareness that if the moves succeed they make the foreign subsidiary that much less attractive. The unions in the host country however find it difficult to establish a line of action. They are probably realistic enough to know that comparable conditions in the short run means no investment and no jobs, although the situation may change once the enterprise has built up a substantial stake in the host country and cannot pull out without heavy loss. The problem of the national trade unions is simply this. They can oppose any move which takes investment and jobs away from them: but will they oppose the obverse side, namely when the investment and jobs are coming to them? American and British car workers object to the multinational corporations setting up production lines in Spain, but will Spanish workers? And if circumstances later compelled the Spanish plants to be closed with production concentrated back in the home plants would American and British workers strike in protest? In practice trade union members in foreign subsidiaries are more often directly concerned in comparisons of wage levels with other industries in their own country, than with the wage level of workers in other national subsidiaries of the enterprise. It is relatively easy to compare wages and working conditions within an economy but meaningful comparisons across national or cultural frontiers are much more difficult.

This is not to say there is a complete diversity of interests between the labour force in one country and that of another. Particularly in crises they will co-operate in the short term — by 'blacking' suppliers, or refusing to increase production to fill in a gap caused by industrial action at a foreign plant. But when the response of management to an unsatisfactory labour situation is not to go for a confrontation, but merely a longer term change of emphasis on where new investment will go, the trade union reaction is muted and confused.

THE WEAKNESSES AND STRENGTHS OF INTERNATIONAL TRADE UNIONISM

The weaknesses. The major weakness has already been mentioned, namely that there is no overall supranational control of the unions as there is for the international enterprise. There are however other weaknesses which in total are at least as important.

The first is that there is no agreement about trade union aims on an international basis. There are for a start two major international trade union organizations. One of these, the World Federation of Trade Unions (WFTU) is communist dominated, the other the International Confederation of Free Trade Unions (ICFTU) is not. But even within these two groups there are splits: the fact that one country's Trade Union Congress adheres to one of these organizations rather than the other says something about the balance of power within the Congress, or the ideology of the government. It does not represent unanimity of view. For example, both American and British trade unions subscribe to the non-Communist dominated organization, the ICFTU. But clearly the American unions are by and large non-political; certainly they are non-ideological. The British unions in most instances are officially socialist in outlook, and support and finance the British Labour Party. Both American and British unions, however, contrast sharply with those European countries which have more rigorous ideological and religious overtones, i.e. with unions dominated by Communists, Social Democrats or Catholics who may co-operate with each other from time to time to oppose government or employer, but who normally are in rivalry with each other for the loyalty of the working class.

A variant on religious or ideological splits within trade unions, both internally and internationally, can be found in colour, caste or nationalism. A 'whites only' South African trade union will oppose bitterly any move to give equal status to a black worker. In a caste divided society like India, the problems of securing equal working conditions is virtually impossible: jobs may have to be allocated by castes. And finally, where countries have a long tradition of mutual hostility, patriotic feelings follow strictly nationalist lines. The day when Arab and Israeli trade unions co-operate will be a truly significant one for the Middle East.

Secondly, there is the fact that some unions are strong, both in financial terms and in their political acceptability to national governments; others are weak, poor, and possibly corrupt. In some authoritarian countries whether of the right or left, free trade unions simply do not exist. By contrast a powerful trade union can enjoy a close relationship with the government, e.g. in a Scandinavian Social Democratic state. In other countries the management's problem may not be excessively strong trade unions, but the opposite —the situation where they are anxious not to be associated with the repressive activities of an authoritarian government.

Finally, arising out of the lack of overall direction, there is simply a lack of information, or at least pooled information about conditions and company plans. Trade unions are both better informed and more interested in their relative status within their own country than in the situation in foreign plants of the enterprises in which their members work. They can readily compare wages with other trade unionists in their own country. Wage and working conditions in other nations are of relatively less consequence, a situation which strengthens the hand of the management of an international enterprise.

Strengths. The main strength of the trade unions is their willingness in the short-term to react to crises affecting foreign plants. Unions are, theoretically, in a strong position to act internationally only when there is an element of vertical integration in the enterprise —a *Category II* situation, because action by one can bring foreign subsidiaries to a standstill for lack of parts. So far, however, unions have only intermittently tried to exploit this situation.

AREAS OF CONFLICT WITH MANAGEMENT

Aside from the usual conflicts on wages and conditions of service, there are several areas of conflict peculiar to the relationship between labour and the international enterprise. The first is one which has been alluded to already, namely the room for manoeuvre in dealing with unions (as with national governments) the enterprise has, precisely because it is international. Particularly when the national government is broadly favourable to the trade union interests (i.e. in a Social Democratic government) it is galling for nationally based unions to realize how difficult it can be to make use of political strength. Even where the government is not particularly sympathetic to the unions it remains a fact that the latter are often more nationalist in outlook than business, especially international business.

For the term nationalist, one could substitute either of the loaded words patriotic or chauvinist. Trade unions object very strongly to the erosion of national powers produced by the existence of the international enterprise.

At the internal political level their interests may clash with the enterprise. Most unions outside the U.S.A. have a very close link with the political left, whether social democrat or communist. In theory, at least, they are in favour of central planning by government. Such central planning implies a degree of control even over private enterprise. International enterprises are a good deal less easy to control than domestic ones.

Another major source of friction is the difference in management styles from one country to another. American management at one extreme has an already noted reputation for the 'hire and fire' policy; American trade unions are often willing to go along with substantial cuts in the labour force, provided that those kept on get their share of any extra profit from increased efficiency. Japanese management at the other extreme is paternalistic, almost feudal in its sense of rights and duties in respect of employees. The problem which arises is that an international enterprise may try to apply its domestic policy in an inappropriate situation. The takeover of a European company by an American corporation produces very mixed reactions from the trade unions, i.e. from an expectation of getting American wage levels to a fear of massive dismissals.

EMPLOYEE PARTICIPATION IN MANAGEMENT

A recent development in European management, particularly in Germany, has been the representation of workers on supervisory boards and the whole issue of 'codetermination'. The supervisory board is the first half of a two-tier system and appoints the second tier, the management board. Up to half the supervisory board may consist of employees' representatives. Like the other members of the supervisory board their primary duty is to the company rather than sectional interests. Something of the same pattern has been followed in other European countries.

The Commission of the European Economic Community has been considering the harmonization of European Company Law, and produced its proposals as the so-called Fifth Directive. ·

The Fifth Directive would require each member state of the European Community to adopt a two-tier system in their company legislation, based on the German pattern. The same pattern would also apply to the European Company (The Societas Europea, SE) pattern discussed in an earlier stage. At the time of writing the proposals for amendments to national company law are being considered by the legislatures of the members of the Community which have not already made such provision.

The attitude of both European management and labour to the Directive is ambivalent. So far as European management is concerned, reaction is mixed: the advantage of making the labour force feel a sense of responsibility for the success or failure of the enterprise being balanced against a reluctance to let a sectional interest, hostile in many instances to the idea of capitalist enterprise, have a say in the operation of the firm. So far as the unions are concerned the attitude is in many instances even more confused. The slogan of workers' control of production facilities sounds well as long as it is not associated with the problem of actually making an enterprise operate at a profit. Workers' representation, and therefore responsibility, may have to be reconciled with a conflict between the interests of labour and that of the enterprise as a whole. Trade unions, like everyone else, prefer to follow a policy of having their cake and eating it—of wanting more say in the running of enterprises without necessarily accepting responsibility for success or failure.

What is the likely end result? The tide appears to be running in favour of employee participation along the German lines—and after all, West German industry in the postwar world has a success story to tell, whether or not that fact is relevant to employee participation. If, then, there is general acceptance within the European Community of employee participation in management, it is unlikely to be confined to that part of the Western developed world, or those other areas of the world in which the international enterprise operates. If participation in management is to be the norm in the parent company it will equally be the norm in the host countries, developed or underdeveloped.

8. *Finance and Taxation Issues*

INTRODUCTION

Financial and taxation issues are among the most sensitive areas for the international enterprise in its relations to the general public and national governments. The short-term effects of financial decisions by the enterprise are readily observed and measurable, but decisions on product policy or technology level are not so apparent.

The enterprise. In a multicurrency situation the enterprise will have to reduce its financial operations, for presentation, to a standard currency, namely its own. The fact however that its balance sheet shows its assets and liabilities in this form does not necessarily imply that its own currency is the actual as opposed to the nominal unit of account in everyday transactions. Nevertheless, a prerequisite of operating on an international basis is probably that the parent country currency is reasonably 'hard' and acceptable on the international front. The possibility of an international enterprise operating officially in a suspect currency for any length of time is highly unlikely. The enterprise would perforce have to adopt a new national unit of account and in the process either run foul of its own government or change nationality.

Where currency controls are the rule (and that means almost everywhere) the larger enterprise may have reached an agreement with the parent government to convert financial cash flows into the national currency, when convenient, in return for an assurance that reconversion facilities will be freely available. Nevertheless, where the national currency is depreciating steadily, there is an ever-present temptation to put the company's interests before national interests.

The national government. The general principle applied by governments is that capital transactions require approval, current account transactions do not. In other words, a decision to set up a foreign subsidiary would require consent insofar as it would almost certainly involve heavy foreign expenditure, while sale of products between one branch of the enterprise and another in a foreign country would not.

It can be difficult to distinguish between a capital and a current transaction. Since it is not, in practice, necessary to price such products 'at armslength', i.e. as though they were being sold to an outside customer, it may be possible to use this system to transfer resources from one country to another free of capital controls. This situation causes problems for other governments than merely the national government exercising power over the parent company. Host nations, trying to limit or stop a vital drain of foreign exchange resources by preventing the repatriation of foreign investment capital, may find it trickling through their fingers as transfer price goods nominally being sold to the parent by the subsidiary but in practice being substantially undervalued.

THE EFFECTS OF EXCHANGE RATES

Variations in Exchange Rates constitute a major financial problem for the international enterprise. Where the prevailing international policy favours fixed exchange rates then the danger facing the enterprise is being caught holding substantial amounts of a devalued currency. Unfortunately, any action by the enterprise to protect itself in a crisis worsens the crisis and attracts the hostility of the government whose currency is under attack. Direct transfer of assets out of the endangered currency is the most obvious example. Just as prevalent is the temptation for the enterprise to contribute to the 'leads and lags' phenomenon, i.e. accelerate payments out of the threatened currency by paying accounts before they are due, on the one hand, and delaying payment in the threatened currency for as long as possible, on the other. This behaviour is particularly easy for the international enterprise if payments are being made on a transfer basis from one national subsidiary to another, or to the parent company.

The situation where currencies are being allowed to float is rather different. There is a less obvious clash of interest with national governments but a more complex problem for the enterprise. Where a floating currency is depreciating on the foreign exchange market, the most likely cause is a relatively faster rate of inflation within the country. The enterprise may have considerable difficulty in deciding where to hold its major assets, and where and in what currency to raise working capital.

162   *The International Enterprise*

APPRAISING INVESTMENT OPPORTUNITIES

Any national enterprise has a constant problem of investment appraisal between competing use of its available funds or credit resources. To cope with the problem of evaluation, a number of appraisal techniques have been developed, the most widely quoted probably being the Discounted Cash Flow technique (DCF).

There are in practice, if not in theory, very great difficulties in applying such techniques to the real life situation which faces the international enterprise. As in so much else in business, the problem about applying quantitative techniques instead of using intuitive methods, or even hunches, is that the various components have to be quantified before the techniques can be used. One advantage of a nationally delimited enterprise however, is that it can generally assume a number of factors to be constant, as between alternative choices for expenditure. Inflation or tax rates cannot always be foreseen, but they are probably going to apply to all the alternative choices, and so can be treated as a constant within a national framework.

In international business no such assumptions can be made, once the appraisal has to be made of investment projects in different countries. There is not necessarily a pool of funds which can readily be switched from one project to the other: national currency controls see to that. There will also be different rates of tax applying (and possibly different rates of subventions or subsidies) from one country to another. There will almost certainly be different rates of inflation: different rates of exchange depreciation or appreciation: different rates of devaluation or opportunities for upwards revaluations: different political problems and different political risks.

Although it is possible to build up an elaborate model to test out the investment prospects using given capital resources, the problem of translating the exercise into reality becomes almost impossible simply because no one can confidently predict the quantities to be applied to all the inputs. In this situation an elaborate DCF calculation as between two widely differing and possibly relatively instable economies becomes positively dangerous if it persuades the executives concerned that they really are making a decision on objective and quantifiable grounds.

Putting the problem at so simple a level as to be virtually a caricature, how does one evaluate two projects in the same country, one of which gives a complete return on the investment and a small profit in a few years, the other a slower build up but a much higher rate of return over a decade or two? If one expressed the problem in DCF terms for a wide range of assumptions on interest rates, etc. the second project could be shown to have a far higher net present value than the former. Using an even simpler rate of return technique and depreciating the returns over the same interval, again the second project might show a higher rate of return.

Two all too plausible scenarios of national situations which could face the enterprise illustrates problems where conventional quantitative appraisal techniques can be irrelevant. The first is of a politically unstable country with a pro-Western or pro-free enterprise government, but under constant threat of political subversion, perhaps with an active guerilla campaign being mounted against the government. The second is of a national government headed by an elder statesman who led a liberation struggle in his earlier days. Then, when he came to power, the leader moderated his political views in the light of experience. Suppose then that such a statesman is ailing, under imminent prospect of death, with no obvious successor, or with an overtly anti-foreign successor waiting in the wings.

In either of these or other similar situations, projects have to be appraised in the light of the political situation as much as the financial one. A project which paid off modestly in say four years becomes a more realistic proposition than a financially more rewarding one which takes two or three times as long to pay off.

Even these oversimplified examples conceal a further complication, namely that the rate of return on the two projects may not be as predetermined as is sometimes supposed. In other words, the policy may be to extract all returns fast, if necessary borrowing locally at relatively uneconomic rates, or simply failing to maintain the capital equipment of the plant. Often when foreign-owned subsidiaries are nationalized by a host government, which is nevertheless prepared to pay compensation, a quarrel on valuation can turn on whether or not the foreign enterprise, fearing nationalization, had allowed the plant to be run down. Certainly the Chilean military junta which overthrew the left wing Allende regime could scarcely be accused of being overly left wing. But it continued the quarrel with the Kennecott and Anaconda corporations whose assets had been nationalized, using the same argument about the alleged run down state of the nationalized subsidiaries.

QUANTIFYING INVESTMENT RISK

Any type of insurance premium is in the last analysis merely a way of transforming a risk into a financial cost. In recent years,

developed nations which have substantial direct investment overseas
have been moving in the direction of offering insurance not merely
on export credit but on direct investment. Examples of this are
to be found in the U.S. Overseas Private Investment Corporation
(OPIC) and the British Export Credit Guarantee Department
(ECGD) policies, which cover direct investment. As in the case
of insurance on export credits, if an organization like this refuses
to extend a guarantee to investment in a particular country at
a particular time, it would be a bold enterprise which would take
the risk of investing, regardless.

INVESTMENT INCENTIVES BY HOST COUNTRIES

Host countries which are anxious to attract foreign investment
in manufacturing plant may be prepared to offer investment incentive
to international enterprises. The form these incentives take should
depend on the motive for wishing to attract foreign investment.
There are times, however, when these motives are mixed, even
contradictory, and the concessions may not therefore produce the
desired results.

There are three main motives for seeking foreign investment:
  a) to encourage the introduction of new technology
  b) to create more employment
  c) to earn or save foreign exchange

Almost certainly there will be elements of more than one of
these present on any particular occasion. For example the technology and employment motives may be sought, and yet clash.
Industry, based on new technology, is likely to be capital intensive
and create very few new jobs directly; indeed by making traditional
local skills obsolete it may reduce employment overall. If the
emphasis is to be on technology, concessions ought to include
capital equipment grants and generous capital depreciation allowances. If the emphasis is on employment, concessions ought to
lower the cost of hiring labour and possibly even discourage the
use of labour saving equipment.

There is another dimension to a possible clash between the technology and employment motives: that is a desire to steer new
developments into depressed regions where existing industry is dying
and new industry and industrial opportunities are needed. If the
intention is to steer industry into particular regions the investment
incentives are not necessarily limited to or even primarily intended
for foreign companies. A major target may be domestic enterprises,
which can be persuaded to relocate or at least set up branch
factories in designated regions. In the postwar period, for example,

the British government has poured large sums into the poorer regions, Wales, the North of England, Scotland and Northern Ireland in the form of investment grants or allowances and wage subventions. In very many instances it has been foreign firms, mainly American, but also German, Dutch, Swedish and Japanese who have taken up the investment incentive, rather than the British companies based on the Midlands and the South East of England. Even so, it has not always been clear which objective was paramount, more employment or new technology, and this confusion has been evident in chopping and changing, between investment grants, which are outright subsidies, investment allowances which encourage capital intensive firms, and a regional employment premium which subsidizes wages and so favours labour intensive industries. Nor is this confusion limited to British regions. It can be seen in the confusion of concessions by central governments to industry all round the periphery of the European Common Market, in the Republic of Ireland, Brittany and Bordeaux, Southern Italy and Sicily.

The other major objective is to encourage import substitution or actual exporting by new firms. Here it may be desirable to give tax concessions on the import of the initial capital equipment; or on raw materials; or to be very generous on the repayment on exports of the tax content of the inputs. This is readily done under a Value Added Tax system where in theory all tax elements can be identified and repaid to the exporter. The most generous tax concession of this type will be a complete fiscal exemption on export earnings for a period of years, a system offered to foreign investment by the Republic of Ireland.

Most tax systems inevitably operate in favour of one of the three types of enterprise to be attracted, namely the capital intensive, the labour intensive and the exporting firm. Unless the host country has a clear idea of what it really wants from foreign investment it may find investment incentives actually hinder rather than help. Perhaps only a tax holiday is neutral in this respect — or rather an indication that the government has not really clarified its own objectives in encouraging foreign investment. Conversely, if any international enterprise is bargaining with a host government for tax concessions, it would be advisable not merely to compare what one government is offering with another, but also what type of tax concessions would give a maximum return on its own particular strengths and weaknesses.

The Form of Investment Incentive

Although governments and businessmen tend to equate investment incentives with tax concessions, the latter is only one method. The other main method is outright subsidy, i.e. by investment grant rather than tax allowance.

There is a strong case for either subsidy or tax concessions. With a subsidy, both enterprise and host government know the exact value of the incentives, and there is therefore less reason and opportunity for the enterprise to indulge in transfer pricing as a means of increasing any tax concessions. As against this however, an outright subsidy of this nature puts no premium on efficiency or indeed long-term investment. The pros and cons of tax concessions are simply the reverse of the above. The most controversial aspect of the issue is transfer pricing and its influence on projects which may be exempted from tax.

THE FINANCING OF SUBSIDIARY COMPANIES

A common situation in a foreign subsidiary is that fixed capital is provided by the parent enterprise and working capital is raised through appropriate local channels. In the early stages particularly this clear cut division may not exist, and it is worth considering how and where finance may be raised. Essentially there are three possibilities a) raising finance in the parent country; b) raising finance in the host country; c) raising finance in a third country or through the international financial markets.

A. FUND RAISING IN THE PARENT COUNTRY

The most obvious source of difficulty has already been alluded to, namely that permission may have to be obtained from the government or central bank to export capital. Capital exports create a situation where foreign exchange earnings from exports are likely to be lost, and a drain on the balance of payments capital account substituted for these earnings. Generally, where controls are severe, a case may have to be made out of the benefits to be derived from the new venture—or at least its inevitability in face of pressure from the foreign market.

How then to prove a benefit, when the most immediate result is likely to be a loss of export earnings? One method may be to convince the authorities that the export of capital will generate a demand for capital equipment to be supplied from the parent country. The ideal situation will be that if an assembly or manufacturing plant is to be built abroad, the capital equipment, either new or second hand, will come from the parent country.

ALTERNATIVE METHODS

1. *Extended Credit by the Parent Company*

A stop-gap method which does not require currency control permission is simply to vary the credit terms and interest charges. Goods and services which are then being officially sold to the overseas subsidiary are covered by what is effectively a loan. The major complication, if any, comes from the host country which may place legal limitations on credit terms, to discourage imports, or it may insist on a deposit of the value of the imports being lodged with the central bank before the imports are allowed entry. Such requirements are generally speaking designed to reduce an import bill by hitting at luxury imports but the administrative machinery in an underdeveloped country may not be selective enough to discriminate successfully.

2. *Export Credits as a Means of Finance*

If the equipment is new and has to be built to specification it may be possible to use conventional export financing as a form of capital financing. The equipment could then be ordered by the new created subsidiary, to be paid for by conventional credit arrangements. Most industrial countries offer such long-term finance, backed by export credit guarantees. For example a U.S. corporation subsidiary might attempt to finance the sale of equipment through the Export Import Bank and the Foreign Credit Insurance Association (FCIA); a British company through financial guarantees to commercial banks covered by an Export Credit Guarantee Department (ECGD) insurance policy; and so on among all countries subscribing to export credit rules as laid down by the so-called Berne Union, which regularizes conditions under which credits may be extended.[24]

A curious anomaly which arose in the middle 1970's was that credit was being extended at a negative rate of interest. It is very desirable to have fixed rates of interest for long-term credits over say five to fifteen years, and most ·nations had let the rate settle around five to six per cent. The logic of this was that it represented about the average interest rate experienced over a number of years. Unfortunately, when inflation rates climbed well beyond the official interest rates, credit at five to six per cent was effectively being subsidized. Although most trading nations raised credit rates gradually, these tended to lag behind the rate of inflation. No nation appeared willing to take the risk of raising the credit rates to a realistic level. Apart from losing sales by so doing, it would have conceded that inflation was a long-term condition. At the same time, in spite of the efforts of the Berne Union to limit the length of time for which credit could be given, this tended to go on extending. The main benefactors of this largesse were probably the Communist countries trading on credit. There was, however, no reason why international enterprises should not benefit as well.

3. *Capital Value as a Key to Profit Repatriation*

If the equipment is reconditioned after having been replaced in use by plant in the parent company there are a number of factors to be considered. The system will be cheaper for the enterprise than having to find finance to buy brand new equipment. The parent government, however, will perceive that the loss of export earnings is not going to be balanced by exports of newly manufactured capital equipment and will be even less enthusiastic about the move by the enterprise to move production facilities elsewhere. But most important may be the valuation of the reconditioned equipment accepted by the host country, for this valuation may be important in fixing the level of subsequent profit repatriation, where exchange controls exist. Thus, for example, the Cartagena agreement of the Andean Pact (discussed in detail later) permits profit repatriation at the annual rate of fourteen per cent of the agreed capital value of the plant: the agreed capital value need not be the amortized book value of the equipment when it has been pulled out of production in the parent country.

4. *Direct Borrowing*

Direct borrowing may be possible from home banks. Leaving aside the requirement for permission to export capital, there are some serious problems. The most obvious is that such heavy borrowing from home banks or other financial institutions may be easy but it also ties up the amount of credit available for domestic operations.

5. *Self-financing Operations*

For many enterprises especially the smaller ones which find credit raising difficult for foreign ventures it may be necessary to finance the project from internal resources. The major problem is that few enterprises are likely to have such liquid funds available; and even if they had, it would perhaps be difficult to justify the foreign operation as the best use of resources.

Finally, in this review of methods of financing from the parent country, it is probably true to say that, after the initial funding required to set up the subsidiary, the transfer of substantial capital funds from the parent company to the subsidiary is likely to be the exception rather than the rule. In the past quarter of a century most of the world's currencies have varied enormously in their hardness and it cannot be said that any major country is likely in the near future to dispense entirely with capital controls. Large outflows of capital which are apparently taking away jobs and knowhow from even the richest countries are increasingly unpopular. Further investment however can still be carried on discreetly, by selling to subsidiaries at very low transfer prices, or by extending credit arrangements of the type discussed above.

B. FUND RAISING IN THE HOST COUNTRY

There are two possibilities, the raising of loans and the issue of equity stock.

Loans

A number of problems have to be considered. The major one may be whether there are adequate financial institutions to make such loans available at reasonable rates. In many developed countries a form of industrial banking, perhaps by a Societé Generale or some other financial institution, may be the obvious source from which to borrow in the absence of conventional commercial banking institutions such as are found for example in the U.S.A. or Britain. It may well be that the organization will not be content merely to lend capital but will press for a joint venture status. Thus it is possible, for example, to find that in Brazil, an insurance society becomes a partner in a joint venture with a foreign company, largely because such a company is one of the few financial institutions in Brazil able to finance the building of a foreign subsidiary, but unwilling to do so merely on a loan basis.

A second point has been mentioned in another context, namely that in really underdeveloped countries affluent individuals simply do not consider putting money into local financial institutions. They might buy gold, jewellery, land or property on their own account: they would not dream of using it to finance a foreign enterprise. This reluctance to put money into the banking system is not easily overcome, particularly where the reliability of newly created banks is suspect or where there is a substantial and varying rate of inflation.

The same issue of inflation poses particular difficulties to the enterprise. It is possible to consider borrowing locally at say thirty per cent interest when there is a steady rate of inflation of say twenty per cent. But what if the rate of inflation is, say, one hundred per cent annually (and quite a few underdeveloped countries have reached such a figure). Any borrowing on more than a week-to-week basis is impossible because all that is certain is that the rate of inflation will not remain static—either it will be brought down drastically, with ruinous consequences to debtors, or the currency will collapse, with ruinous effects to the lender. Finally, there is the problem of whether or not the parent company will provide a financial guarantee on loans negotiated locally. There are. of course, pros and cons in the situation. Essentially however the non-guarantee approach emphasizes the necessity of the subsidiary to pay its way in the world.

Equity Shares

Again there are two possibilities a) Equity shares in the subsidiary and b) shares in the parent enterprise being quoted internationally.

A. Local equity shares.   This is a solution which appeals to many nationalistic governments in the underdeveloped world, who wish to see a majority share of a subsidiary, and therefore its control, firmly in national hands. The enterprise is then expected to issue shares, retaining for itself whatever maximum is permitted under the current legislation (often only 49 per cent) and by selling the rest to raise local capital.

Most countries have no stock exchange and it may be necessary for the government (often committed to Socialism) to assist in the creation of a Stock Exchange, whose very existence is anathema to pure socialist doctrine. But, as has been noted, even where a stock exchange does exist only a small section of the community may be attracted to it (and those, the relatively well-to-do, may be the natural enemies of the regime). The man in the street would as soon buy shares in the moon as pieces of paper in such an organization.

Some stock exchanges do flourish in areas like Hong Kong but virtually as a variety of gambling house rather than a serious attempt to solve the problem of funnelling local capital into industry or commerce. It is probably accurate to say that in the one hundred or more countries which permit private ownership of industry or commerce, not more than a tenth have a significant stock exchange system, or indeed any method of making possible the buying and selling of equities on an open market. Although several governments, which a few years previously would have denounced the stock exchange as an excrescence of capitalism, are now endeavouring to promote one locally, a mere government fiat that it is now approved will not change the grass roots situation. In the industrial

West only a small minority in any society are equity holders: in the underdeveloped world the numbers are miniscule. Gold, jewels, land or cattle are instinctively preferred.

B. Equity shares in the parent enterprise. The second possibility is that equity in the international enterprise should be issued, if the existing shareholders are agreeable. Again, in theory there are considerable advantages: an international enterprise logically implies international ownership as well as international markets, and it is increasingly the practice for large enterprises to have quotations in major foreign stock exchanges, as well as in domestic ones. Indeed, some definitions of a multinational enterprise would claim that international equity hold is an essential condition.

The problems remain formidable. The first is to persuade local nationals to buy them, if they are not used to a money and credit economy. Almost certainly the task is much easier than for shares in the subsidiary but the dangers even are greater. The shares become more attractive to those who want to get their money out of the country, again the natural enemies of the regime. Supporters of the regime too, government officials and politicians are often corrupt and might ensure that only they or their friends could buy in—an arrangement with obvious advantages as long as the government does not change. If there are currency controls, a premium can arise and the whole market in equities be distorted to the embarrassment both of the enterprise and the host government, and with the probability of 'stock drift', i.e. shares moving out of the currency areas to which they had been allocated.

The other side of the problem is that the parent company government may choose to impose capital controls. Virtually all developed countries do, and the issue of equity shares on this basis would require at least as much justification as the export of capital.

Notwithstanding the difficulties, it is probable that international enterprises may be forced to think along these lines, even at the risk of exacerbating conflicts of interest. Equally, those governments of underdeveloped nations which are hesitatingly moving towards a stock exchange system to secure local participation in subsidiaries may in time conclude that the best way of preserving national interests is in the shareholders' meetings (and possibly the board rooms) of the international enterprises.

C. FUND RAISING IN A THIRD COUNTRY OR THROUGH INTERNATIONAL FINANCE MARKETS

There are a variety of theoretical methods of getting access to funds made available through the World Bank, the International Development Agency (IDA) and similar international bodies which exist to further the flow of capital into the underdeveloped world. For most purposes, however, fund raising in third countries means recourse to Eurocurrency sources, namely Eurocurrency and Eurobond markets.[25] To a large extent these exist to make use of currency resources available to financial institutions outside the national territory where the currency is the official 'money'. The Eurodollar is literally the dollar available in a dollar account in a European country and by that reason free from any normal U.S. capital restraints. The size of the funds available varies with the degree of restrictions imposed on capital transfers and the amount of funds emanating from sources not overly friendly to the U.S. government, but willing to hold dollars outside the immediate control of the U.S. monetary authorities. It may be possible to borrow currencies such as the dollar for investment purposes at reasonable interest rates, in London or other non-U.S. centres.

Finally, as in most aspects of international business, it is the large enterprise which has most freedom of access to funds within its own home territory, in the host country, or elsewhere. The small company with a limited equity issue quoted perhaps in a single stock exchange has much more of a problem.

PROTECTING THE ENTERPRISE AGAINST DEPRECIATING CURRENCY

Any international enterprise is likely to find its assets and liabilities expressed in at least two currencies. If one of these is imminently likely to be devalued and to depreciate substantially, then the whole valuation of the enterprise is liable to be changed arbitrarily overnight.

Common sense suggests that the enterprise will limit its assets and preferably extend its liabilities in the threatened currency. This is essentially what the various measures to protect the enterprise are all about. The simplest technique is the Exposure method. Assets which are valued in the threatened currency are regarded as 'Exposed', i.e. they will lose value in the event of a devaluation/depreciation. Assets which are expressed in a hard currency which will not lose value are regarded as 'Neutral' of 'Unexposed'. So, tentatively, may be tangible assets expressed in the threatened currency whose value might in time be expected to adjust upwards, even if an immediate paper loss were incurred by devaluation/depreciation. The third possible condition is 'Covered' assets. Here the enterprise will actually gain from a devaluation, because liabilities which the enterprise has incurred are expressed in the threatened currency, and will be reduced in terms of the other currency in the event of devaluation.

All that is involved in the so-called 'Exposure technique' is that the enterprise's assets and liabilities are laid out in the currency in which they are legally expressed (or, in the case of fixed assets, locally valued). Then, as far as possible, items will be moved from the exposed at least to the neutral status, and preferably to the covered status. This is rather a roundabout way of saying that any assets should be moved into the hard currency valuation and any liabilities into the soft currency.

Even in the very simple two currency situation, one hard, one soft, there are practical limitations. The most obvious is that the enterprise's assets are often someone else's liabilities, and the enterprise's liabilities someone else's assets. That individual or company will be attempting to achieve the reverse situation so that they gain from devaluation.

The other major problem has been touched upon in the definitions. Some fixed assets which are valued in the threatened currency cannot be moved or revalued meaningfully overnight. They are at best unexposed. The hope of the enterprise must be that, even if their value drops arbitrarily in terms of the other currency, the inflation which so often accompanies devaluation will gradually raise the value of the assets again.

A few variants can be perceived, i.e. attempts to borrow on the strength of unexposed assets and use the credits raised to purchase hard currency. But these tactics are effectively merely speculation, and best left to experts in the field: they are not the raison d'etre of the enterprise whose tactics are more or less defensive.

The Exposure technique has always been practised instinctively by international enterprises, but was first definitively outlined in the 1950's as a method of formalizing tactics for American enterprises threatened with devaluation elsewhere. The tacit assumption then was that the hard currency was the national currency of the parent company, i.e. the dollar. There was thus no conflict between the interests of the company protecting its assets, and the U.S. government. Since this time, however, the hardness of the dollar can no longer be taken for granted. U.S. enterprises have therefore found themselves at times in the situation facing European international enterprises from the 1940's onwards. What happens if the threatened currency is the enterprise's own national currency? The same principles apply, but this time the efforts of the enterprise to protect its assets are working against the interests of its own government if the latter is trying to prevent devaluation or depreciation. This presents a much more delicate problem for the enterprise which will probably be less anxious to offend against the interests or indeed the financial controls of its own government, than those of other governments.

The Effects of Floating Exchange Rates

The Exposure technique is best designed to meet an identifiable financial crisis: that was a fair description of any of the European devaluations of the 1940's and 1950's. Then, under a regime of fixed exchange rates, a national government whose currency was threatened was expected to defend the existing parity by internal measures, the use of its gold or convertible currency reserves, and swap or borrowing arrangements with other governments, the International Monetary Fund and associated groupings. If all of this failed then devaluation was decisive, probably well over ten per cent, and possibly leaving the currency slightly but not decisively underdevalued rather than the reverse. It was necessary to do this to remove uncertainty. A small devaluation might mean another devaluation shortly and speculation could continue: a very large devaluation would bring about other currency devaluations which might defeat the object of the original devaluation. If the devaluation were pitched at the correct level, the international enterprise would find it possible to go back to whatever happened to be the most useful disposition of assets in national currencies, for everyday business, not for defence against a devaluation crisis.

The situation was changed by the U.S. dollar crisis in 1971 when the dollar was not decisively devalued, but allowed to float downwards to find its own level. This created an entirely new situation, not merely for other currencies but for the international enterprises.

The reasoning behind the U.S. government's decision to float, rather than to devalue was simple. The U.S. dollar was the major currency in the world. If the U.S.A. devalued, other nations would also be inclined to devalue as well and no one could readily foresee what the end result would be, or whether the U.S. decision would not simply be frustrated. The American government's conditions for a return to a fixed parity were that the other nations would agree collectively, which currencies would be revalued upwards or downwards and by how much. The Smithsonian Agreement at the end of 1971 saw such a settlement, the main point being a substantial revaluation upwards in dollar terms for Germany and Japan, and lesser revaluations for other currencies including the Pound Sterling. The Smithsonian Agreement broke down because Sterling could not be conveniently sustained at the new level and floating rates returned.

So far as the international enterprise is concerned the results were to make a comparatively simple problem of defensive tactics far more complex, for two reasons. The Exposure technique is essentially a defensive posture for an emergency rather than a long-term financial strategy. It worked well when everyone could see there was a crisis and equally could agree when the crisis was over. In this situation, floating exchange rates represent a perpetual state of crisis which is not obviously going to be resolved overnight by a once for all devaluation. The second point is that it is apparent that if any significant currency is under threat, then the government concerned will probably follow the U.S. example in 1971 and the British example in 1972, i.e. to let its currency float and refrain from refixing rates until it has got agreement with other currencies about relative revaluation. This means that there is no longer merely a two currency problem, one of which is liable to fall in value, the other to remain constant. In future, such a crisis will mean that some currencies may rise relative to the enterprise's national currency, others may fall. Such a situation is not entirely new—even under pre-1971 conditions a devaluation of a major currency could bring varying degrees of revaluation elsewhere, but what previously *could* happen almost certainly *will* happen in the future.

Finally, in theory, floating exchange rates are supposed to be temporary measures; there is often nothing more permanent than a temporary measure and international enterprises may just have to learn to live with floating exchange rates as they have to live with varying rates of inflation.

Monetary Correction—the Answer to Inflation?

The international enterprise exists in an era of 'funny money'. It is not easy to say whether inflation is a temporary and curable condition or a persistent state which can be moderated but not eradicated. Since the end of World War II, inflation has been a persistent factor. Since the middle 1960's it has been one of the dominating factors in international finance.

One method which has been considered as a means of reducing its impact has been the concept of monetary correction factor such as has been developed in Brazil. In its simplest form this is a system whereby the face value of loans is raised over time to keep pace with the falling value of currency, i.e. what matters is the real value not the monetary value. At its very simplest, if the cost of living rose by twenty per cent in a year the face value of any loan would be written up accordingly.

There are two major advantages: firstly, interest rates for borrowing would be more realistic since they would not have to include an inflationary element; secondly, more stability would be introduced into an economy. After all, in a highly inflationary situation there is no incentive to lend and every incentive to spend.

The disadvantages are the practical administrative problems of revaluing loans at least annually, and the fact that the correction would probably help to perpetuate inflationary processes. Psychologically, too, the danger is that such policies might be taken as signifying that inflation was a permanent feature. The widespread adoption of a monetary correction factor might pose considerable accounting problems for the international enterprise. Overall, however, the merits are in practice considerable.

BARTER AND BILATERAL TRADE

The subject of Barter is not one which fits neatly into any scheme of treatment in international business. Nevertheless it has to be considered both because of its importance in world trade, and because the international enterprise is particularly likely to be involved in it. It may be convenient therefore to deal with it in an addendum to a section on finance, at the risk of digressing temporarily from the main theme of this chapter.

Barter is often seen as the most primitive state of exchange, to be replaced at a very early stage in any society by a more convenient system involving money as the medium of exchange. On the international scene however, barter is by no means primitive and it is certainly not being replaced by monetary exchanges. Indeed if one includes with barter its slightly more sophisticated version of bilateral trade, on one definition at least, it comprises well over half the world's trade.

Why then is barter so widespread, when financial deals appear to be that much simpler? Briefly it is because most countries in the world are to a greater or lesser extent short of foreign exchange —of other nations' currencies. Foreign exchange reserves in this sense might be regarded as a lubricant—not all that much is needed considering the power involved, but too little can cause any machine to seize up. A nation with inadequate reserves of foreign exchange may be paying its way in the world, but still could find its foreign trade hampered by a shortage of 'ready money' at any time.

The tendency for many nations to be chronically short of foreign exchange has been exacerbated at times by an overall shortage of foreign reserves, i.e. an acceptable international currency. It is unnecessary to go into the details of why and when there has been an overall shortage of world liquidity, except to say that if the increase in world trade is not more or less matched with an increase in the quantity and value of gold or an acceptable substitute, then multilateral buying and selling by all nations becomes an impossible ideal. A nation may be forced into straight barter deals with another, or a treaty involving a bilateral trade deal because neither can afford to run a deficit which would have to be paid for by gold. Trade, then, more or less has to balance if no currency is to change hands.

The above is an enormously simplified version of a highly complex issue but it does serve to illustrate the type of country which might choose to deal in barter or bilateral trade. These are essentially two. Firstly the Communist countries which are overall short of the relatively hard convertible currencies of the West. In trading with Western countries they may have to resort from time to time to barter or partial barter deals, in the manner described in Chapter 2. Even as between each other there is still a measure of barter because of currency inconvertibility.

The other major group of nations which indulge in barter deals are the less well off of the underdeveloped nations, chronically short of foreign exchange. Sometimes there will be bilateral deals between each other or with Communist trading partners, less frequently with individual companies in the West. A typical pattern of trade may be as follows. Raw materials fluctuate notoriously in price, doubling or halving in price, often within a year. It sometimes happens that an underdeveloped raw material producing nation will enjoy a windfall because of vastly inflated prices and will then spend its newly acquired foreign exchange recklessly. But by the time the bills start accumulating the commodity boom has collapsed and the nation simply cannot meet the cost. What sometimes happens then is a moratorium agreed with the nation's creditors for debts to be paid off over the years. During such a period any further trade is likely to be a cash on the nail affair, or if foreign exchange is not available on that basis, the country may offer to pay in commodities for imports. Barter trade becomes a necessity until the debt situation is resolved.

In recent years a new barter situation has emerged, not from scarcity but from excess. The oil producers, finding themselves with vast quantities of foreign reserves, which they could not usefully spend and which were visibly depreciating under inflationary conditions, signed long-term deals, exchanging specified quantities of oil, not for more foreign exchange, but for quantities of manufactures or commodities regardless of the relative changes in price. This sort of deal is of very dubious value in the long run. It poses too many questions about fluctuations of prices particularly prices of raw materials. In a long-term deal based on predicting and averaging the change of prices of raw materials, one party or the other is liable to be badly burnt. If inflation can be overcome, or a satisfactory method of credits can be agreed this barter from excess may well disappear.

Bilateral Deals

So far the principle of the bilateral deal has not been examined. It may best be seen by an imaginary example that bears a resemblance to several actual deals. Israel and Turkey are two countries which are likely to suffer a chronic shortage of foreign exchange, and might therefore choose to set up a bilateral agreement. This might provide for U.S. $10 million of trade each way in a year.

The first point to note is that neither country proposes to pay out any dollars to the other. The dollar is a unit of account only. Once the deal has been completed, any Israeli businessman who wished to buy goods from a foreign source would require to get permission from the Israeli Central Bank to change Israeli currency. If it appeared that he could buy an acceptable version of the product from a Turkish source, he might find that he was refused permission to acquire currency to buy the goods elsewhere, say in the U.S.A. or Western Europe. Reluctantly, no doubt, he would settle for a Turkish supplier. When he came to buy, however, he would simply be required to pay into the Israeli central bank the value calculated according to the agreed exchange rate but in Israeli currency. The Turkish supplier would be paid in Turkish currency through his central bank and that transaction would be debited against the Israeli credit with Turkey. A Turkish buyer would go through the same procedure, and an overall total of up to $10M dollars of trade each way on a bilateral basis would be possible.

It is probable of course that towards the end of the year one country would still have a net credit with the other. It could not be expected to receive dollars in settlement but might be prepared in effect to sell its currency quota at a discount to a foreign trader who wanted to buy in the other country and might find the 'leftovers' of the credit cheaper than paying in a Western hard currency.

Probably too, the majority of buyers on both sides would not be entirely satisfied, but from the national point of view the two central banks would have conserved foreign currency by discriminating in favour of the other partner and against other nations. The next stage might be for a clearing house arrangement whereby several bilateral deals between two partners could be balanced off, still with no actual settlement in hard currencies. Such arrangements were the norm in Western Europe for a few years after World War 2, when the European nations effectively discriminated against the dollar and in favour of each other—the entire arrangement having the agreement of the U.S. government which saw that the alternatives were more dollar aid or less international trade. Once the immediate postwar crisis had passed, multilateral trade, dependent on freely convertible currencies, returned. This period of non-convertibility was, as it happened, the stage in which U.S. corporations chose to manufacture in Europe, because they could not readily get paid for exports (see Chapter 1).

The Problems of the Second Best Deal

If bilateral or barter deals enable trade to take place without valuable hard currency being lost, why go on to multilateral trade and convertible currencies at all? The answer briefly is that such bilateral deals are almost inevitably second best, as two historical examples may show.

In the early 1960's under the Sukarno regime, Indonesia was moving closer and closer to the Communist world in political terms. In economic terms the Indonesian government's domestic and international extravagances had produced rampant inflation internally, while exhausting foreign exchange reserves. Economically, the country was virtually bankrupt.

The government then set about negotiating a series of barter deals with Communist countries: a typical one was with Yugoslavia and involved the trading of oil, ores and raw materials from Indonesia for manufactured goods and textiles from Yugoslavia. On the face of it the arrangement was a neat solution to some of the most pressing economic problems of both countries. In little over a year, however, the arrangement collapsed amid mutual recrimination. Both parties loudly accused the other of failure to live up to the terms of the agreement, and the specific complaint was the same on both sides. It was that whenever an opportunity arose to sell any of the listed products for hard currency to a third customer, then that customer got the goods, not the barter partner who had to wait and take what he was offered. It is unimportant in the present context to make a judgement about which party was at fault, or whether both were. But the case illustrates the important point that, in many cases, if barter deals are a second best, then the participants are liable to get second best treatment from each other.

The Yugoslav experience was repeated with other partners in the Communist world with more or less the same results, and Indonesia found itself in the almost unique situation of having virtually no credit rating with either ideological camp, and so reduced to virtual cash on the nail trade. With the fall of the Sukarno regime, the Indonesian economy was drastically overhauled by the new government which re-established friendly links with the West and reversed its political as well as its economic policies.

The second example is of an earlier and rather less well defined problem arising from barter. In the late 1950's Egypt swung towards friendship and dependence on the Soviet Union after the Suez War of 1956. Traditional trading links with the West were severed and the Egyptian regime, officially 'Arab Socialist' concluded barter deals with the Soviet Union—again both partners being very short of foreign exchange. In this case too the trouble arose because of the superior attractions of Western trade for hard cash, this time for high quality Egyptian cotton. By an ironic twist, however, it was not the Egyptians who were at fault—it was the Russians who, finding themselves having to absorb vast quantities of Egyptian cotton, began to sell the surplus in Western markets, and in the process spoiled the market for the original producers.

The problem of the second best aspect of the barter deal runs through the whole concept. Either the goods which are being traded are in some way inferior, and not therefore the first choice for the buyer; or if they are of high quality to sell on the open market for convertible currencies, then either the producer or the consumer in the deal may be tempted to sell the products around outside the deal.

This same situation is seen in barter deals with the Communist countries where, as has been observed, foreign trade organizations may wish to pay part of the deal in kind rather than cash. Many exporters to Communist countries regard this as an unmitigated nuisance, and the foreign trade organizations seem to accept this point because they tend to offer the commodities at a discount. In some instances, therefore, what may look to the Communist Foreign Trade Organization like a smart deal at the expense of the capitalist world, may spoil the market for sales of the bartered commodities for hard cash.

The next stage in barter. The attachment of Communist countries to the barter deal has been seen in many agreements with Western enterprises. The Occidental Petroleum Corporation's contract to build fertilizer plant in the Soviet Union, against partial payment on such products as phosphates and urea has an estimated $8000M dollar value over twenty years. The same pattern has been repeated by Shell (U.K.), Montedison (Italy), Krupps (West Germany) and many other international enterprises, in most East European countries.

The implications will be explored in more detail later on.

National attitudes. The attitude of Western nations to barter deals is mixed, but very often suspicious. Insofar as there is any American attitude it is still that of reluctant acceptance. In part this is historical, in part shrewd calculation. Historically the U.S. government has had good reason to fear discrimination against the dollar when the dollar was the world's most desirable currency. Discrimination was reluctantly accepted as necessary in the immediate postwar European situation, but the U.S. government pressed vigorously for the removal of discriminatory currency practices as rapidly as possible. In the contemporary world the problem is not quite the same dollar discrimination, but the use of methods which limit the use of the dollar in international trade and the use of U.S. financial institutions in general. In spite of the vicissitudes of the dollar in the 1960's and early 1970's it is still the only world wide international currency which remotely compares with gold for international acceptability. If multilateral trade therefore means less dollar discrimination in any sense than barter or bilateral trade, then the U.S.A. presses for that. At the same time, it is aware of the realities of the massive U.S./Soviet Trade Deals. The alternative to payment in kind would be huge U.S. credits to the Communist world and this is not a course which commends itself to President or Congress.

The British attitude has probably changed more drastically than the U.S.A. While sterling was the third international currency after gold and the dollar, and much world trade was carried out in sterling, then the official attitude tended to discourage barter deals. The collapse of sterling as an international currency has transformed the situation, and the balance of advantage or disadvantage is no longer so clear. British banks still finance a great deal of world trade — and the European dollar market is dominated by the British, not the American banks. There is therefore advantage in multilateral trade to a trading economy like Britain. On the other hand, the vast facilities for commodity trading in London, again the commodity centre for the world, means that barter deals in commodities can be more easily converted into hard cash in London than anywhere else.

Other nations have shown themselves more ready to experiment, and the Dutch and Swiss play a role in barter dealing out of all proportion to their size.

Switch Traders and Trading Houses

The fact of barter on a world-wide scale has created opportunities as well as problems, for individuals and companies. The profession of switch trader is virtually a postwar phenomenon. The switch trader attempts to marry up commodities and wants, buying up commodities included in barter deals, taking over the remaining credits towards the end of an international bilateral deal of the type described above, or putting together a multilateral barter deal matching commodity and demand among several, perhaps many, buyers and sellers.

Conclusions

So far as the international enterprise is concerned, the implications of barter can be seen either as an obstacle or an opportunity. Some large organizations find it convenient to set up organizations to dispose of commodities acquired by barter. Others may go further and convert the barter situation into a new enterprise, as a trading house. One of the major advantages of the international enterprise to the underdeveloped nation is that it can give the nation's products access to developed markets: the same can be said of bartered commodities. If any organization can readily absorb and dispose of these at a profit, it is the international enterprise.

TAXATION—THE ENTERPRISE VIEWPOINT

Taxation poses two major problems for the international enterprise:
  a) it complicates the issue of deciding what is most profitable on an international basis
  b) it poses problems of how to minimize payment.

A.   Measuring Efficiency and Profitability

Some of the problems of rational investment appraisal have been discussed earlier in this section. The main point is that taxation (and its obverse, subsidy) can change the order of choice. In the domestic market, profit can be used as a measure of efficiency. In the international market the most profitable project may be that which attracts least tax or most subsidy. Efficiency and profitability are not necessarily the same. When a Japanese ball-bearing manufacturer is looking for a site in Europe, it is at least as interested in the relative subsidies offered by various governments as by wage rates and productivity. Equally Ireland does not immediately conjure up the same vision of efficiency as say West Germany. But comparing the relatively meagre incentives offered by a German government with the few problems of employment and none of foreign exchange earnings, with the very generous subsidies plus tax exemptions on exports offered by the Irish government, a decision to invest in Ireland rather than Germany may make sense.

B. *Minimizing Tax Payments*

The enterprise has to deal with at least two tax levying authorities, the host and parent governments. It has to a limited extent some discretion about how it will move its tax liabilities between these two authorities; it cannot simply transfer all liabilities to one government or the other, but there is generally some room for manoeuvre; with the implication that it will normally seek to minimize its liabilities.

If, for example, profits earned by a subsidiary are left with the subsidiary, and not repatriated, it may be able to avoid paying the parent government's taxation on these profits, and so pay only the host government's taxation. But if the subsidiary wants to reinvest these profits at home, or has to use them to pay dividends at home then it will incur more tax liabilities at home. In general therefore it can be said that, particularly if taxation is lower in the host country than at home, there is no obvious incentive to repatriate profits to face taxation, if there is any possibility of the funds being invested profitably by the subsidiary. The tax penalty which may be incurred by moving profits from one country to another qualifies the notion that an enterprise may have financial assets which can be moved freely from one part of the world to another.

So far in this section it has been assumed that pricing policy is 'neutral' so far as taxation is concerned, i.e. that it has been determined by one of the methods described in Chapter 6. But the enterprise may use a transfer pricing policy as a means of minimizing taxation. Transfer pricing is not used merely for this purpose: other uses, namely in respect of currency or customs duty transactions, have been noted. But clearly transfer pricing can be used to minimize taxation by moving the tax burden to wherever the tax rate is lightest on profits.

There are two problems about transfer pricing. Firstly, although its importance is probably exaggerated, that does not prevent its existence being used as a stick with which to beat the enterprise. Studies which have been carried out on the issue suggest that enterprises do not seek to exploit transfer pricing exceptionally or act in a way which will always minimize taxation on a world wide scale. [26] Possibly they are aware that a proven abuse in the form of tax evasion would bring a scale of response which would make the risk simply not worthwhile.

The other problem is that transfer pricing for taxation avoidance might produce the diametrically opposite policy to transfer pricing for either currency or customs duty purposes. Generally, taxation in subsidiaries is at a lower level than in the home industrial territory —which would suggest the need for exporting profits as well as products, but if the plan is to recover costs or repatriate profits fast in an uncertain foreign market, this produces a conflict of aims. The reverse applies to customs valuation where attempts to minimize taxation at home can affect tariff payments abroad.

Dividend Payments by Subsidiaries

It would appear then that the dividend policy of a subsidiary may be different from that of the parent company. This is likely to be particularly the case when the subsidiary is not wholly-owned but has local partners or shareholders. The dividend policy of the subsidiary might be to pay the largest possible dividends in order to recover the initial cost as quickly as possible. The difficulty of such a policy might be limitations on remittances of profits. At the other extreme it might be deemed inexpedient to plough profits back with little or no dividend being declared for years —always assuming that there were no local equity holders or partners to be appeased. In general, if there is a degree of uncertainty about the reactions of tax authorities, it makes sense to have a regular dividend and profit repatriation policy, if only to establish that the enterprise is not attempting to evade local control in an emergency.

Multilateral Transactions

So far the assumption has been made that the decision is simply whether to let tax liabilities accrue to the subsidiary or the parent company. It is perfectly possible however to have more than two companies involved. Thus American multinationals have been known to build plant in Britain or another relatively low cost area to serve the entire European market. But although costs might be lower in Britain, tax rates could be lower still in Belgium, and a European regional headquarters established there. Thus, sales from the British plant to a German customer, for example, are routed through the Belgium company and the mark-up takes place there. The situation costs the British government tax revenues and foreign exchange, and is scarcely likely to be welcomed by it. But short of evidence of blatant transfer pricing there is little the latter can do about it.

The Profit Centre Concept

The limited ability of the enterprise to move its liability for taxation to low tax areas means that an important control and measure of performance is lost, in the effort to establish a profit centre.

At the risk of oversimplification, the subsidiary with the best profit record indicates a possible area for further investment or indicates the quality of local executives or the work force. But once profits can be moved about in a rather arbitrary manner it becomes difficult to rate the performance of subsidiaries, or their staff whose performance may be up or downgraded by the enterprise's reactions to the prevailing tax rates.

It might seem an obvious point to avoid such judgements: it is however very easy to assume that an enterprise has an overall taxation policy, and has worked out all the other implications. Many enterprises however do not seem to work them out on a systematic basis, and profit centres are established by local decisions, i.e. executives aware that their career may be judged on profit records, attempt to establish their own areas of profitability regardless of the overall interests of the enterprise. This however is not a phenomenon confined only to tax policy.

TAXATION—THE NATIONAL VIEWPOINT

The problems of the national authorities are the reverse of those facing the enterprise. In general, however, it can be said that the problems of the host government are more difficult than those of the parent government.

The Host Government

The difficulty of the host government in getting information from the parent company in another country has already been discussed. Such information may be essential in determining whether pricing policies are being used to limit tax liabilities to an unacceptable degree. Nevertheless, and not withstanding the practical limitations imposed on the tax authorities of the host country, the subsidiary will be liable to tax on its declared local profits just as any other locally registered company.

There is however a potent political factor in the situation. Many subsidiaries are located in countries which are politically unstable or where anti-foreign sentiment is easily aroused and exploited. 'Tax the foreigner' is a common slogan, even if it is not clear that the ultimate tax burden falls on the foreigner and is not passed on to the local customers.

The other side of the taxation issue is the extent to which fiscal measures can be used as a method of encouraging foreign investment. Some possible forms have already been briefly touched upon: investment grants and allowances which effectively reduce and perhaps neutralize the tax burden for at least the early years of the subsidiary's existence; and complete tax exemption on export profits.

It is even theoretically possible for subsidiaries, subventions and tax holidays to exceed the total tax bill. This is not generally an intended result, but may occur if transfer pricing on capital equipment imported or products exported are sufficiently at variance with their true cost.

The Parent Government

The tax policy of the parent government will be affected by its attitude to overseas investment by its national companies. It is obviously not always likely to be pleased at the intention of an enterprise to transfer capital industrial capacity and jobs abroad, by the setting up of foreign subsidiaries. It is likely to be even less enthusiastic if it appears that the decision to set up abroad is based, not on an objective comparison of investment opportunities at home and abroad, but on the payment of subsidies and tax holidays by other governments. Tax concessions, if they tempt enterprises to move production facilities, are arguably an involved way of exporting unemployment by subsidy.

Two policy decisions on taxation have to be made by the parent government:

a) The first is to decide whether to tax profits made by the subsidiary; and if so whether to treat taxation already paid to the host country as a tax credit or simply as a deductible item. If the decision is not to tax the earnings of subsidiaries, this will be an encouragement to foreign investment. Such a policy makes sense particularly if the economy has overfull employment at home, or an embarrassingly large foreign exchange surplus. If the tax credit policy is followed the tax levied by the parent government will be rather marginal, i.e. it will be necessary to calculate the notional tax on the net (after host tax) profit and then deduct the host tax from the amount of tax payable. Such a policy is broadly neutral in respect of foreign investment by national enterprises. If the tax deductible policy is followed, then the enterprise has to pay double taxation: first the host country tax; then the full parent country tax on the after host country tax profits. Indeed, if the parent country intends a punitive tax level it can levy tax on net after host country profits plus a notional profit based on the value of subsidies, etc. paid by the host country. Such a policy is clearly intended to make investment abroad very unprofitable. It carries the implication that subsidiaries will be closed down or sold off. It also carries the risk that the enterprise may be tempted to change nationality, perhaps to that of its most profitable subsidiary.

The double taxation proposition poses a very serious threat to the international enterprise and is of course a weapon used by opponents of foreign investment and 'runaway' industries, i.e. domestic trade unions of the parent country who see employment opportunities being transferred abroad tend to favour such action. The Hartke-Burke proposals to the U.S. Senate were intended to achieve just these results, and enjoyed the support of the U.S. labour movement.[27]

Finally, in this subsection it has to be emphasized that there is a danger in setting up such precise categories of policy, as shown above. In real life, governments may be rather more confused about their priorities and motives. They start on one policy and are likely to carry on with it even if circumstances alter, until a new interest forces a change.

b) The second policy decision is whether taxation will be levied in the year in which profits are made, or only if and when profits are repatriated. Again, the decision turns on the question of how anxious the government is to encourage or discourage foreign investment.

ACCOUNTANCY STANDARDS AND PRACTICES

There is a wide variety of standards and practices in financial matters even within developed societies; and when the comparison is extended to underdeveloped nations, the variation is even greater.

There are three elements which help to explain the variety:

a) the degree of financial disclosure required by the fiscal authorities;
b) the degree of sophistication and standards prevailing in the accountancy profession in each country;
c) the national attitude towards paying taxes.

a) Some countries require very little disclosure indeed, and it is virtually impossible for the outsider to obtain information on costs, profits, pricing policy, etc. Generally, where there is a wide measure of equity holding in the general public, the financial accounts are likely to be more open and comprehensive. Most developed countries have a greater dependence on bank and other long-term financing,

FIGURE 3

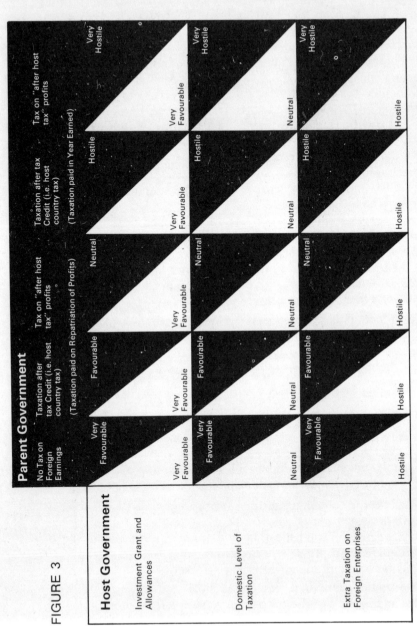

Parent Government / Host Government matrix

Host Government	Parent Government				
	No Tax on Foreign Earnings	Taxation after tax Credit (i.e. host country tax) *(Taxation paid on Repatriation of Profits)*	Tax on "after host tax" profits	Taxation after tax Credit (i.e. host country tax) *(Taxation paid in Year Earned)*	Tax on "after host tax" profits
Investment Grant and Allowances	Very Favourable / Very Favourable	Favourable / Very Favourable	Neutral / Very Favourable	Hostile / Very Favourable	Very Hostile / Very Favourable
Domestic Level of Taxation	Very Favourable / Neutral	Favourable / Neutral	Neutral / Neutral	Hostile / Neutral	Very Hostile / Neutral
Extra Taxation on Foreign Enterprises	Very Favourable / Hostile	Favourable / Hostile	Neutral / Hostile	Hostile / Hostile	Very Hostile / Hostile

Note: It would be logical to assume that the policies of both Parent and Host Governments were reflected in their tax concessions or investment incentives. In practice this is not always the case.
a) Policies are often made on a particular situation but persist long after the original circumstances change, unless there is positive pressure to change. "An old tax is a good tax" applies to the treatment of international enterprises.
b) Tax concessions and investment incentives are often directed, not to encourage international enterprises per se, but to encourage regional development. There may be confusion over aims or priorities.

and so do not regard it as necessary to make detailed accounts available to the general public. There is also an additional dimension which might be termed management style. Some like the Americans are very open, others are not.

b) So far as accountancy practices are concerned, it would perhaps be invidious to single out nations with somewhat rudimentary accounting practices, but these exist even in developed societies. An EEC Draft Directive has attempted to standardize accounting procedures within Western Europe and, by implication, raise the accounting standards of some member states. It appears however to have achieved limited success.

c) Finally the attitude towards paying tax varies enormously: some societies practise tax avoidance; others tax evasion. In some countries the U.S.A., U.K. or West Germany for example the idea of two or more sets of accounts showing different figures, one set for the authorities, another for internal financial control, and perhaps a third for publication, would be regarded as fraud. In other countries it is taken for granted that a set of accounts prepared for tax purposes is more in the nature of an opening bid than a statement of fact. It is difficult to generalize but it can be said that Southern European and Latin American societies have a rather more casual approach to accuracy than that which prevails in Northern Europe or North America. In parts of the underdeveloped world payment of taxes is almost a voluntary activity, and the willingness of postal workers to stamp on a letter from the tax authorities 'addressee unknown' ensures a useful supplementary income.[28]

In societies where rapid inflation prevails, the temptation at the very least, to delay and dispute tax payments is very strong: indeed in a situation of runaway inflation most taxes, unless levied and paid almost immediately, become almost meaningless over time.

The problem which this poses for the international enterprise is that it may adhere to very high standards set in the parent country and in so doing attract more taxation than if they had adhered to local practice. It is alleged in some countries however that tax authorities, by experience, have been known to adopt a different line in dealing with a foreign subsidiary with eccentric notions of how to make tax returns. They assume that subsidiaries of foreign enterprises are prima facie, giving accurate figures, while local enterprises, prima facie, are not.

9. Culture and Ideology

INTRODUCTION

Till now, international enterprises have developed from a base within Western society. The conventions, rewards, and sanctions are therefore Western in nature and these conventions have, initially at least, been carried over into other societies as subsidiaries have been set up in these societies. The success of this transplant to other societies has been rather mixed.

There is now a prospect of the non-Western international enterprise as the Japanese multinational corporation emerges. But the change in conditions for the Japanese multinational does not express itself through the subsidiaries in other Asian cultures, but in the West where the cultural contrast is most marked. So far Japanese ventures in Western society have been small in scale and problems have rarely arisen. But what happens when large scale Japanese owned and run plants appear in the West is a different matter.

Other cultures are likely to produce international enterprises and this includes the Communist world. The tacit assumption which is so often made is that international enterprises are going to play a dominating role in world trade and industry. National governments, particularly of the underdeveloped world have very ambivalent feelings about these enterprises, sometimes welcoming their subsidiaries as bringing in jobs, new industry, or the prospect of foreign exchange earnings, sometimes denouncing their activities as economic imperialism and neocolonialism.

But, whether national governments welcome new enterprises or denounce them, there is an assumption that they are immensely powerful, beyond the effective control of individual national governments, and growing in significance all the time. Attempts are being made at the national and international level to impose more constraints. There are however some indications that the growth of the multinational is producing a natural, as opposed to a deliberate reaction, a countervailing power to use current jargon. This reaction is almost instinctive in national culture, and is most noticeable when the multinational corporation moves into a non-Western culture.

Before considering in detail the nature of this reaction, it would be useful to review in a broad sweep what has been happening in three major groupings of countries, in part summarizing comments already made, in part anticipating points to be developed in more detail later. The three major groupings are a) the Western World b) the Communist World c) the Third World. This is not exactly the division used in Chapter 2. The Western World includes both Western developed and developing countries but excludes Japan. The Communist world is as defined in Chapter 2; and the Third World comprises most of the underdeveloped countries, together with Japan. The reason for the reshuffling of the groups is that what matters in this context is as much culture as politics or state of development.

Western society. In spite of the Gaullist reaction of the 1960's to American investment in Europe (a reaction most overt in France but by no means confined to that country), the multinational has now taken root in this third of the world. What has muted the anti-American feeling has been growing self-confidence among the Europeans, and an awareness that direct investment is a two-way traffic with substantial European investment in the U.S.A. It is no longer appropriate to make the facile assumption that multinational and American multinational mean the same thing. American corporations are by far the most important and numerous, but they are not unique. For that reason they are less vulnerable to political action than they were a few years ago.

The Communist World. The Communist World has learned to live with, and at times co-operate with the multinationals. So far, joint ventures in Communist countries are still the exception, wholly-owned subsidiaries almost a pipedream.[29] Nevertheless the scale of deals now being negotiated are immense. Licensing, turnkey operations and similar deals, exchange Western technology for raw materials or manufactured goods.

The Third World. It is, however, largely in the Third World that the most subtle problems are being posed for the multinational and where it may be facing most prospects, if not of failure in the conventional sense, of frustration; not for obvious political or economic reasons but for more subtle reasons. And yet, it would appear that it is in the Third World, or the vast majority of underdeveloped nations in the group, that the multinationals could do most to transform the economy by introducing new technology and even providing access to the mass markets in the West which any new industry needs. Trade unions in the Western world may decry the motives of 'runaway' industries exploiting cheap labour and tax concessions in the underdeveloped world. But they provide that world with jobs, skills, and above all markets. In that sense the self-interest of the multinationals may serve the material interests of the Third World far more effectively than political pressure or idealism in the UN on its associated bodies.

The problems which face the multinationals in these areas are ill-defined: but they are beginning to look remarkably like the problems of international Marxism. What has happened to Communist theory and practice over the last thirty years may give an indication of the development in international business in non-Western cultures.

To suggest that Marxism and the multinational corporation have much in common might seem to be playing with words. But in one issue, and it may be the vital issue, they are similar. Both are essentially Western concepts arising out of Western experience, and they are now facing non-Western cultures. The argument developed here about the future of the multinational corporations is therefore based on the analogy of what has happened to Marxism. There are notorious dangers of arguing by analogy, but these can be limited if the concepts to be used are defined. Let us look at *culture* and *ideology*.

A *culture* can be defined as that body of economic, political, and ethical beliefs which have historically evolved in a society. An *ideology* can be defined as that systematic body of economic political and ethical doctrines which are adopted by a society or imposed on it by the ruling establishment. The term 'doctrine' has been substituted for 'belief' in the second definition because the elements may be more precisely defined in an ideology than in a culture.

Culture will have been influenced by factors such as foreign, political, military, or economic influences: and by ideologies which in time are either largely absorbed or rejected. In either of these events the culture is to a greater or lesser degree modified.

The proposition put forward in this section is that in the short run what matters is ideology; and in the long run, the culture which gradually absorbs it. If an adopted and imposed ideology is to remain substantially unabsorbed it has to be sustained or reinforced over time.

If this hypothesis is valid then the significant point about the Third World is not that it is relatively economically underdeveloped and technologically backward. Rather, it is culturally different from the background which produced both Marxism and the multinational. And on that basis, Japan, one of the most highly developed economies, can be grouped with the other non-Western societies.

What then has happened to Marxist ideology? Marxism derived from Karl Marx's German background and his researches into nineteenth century English economic conditions. It was adopted, somewhat unexpectedly in one of the least capitalistic states of the West and evolved into Russian communism. Marxism became Marxist Leninism. As long as Moscow remained the Rome of Communism then Communism and Russian Communism were for most people the same ideology. This was the situation in the interwar years, and for a few years after World War 2, until the quarrel with Yugoslavia, and, far more significantly, the triumph of Chinese Communism.

Today the situation is vastly different from the 1940's. There is now Russian, Yugoslav, Chinese and Cuban Communism, with other varieties evolving elsewhere in S.E. Asia. Only in those parts of Eastern Europe where Russia still dominates can Russian Communism be equated with Communism; and even here it has significantly changed—as far, that is, as the Soviet Union will permit these changes, in the light of its own development.

It is with the Chinese experience of Marxism that the greatest significance lies. The Yugoslav and Cuban varieties have risen in other Western societies which are different admittedly from that of Russia, but of the same broad cultural pattern. China, on the other hand, a profoundly non-Western culture and civilization, has adopted and adapted a Western concept in about two decades, in the process producing a society very different from that of the original Russian model.

If this description of what has happened to Communism is valid (albeit simplified to the point of caricature) what are the implications for that other very Western concept, the multinational?

Briefly, the multinational corporation reflects Western values, indeed ethics, and Western rewards and sanctions for its personnel. In a limited sense, at least so far as its employees are concerned, it can be regarded as an ideology in its own sphere, i.e. a Western ideology now being applied to non-Western culture.

In these cultures some virtues and vices may be reversed, others become irrelevant. A reversal of roles may be seen in an example already quoted, namely nepotism—officially an unacceptable practice in the West if carried out very obviously. This is not to say that it is not practised, but it is not approved of, particularly at the executive level.

In most non-Western cultures the duties and obligations of the individual cover not merely to his own immediate relatives but to his extended family.

Family duty is then a measure of worth. Anyone in a position to give out jobs has a clear duty to favour even the most distant relative before any outsider. The blood relationship may be far more important that efficient personnel selection. In those Western cultures where the multinational corporations have originated, an accusation of favouritism by family would produce an indignant response—the more so if the charge happened to be true. In the non-Western society the charge would cause not so much indig- nation as incomprehension in that the person concerned was being accused of doing his natural duty.

The example of nepotism is interesting because it points to an element of hypocrisy in Western society, at least so far as close family members are concerned; and it is an example of the inversion of vices and virtues as between cultures. But there are other examples where practices are regarded as clearcut wrongs. Discrimination occurs in terms of sex, race, religion, the colour of a man's skin, and it would be a rare individual in Western society who would defend the practices. In some non-Western cultures any or all may be common, and acceptable. The practices are not regarded as virtues, as nepotism would be, but simply as a natural fact of life, even by most of those who are discriminated against. Western multinationals operating in these cultures may try to moderate these practices. They are asking for trouble, however, if they try to impose Western policies.

The examples above illustrate practices which would be regarded as undesirable in Western eyes. There are, however, admirable qualities to be encountered which are nevertheless difficult to combine in the values of Western multinationals because the conflict with competition and personal ambition. Group, or team loyalty which is associated with the countervailing powers of trade unions in the West may be a more integral part of the whole company set up elsewhere, most noticeably perhaps in Japan.

These then are illustrations of how Western values may seem inappropriate in other societies. The major problems this poses are to what extent are these values essential to the Western multi- national and, secondly, can subsidiaries in what might be called a transcultural situation, adhere to Western values recognized as normal by the parent company? What happens if the subsidiaries do not accept the values, but continue to adhere to the values of their own cultures which are far more relevant to the personnel of the subsidiary? Before attempting to answer these questions, it might be expedient to dispose of the twin issues of why the problems have not risen before now, and why they may be expected to become more acute in the future.

The early transcultural corporations operating in the non-Western world in the nineteenth and early twentieth century were extractive concerns (*Category I* enterprises as defined in the first chapter). But their executives were expatriates, who, though they might spend their working lives abroad, were drawn from, and intended to return in retirement to, their own cultures. They had no difficulty in adhering to the values of their own culture. Indeed their very isolation tended to reinforce the tendency.

Today, however, the expatriate executive is the exception rather than the rule. In an era of increased nationalism and newly independent states loudly proclaiming their fears of economic imperialism and neo-colonialism, the Western multinational increasingly depends for local acceptability on its publicized willingness to train up local executives. The expatriates are tolerated only for as long as it takes to train their local replacements. In the past decade or two local executives who are not going to move about the world as did the older expatriates, have become the norm. The problem, therefore, is not so much dealing with the individual questions posed above, but what happens if and when the local culture begins to absorb what we have called the ideology of the Western multinational, and transform it into a more acceptable local set of values.

The results could be summed up simply as the danger of loss of control by the parent company, a loss of control going so deep that it would not be rectified by displacing the top executives (even if this could be justified) because the fault is not deliberate defiance of the conventions of the parent company by individuals. All the executives suffer from the same fault, indeed the more junior probably more so than the seniors. The loss of control does not necessarily imply loss of ownership: merely a situation where the parent company would effectively have little more power than the individual shareholder. The role of global strategy for the multinational with each subsidiary playing its own alloted role would then be impossible. Subsidiaries would be all but autonomous not only in policy, but in their very philosophy. It is already arguable how far, for example, Japanese subsidiaries of non-Japanese multinationals with wholly Japanese management can really be said to be under the control of parent companies. It is probable that the Japanese pattern will spread to underdeveloped countries with non-Western cultures.

The situation is rendered more difficult by the insistence in many of the Third World countries of local participation in a joint venture. The joint venture may turn out to be a partnership of Western technology and non-Western culture.

There are some methods of limiting the effects. One might be to insist on Western oriented training, perhaps an MBA or similar course at a Western business school and company experience in a Western society. But even if every executive were a Harvard trained MBA with headquarters experience, the two or three years immersion in a Western culture would at most sensitize him to the differences between his culture and the company's. It would not transform him once he went back home. At worst, it might make him what the French would call depaysé, and as a result an alien in two cultures. Other possible restraints might be to set up a parallel structure of Western advisers, with these executives attempting to keep the indigenous line management from straying too far from Western conventions. Even so, such a parallel system, in effect a tandem management, is in the last analysis ineffective because the executive who matters is the one who makes the decision.

It is perhaps easier to pose the problems for the multinational corporation than suggest the answers. This progression to other cultural conventions is a logical end to the ethnocentric organization described by Professor Perlmutter in an earlier chapter. Nevertheless, some solution combining respect for cultural differences with mutually agreed conventions may have to be found if anything approaching a truly transnational corporation can be maintained in a transcultural situation. It remains to be seen whether the multinational can prove more flexible than Marxism.

This discussion has been posed in terms of the Western multinational and Japan has been cited as an example of a host country situation which may be duplicated elsewhere. But such evidence as there is suggests that the Japanese multinationals in turn are finding it difficult to transfer their particular strengths of consensus decision taking to other parts of the world. Even in the neighbouring countries of South East Asia the cultural difficulties appear to be almost as formidable as those facing Western multinationals.

Finally it is worth pointing out that the difficulty in the transcultural scene appears to be a function of size. A small subsidiary seems to present few problems even if different conventions apply. It is only when the company reaches an autonomous stage that problems seem to emerge. Reversing the roles once again, the

Japanese subsidiaries in the West tend to be very successful when small. The question is whether their management style will survive growth.

SOME RELEVANT FACTORS IN CULTURE

The culture of a community is an all pervasive factor and it is difficult to judge which of the various aspects of culture are significant to the international enterprise. A few however stand out, and are discussed below.

The role of the business executive.   The valuation put on business careers varies significantly from one culture and another. At one extreme Americans tend to rate businessmen very highly, in another culture they may be regarded as very low in the social order. The social rating given to business clearly affects the calibre of the local executive. If it is taken for granted, for example, that the national elite do not go in for business the effects may be serious, not so much on account of lower quality management (there is probably adequate calibre of personnel outside the accepted establishment of any society), but in their ability to reach and influence the key decision makers in the society. The situation is complicated by the prestige or lack of it attached to working for a foreign company. In some instances a foreign company employee automatically acquires prestige; in other societies the implication of joining a foreign company may be that the individual is unlikely ever to find a place in a domestic enterprise. Employment by an international enterprise may be a form of national exile, even though the employees never leave their own country.

Community aspirations.   It is an interesting social phenomenon that the poorest countries are rarely the most politically unstable, and that, for a number of reasons. One of the most potent may be that the cultural or religious *ambience* of that society induces a fatalism which resists the most inequitable conditions or the most revolutionary doctrine. Injustice may simply be accepted as a fact of nature.

From the point of view of the international enterprise it is by no means certain that a stable society in this sense is a better investment area than an unstable one, or indeed that the individual in society who accepts the status quo is a better source of managerial material than the revolutionary. After all, the latter has some points in common with the international enterprise as an agent for change, and it may be that the enterprise, if it can channel the drive for change to its own ends, will find a use for the activist. The problem therefore is to judge whether the revolutionary extremist who, as a student, was in the forefront of resistance to foreign investment has moderated or merely concealed his views. But sticking always to the least disruptive elements in a society may merely ensure that the enterprise itself becomes absorbed into the culture; unable either to meet its own internal needs, or indeed any of the long-term needs of a fatalistic or stagnant society.

Social and family responsibility. A characteristic of advanced industrial societies is that they combine a shrinking sense of family responsibility with an increasing sense of social responsibility. Thus Western society would expect parents to accept responsibility for their children in the early years, but only to a limited extent responsibility for aged parents, in the sense that the state will provide social security benefits, if not on a generous scale, at least sufficiently to ensure minimum comforts. So far as other family relationships are concerned they are almost non-existent in terms of social responsibility. Individuals have no legal responsibilities to brothers and sisters. And yet Western society would regard as appalling the idea that anyone should be allowed to starve to death on the streets.

The moral imperatives may work in opposite directions in under-developed societies. The individual has responsibilities and rights not merely as far as his parents and children are concerned, but with every blood relation however remote. Conversely, however, he has no moral responsibility for anyone in society outside his family. While there may be personal merit in giving a coin to a beggar, there is no responsibility for starving in the community.

This factor has been discussed in terms of finding posts for blood relations, but the whole issue may go much further in an underdeveloped society. 'Everybody's business is nobody's business' is a cliche in Western society. It may be a fact of life in other societies. Social issues, pollution, environmental considerations in building, siting advertisements, etc. are often much less of a problem for the enterprise in the underdeveloped economy than in the developed. In a sense, nobody cares, because a community sense is underdeveloped relatively to family sense.

Class structure. It is a conventional morality in the West that a class structure which prevents upward mobility is both wrong and imprudent. England is commonly accused of being class-ridden, but what enabled the English upper classes to survive, and be accepted when their apparent role in society vanished, was their readiness to absorb the thrusters from beneath.

In some societies, class structure, expressed perhaps in terms of caste or colour are combined with non-absorption. A Hindu Untouchable becomes a Harijan — a 'Blessed One' — but he remains unacceptable in a wide variety of roles: the black man has a place in South African society, but nowhere near the top. In a less marked way such a factor as accent may render acceptability very difficult in some societies and be irrelevant elsewhere. Accents are not so important in this context, because they can be changed by enough of the discriminated against to remove the venom from the situation. Other aspects — the unchangeable facts of birth — present greater moral problems for society and very practical problems for the international enterprise. A society preventing upward movement may in time come apart at the seams, but in day to day terms it can make difficulties for the enterprise in limiting its choice of executives to those which will be acceptable in the role to the rest of the community. There may be a tendency in an enterprise to choose for its foreign subsidiaries those who appear most closely to resemble the executive types favoured in the parent company, a policy which may or may not be successful.

Educational values. Different cultures put a different content into the education they give. An international enterprise has to consider whether what is regarded as a good education has much relevance to their needs. Educational content can be extraordinarily irrelevant or conservative. Education in management has been accepted for well over half a century in the U.S.A., rather less than half that time in many European countries, and not at all in many parts of the world. Conventional patterns are hard to change. It was said of the Chinese educational system in the nineteenth and early part of the twentieth centuries that it was designed to enable the brightest boys, regardless of their social background, to compete for the highly prestigious Civil Service — the Mandarin class. The whole Mandarin system was swept away by the Chinese Revolution of 1912 but for more than twenty years afterwards an education designed for an extinct society continued to be highly prized above all others.

Job status. Every society has its own ranking of jobs, professional, business, educational, all have different valuations from society to society — and though this valuation may change in economic terms, in prestige it does not. Many societies have a fairly clear distinction between, for example, middle class and working class. In Britain in very rough and ready terms, clerical jobs no matter how poorly paid are middle class occupations, while manual jobs no matter how skilled, working class. This distinction certainly does not apply to income; a bricklayer may earn two or three times as much as a clerk. In economic terms it would be common sense for a middle class but poorly paid family to encourage the sons to go for jobs with higher wages, but it is social acceptability not wage which determines their decisions. Many more working class families would try to push their children into middle class occupations than vice versa.

In the U.S.A. class distinction is a good deal more blurred. A minority would regard themselves as working class, while most blue collar occupations of any skill rapidly qualify for middle class status. But even here, the pressure is upward in social, if not always material terms.

Some American firms have succeeded in transferring a less rigorous attitude to jobs to other societies. In its early days of recruitment of executives in Western Europe IBM had a reputation of being prepared to promote rapidly from shop floor to top management. Later on, as the societies adapted to the IBM requirements, more orthodox sources of executive material could be tapped, but IBM appear to have had remarkable success with their policy, even in cultures where shop floor upgrading was very exceptional.

Other societies have their own nuances: in some, manual work is unthinkable for anyone of any social status. In this situation wage offers will not necessarily tempt people into jobs which are below their perceived social status. Even in the so-called classless societies these nuances exist. In some jobs in the Soviet Union, wearing a tie to work is a social distinction.

The Japanese phenomenon may owe a good deal to success in detaching job function from status. The idea of demarcation disputes is virtually unknown, and it can literally happen that a man may be reallocated from being a skilled machinist in one factory to being a floor sweeper if the needs of the company require this. The point of interest is that such a dramatic transfer would not bring diminution in status or pay in what to Western ideas might seem a downgrading in every sense.

It is possible to cite many instances of apparently irreconcilable aspects of any culture concealing hidden traps for the international enterprise. Often it appears that more money solves problems— pay enough and cultural bias breaks down. So it may, in time. But in the short-term, merely to pay out more money may create more trouble for the enterprise than a policy of identifying the particular cultural values of a society and trying to accommodate them. After all, the enterprise may have enough difficulty in reconciling its own values with those of its employees within the subsidiary, without trying to change a whole culture.

STATE ENTERPRISES IN THE UNDERDEVELOPED WORLD

We have said that most underdeveloped nations profess Socialism, i.e. the public ownership of means of production. Few, however, practise Socialism very successfully, in terms of efficient production. The theoretical advantage of a publicy owned and controlled productive capacity over unplanned and wastefully competitive private production are virtually self evident. The hard fact, however, is that it is exceedingly difficult to run efficiently the vast machinery of control and planning on which public ownership depends, and this difficulty is greatest when, as in most underdeveloped countries, the administrative machine is relatively primitive.

The result is that private and public enterprises may exist side by side, with the latter officially favoured and officially the heirs to the future. Often however they are much less efficient than the private enterprises. Some of the possible results have been pointed out in Chapter 5. Such public enterprises are run by executives who, while acceptable to the political group in power, may have little real grasp of what, for example, marketing is all about. There exists, in many instances, a virtual dichotomy between the central planners and the public enterprises on the one hand and the small manufacturer and trader on the other who operates as his ancestors have done for centuries, regardless of the political complexion of the government. At best there is incomprehension, at worst antipathy between the two groups.

The major problem frankly is a matter of personnel. The successful businessman or trader is not generally the man who ends up running the state enterprise. He is more likely to have been dispossessed in a spasm of nationalization and state ownership. Managerial talent is in short supply and such talent as there is may not be experienced or suited.

One example may illustrate the point. At the time of the takeover of power by President Nasser in Egypt in the early 1950's Egyptian industry was small and privately owned. One of the first moves in the new Arab Socialism was the virtual expropriation of these companies and the expulsion of the owner managers. Where then to find any managerial talent? There were two sources: the small group of intellectuals mostly in education who sympathized with the new ideas, and the Army which had overthrown the former King and his immediate successor. If anything the intellectuals were even worse suited to run competitive industry than the officers. Soon there were tales, hilarious or tragic depending on one's point of view of some of the new executives. One Colonel of Artillery, it was alleged, was promoted, retired, and appointed to run a newly nationalized factory. He had spent most mornings of his adult life inspecting his guns: now he inspected his machines and disciplined workers who had contrived to get them dirty. It is not surprising that President Nasser's successor discreetly reversed his economic policy.

In a situation where all industry has been nationalized the system can persist for a long time on a woefully inefficient level. The whole economy may stagnate, but with a virtual monopoly of the market and limitless access to state finance no business is going to go bankrupt. In most instances however the mixture is of private and public enterprises, with the latter simultaneously more inefficient and more favoured by the state.

This may read like a highly simplistic attack on public enterprise: it is not. It amounts to the proposition that where a publicly-owned enterprise will not be allowed to go bankrupt, while a private one will, then the survivors of the latter group are almost inevitably more efficient. And the situation is likely to be most noticeable in an underdeveloped country because the administrative talent available to the public sector is almost inevitably inadequate overall; and nowhere more so than in business. At the risk of over-simplification, a large number of the administrators are ideologically committed to the party in power, contemptuous of private enterprise and highly suspicious of foreign imperialism in the shape of the international enterprise. If is often a long and painful education for some of those managers to realize that it is not enough merely to decree plans, or even arrange production to ensure that goods of the right quality and price become available to the public: some of them never do.

International enterprise often comes into contact with these public enterprises in one of two ways, in licensing or joint venture partnership. The enterprise may find that it has to give licensing rights to such organizations or simply be excluded from the market, but the standard of product which may be produced is not always likely to enhance the reputation of the licensor. The situation in joint ventures, however, is potentially much more delicate, not only because the objectives of the two partners may be different, but also because generally the two partners find it difficult to understand what motivates the other. The ideal may be for the international enterprise to persuade its partner virtually to give it a free hand on the production and marketing side, while it looks after the political issues. No matter how tactful the two partners continue to be, they are operating different philosophies and their long-term partnership is likely to run into difficulties.

STATE ENTERPRISES IN THE DEVELOPED WORLD

The idea of state owned business enterprises is hardly a new one for the international businessman. What does, however, cause a certain amount of confusion is state ownership or partial ownership through financial or industrial organizations operating a form of state capitalism.

The most famous and one of the longest established is the Italian IRI (Istituto per la Reconstruzione Industriale) which derived from the corporate state philosophy of Fascist Italy. Used to finance ailing companies originally, it now effectively owns and controls about 25 per cent of Italian industry: Alfa Romeo is probably its best known subsidiary. The IRI pattern was repeated in ENI (Ente Nazionale Idrocarburi) the oil and natural gas giant. The same pattern has emerged in another corporate economy, Spain, and France. The pattern is, therefore, fairly widespread over Europe.

These enterprises are generally heartily disliked by the privately owned companies because of their apparently limitless access to public funds and influence. They are a more formidable threat than the public enterprises of the underdeveloped world because they have in their subsidiaries managerial talent as good as that available to private companies and they represent a more potent long-term threat to private enterprises than the more overtly bureaucratic nationalized industries.

It does not follow, however, that there is an open ideological clash between the public owned enterprises and the private. Renault in France operates a very profitable joint venture with the privately owned Peugeot (now linked with Citröen), to produce engines and components for both enterprises in the Societé Francaise de Mechanique. The Peugeot partner incidentally is much smaller but a good deal more profitable than Renault. There is no reason to suppose that international joint ventures with such organizations are less profitable than other joint ventures. In a corporate economy there may be a positive advantage of government favour.

State Paternalism

The concept of paternalism used here is both difficult to define and prove conclusively. It is probably seen at its most developed in a country like France where a close working relationship exists between the bureaucratic machine, and industry and commerce. The result is that aid will be available to deal with foreign competition where necessary, and the advent of the Common Market has not really stopped the readiness of the state to use its powers to inhibit competition from abroad which threatens French companies. When for example corn based whisky or other spirits from abroad threaten French grape liqueurs, legislation makes it difficult or impossible to advertise them; not by a direct ban which would be hard to justify but on alcohol produced from anything but grapes.

When foreign enterprises wish to establish subsidiaries threatening the interests of key French industries, they will find it very difficult to move in regardless of the legal situation. The virtual monopoly in industrial gases enjoyed for years by Aire Liquide of France depended as much on the patronage of the French government as on any obvious technological superiority.

Some of the most blatant examples of state paternalism found in many Western countries are massive subsidies to ailing local industries, not from the viewpoint of any long-term economic or political policy, but because of fears of unemployment if inefficient domestic enterprises are likely to be put out of business by more efficient foreign enterprise.

THE TRANSIDEOLOGICAL ENTERPRISE

The term transideological has been developed by Professor Perlmutter to describe those enterprises which span both Western societies and the Communist world.[30] Strictly the term could be used to cover other ideologies than Western and Marxist, and some alternate ideologies will be discussed later in this section. Nevertheless, the main area for study is likely to be the Marxist countries, which constitute one-third of the world's population.

In the 1970's the prospects for East/West co-operation, and deals between Western private enterprise and Communist Foreign Trade Organizations (FTO's) is increasing rapidly. This development has followed the thawing of the cold war which for over two decades in the postwar world limited trade and transaction over a vast range of strategic materials. Now the strategic embargo has virtually disappeared.

Arguably, of course, this is an error on the part of Western governments in that the Communist confrontation with the West, and their desire 'to bury you' to paraphrase a Kruschev phrase, has not wavered, but has only been concealed. But, rightly or wrongly, Western governments are proceeding on the assumption that trade and aid with the Communist countries will end the period of confrontation. This is a situation which now faces enterprises in all the Western countries, and which provides opportunities for trade and co-operation.

The first point which has to be made is that not all Communist countries are willing to trade and deal with Western private enterprise on anything but orthodox trading terms. There appears however to be a period of development. Newly created Communist societies are highly suspicious and hostile; more mature Marxist states either compromise or conceal their hostility. Thus at the present moment the Russians and Eastern Europe show active interest in co-operation, while China remains ideologically pure and condemns the U.S.S.R. for its policy. In time the Chinese may follow the same line of acceptance as the older established Communist regimes.

What is the present situation of international commerce between the Communist and non-Communist world (including the underdeveloped world)? There are five variants:

Firstly, there are orthodox trade deals of the type described in an earlier chapter with Western enterprises buying from or selling to FTO's.

The second situation is a development of this. A consortium is formed among non-Communist enterprises, either on a national or international basis, to supply capital equipment to Communist markets. This type of consortium is common when a very large order is to be filled, e.g. a turnkey operation, involving perhaps the creation of a vast truck and vehicle factory.

The third type of deal is the barter situation already discussed. This does not normally involve international enterprises, but is a government to government deal denominated in a notional hard currency involving the exchange of goods only, not cash payment. It is the type of deal conducted only with underdeveloped countries where both partners are short of hard currencies.

The fourth and fifth variants which are only tentatively emerging can be most accurately described as setting up transideological enterprises.

The first of these, the fourth variant, is the joint venture arrangement within a Communist country. The principle is much the same as in other joint ventures, with capital and technology being supplied by the Western partner. There are two major problems, one ideological, the other financial. The ideological problem is how to accommodate the principle of a foreign private enterprise operating in a Marxist state. This is a principle which can be evaded, not solved, on the grounds that a certain amount of private enterprise has always been permitted. Lenin used the so-called 'New Economic Policy' of private enterprise to revive Russian industry in the 1920's before subsequently crushing the private sector when the aim had been achieved. A transideological enterprise can therefore be regarded as an expedient to be ended when occasion arises. The ideological problems of the Communist partner might seem irrelevant to the interests of the Western partner, except that it poses a long-term threat to the arrangement. There is always a possibility that the partner will revert to ideological purity, perhaps in the face of criticism from other Communist states, and repudiate the whole deal.

The other problem, the financial one, concerns royalties. A common practice is that the joint venture should export to hard currency areas with the Western partner either taking payment in the products which are then sold, or simply taking a share in the foreign exchange earnings. As has been noted, Rumania has been the forerunner in such deals.

The final and most tentative variant is the joint venture outside the Communist country with co-operation between Western enterprise and Communist partners elsewhere. This is, in many respects, the most profound of all, since it is difficult to square any such activities with Marxist ideology. Either it is a temporary situation, or the mature Marxist states are moving into a phase commercially indistinguishable from Western enterprises.

Major Problems

The transideological enterprise is by its nature an unstable arrangement which can be justified and sustained only by an interdependence of the needs of the Western enterprise and the Communist state.

What then are the needs of the Communist states? At first glance they are variants of those discussed earlier: namely foreign exchange and technology, with in certain circumstances 'non essential goods'. The situation however has some peculiarities of its own.

The foreign exchange aim is easily understood. The emphasis even in importing is to try to link this with re-exports as all the transactions are intended to minimize foreign exchange payments and maximize earnings. The emphasis however must be on *earnings*. What Communist states want is access to Western markets for non-traditional goods, and almost subconsciously perhaps, an understanding of that rather vague concept of market orientation. Communist products are generally cheap by Western standards. Exports of manufactures are almost invariably subsidized, but in virtually every other aspect of the marketing mix apart from price the Communist nations, working on their own, tend to fall down. They hire Western advertising agencies on occasion and accept promotional advice, but instinctively begin by assuming that, at a cheap price, a product sells itself. When manifestly it does not, they seek to master the concept of market orientation, an unnecessary concept in their own protected and starved markets but a vital one elsewhere. The desire for foreign exchange is at a deeper level; possibly the desire to beat the Westerners at their own marketing game.

The second aim is that of technology, and here again as so often in the underdeveloped world, there is a substantial gap between buying technology and successfully absorbing it. The need for aid in bringing technology 'on stream' often conflicts with the obsessive desire for secrecy. Many Western products are bought and installed without the manufacturer even knowing where the ultimate user is located. If the deal is on an installation basis then security cannot be maintained. There is no doubt, however, that there is something in the national or political set up which inhibits rapid transplanting of ideas without on the spot advice on installation by representatives of the manufacturer. A complication which arises from the use of the Foreign Trade Organization is that this particular organization may be in a weak position to bargain. If there is a shortage of foreign exhange what does the FTO have to offer? Ideally, reciprocal technology: this however is the exception, and the deal may have to be 'Teach us the technology and then when we have mastered it, we will be able to pay—and incidentally compete with you elsewhere.' In some circumstances it would be better perhaps to offer raw materials or semi-finished goods, except that the resources which would be of interest to the foreigner may be held by another FTO with its own interests. In the last analysis the FTO may not have the resources to deal with the enterprise without direct state intervention, if necessary at the expense of other FTO's.

The third requirement is for the 'unnecessary' goods, i.e. consumer goods. Some of the motives for buying those from the West have been discussed in an earlier chapter. But there is also the possibility of local manufacture to Western designs, which have been tried and proved in production elsewhere. It is a good deal cheaper and more reliable than, on occasions, local design.

The benefits to the Communist partner are clear, but what has the arrangement to offer the Western enterprise which is prepared to transfer technology? The benefits are substantially the same as the *Category III* type of transaction discussed in Chapter 1, when an enterprise manufactures in a less developed economy, for sale in a richer market to which the enterprise has access. The main advantages are relatively low cost, and it must be said, docile labour: labour forces in Communist countries are even less likely to indulge in industrial action than in other but right wing authoritarian states like Spain or Brazil.

Basically many transideological deals are simply the joint exploitation of raw material resources with payment for the imported technology being made by the actual raw material. The major problem is mutual confidence—rather a greater problem for the international enterprise which cannot recall its technology in the case of a dispute, than for the Communist partner. A typical illustration is to be found in the deals involving the Occidental Petroleum Coy. Inc. which was willing in the early 1970's to negotiate a deal to extract natural gas from Siberia, and ship it in liquid form to the U.S.A. While ownership of the plant and pipelines in the U.S.S.R. could be the subject of negotiation, it was regarded as vital that the natural gas carriers should be U.S. owned and controlled. Implicit in this condition was the argument that if the Soviet authorities subsequently repudiated the agreement, they would not find it easy to ship the liquified natural gas anywhere else. If the U.S.A. lost, so too would the U.S.S.R.

It is not so easy in other instances to provide such guarantees. On the other hand, the threat of expropriation is hardly a new one for international enterprises and the authorities have a far better record of prompt payment than most underdeveloped countries.

Ultimately the intention is to export industrial goods of comparable quality to those produced anywhere else. Here the main safeguard of the international enterprise providing technology is the protection of its patent rights throughout the world and in its control of marketing channels. Again Communist governments tend to be keen to obtain not only technology but also access to distribution channels abroad; and by the same token they are punctilious in honouring any agreement made.

Even where technology is being transferred, it is open to the Communist partner to try to interest the foreign enterprise in payment by its existing range of consumer or industrial goods. Such a proposition is not necessarily so attractive to the enterprise, if the product is easily distinguishable in origin, or if it is not particularly up to date. And after all that is likely to be the situation where technology in the field is being sought—an illustration again of the fact that an FTO with interests in a limited sector of industry may not have the most attractive range of 'contra' goods with which to bargain.

What manufactured products from across the ideological barrier are likely to be most acceptable to the Western enterprise in exchange for technology? The answer is most likely to be found in traditional manufactures, handicrafts, foodstuffs, delicacies and alcoholic drinks—industry where in the strictest sense technology may not be important, but knowhow and prestige is. The classical constituents of Russian vodka are no secret to Western chemists, and any number of vodka varieties can be and are sold successfully. These may be cheaper or even better than the traditional Russian variety, but there is no doubt that the latter can sell well. Pepsi Cola is now being produced and sold in the U.S.S.R., and payment is being made for the process in Russian vodka. From the U.S.S.R. point of view, there is one advantage and one disadvantage. The advantage is that consumer loyalty for Russian vodka may be built up which could survive termination of the original agreement. The disadvantage is the lingering suspicion that perhaps a market for Russian vodka against hard dollar currency is being lost.

An interesting facet of such deals is that there has been, so far, little sign of 'fall out' in Soviet technology, at least so far as Western markets are concerned. The U.S. space programme has produced startling advances in computer technology, microminiaturization, ceramics, and even at the humbler end of the spectrum, cadium batteries with a wide range of usage, in, say, powered garden tools. Technology diffusion has been very rapid. There is no obvious sign of such applications of space technology from the Soviet programme, but it is hard to believe that similar breakthroughs in materials and methods have not taken place. Such applications would then be of attraction in the innovative markets of the West and would be an obvious bargaining counter. The fact, however, that the technology does not seem to diffuse nearly as quickly as in the U.S.A. suggests that the problem of technology transfer in some societies is not merely a question of crossing national frontiers. It may be something more deeprooted. in the system which appears to inhibit the rapid application of technology outside the application for which it was originally developed. If that is so the implications may be far reaching. The so-called technological gap may not merely amount to a temporary lag, but something more profound and perhaps longer lasting.

The Future of Co-operation

It is a paradox that the ideologies·most overtly hostile to Western capitalism are at the same time relatively safe areas for investment. The prospects of arbitrary confiscation by a hostile revolutionary government are considerably less in the Marxist society than in most underdeveloped countries.

There are however substantial problems arising from differing attitudes. The most important of these is simply an anti-marketing bias already commented upon, which is liable to frustrate the efforts of the enterprise to sell abroad. It may be that, in time, the marketing concept will be absorbed into Marxist ideology, but it still remains the situation that failures which the Communists ascribe to inadequate technology are really failures to appreciate the needs of the market. And unless they can absorb some of the urgency of a market oriented enterprise, more and more technology is not likely to suffice. Many aspects of Russian technology, especially those deriving from a military base, are comparable with anything in the West. But which Western country buys them in competition with others?

In a sense this latent hostility towards marketing is but one aspect of the ambivalent attitude of the Communist states to international enterprises. It is virtually impossible to square joint ventures with Marxist ideology except on the convention that they are temporary expedients, so that not only can Communist societies readily absorb the technology, but then surpass their teachers. It is convenient for those in power in the U.S.S.R. and East Europe to ignore criticisms of other left wing states, particularly the Chinese. But the situation cannot remain indefinitely in suspense. Either the ideology changes or the enterprise goes. It would be convenient if the Soviet corporate state became in practice less and less distinguishable from any other industrial state. Indeed there is plenty of evidence that the new Russian middle class, the technologists, the scientists and engineers are almost as non-ideological as their Western counterparts. But the possibility cannot be dismissed of a new Communist puritanism which will denounce contact and co-operation with the West and expel the enterprises. Stalinism may be officially dead so far as much industrial co-operation is concerned. But if Stalinism prevails on the political side then industrial co-operation may suffer the fate of the New Economic Policy of the 1920's. Western capitalism has been the traditional enemy of the U.S.S.R. and its allies. It has been replaced in current demonology by China, but the pattern may revert.

OTHER IDEOLOGIES

This chapter has discussed the transideological enterprise in terms of Communist ideology and in particular Western Russian based Communism.

There are of course other ideologies in the world apart from Western Democracy and Communism.

The major problem is to decide what constitutes an ideology. Two important additions to any definition are internal consistency and persistency. The intellectual appeal that Marxism has to many Western intellectuals has been that if one accepts its initial premises then it is possible to explain or interpret economics in political events in its own terminology. It is, therefore, internally consistent and has stood the test of time.

Whether or not the same can be said of many of the distinctive regimes of much of the Western and underdeveloped world, is more difficult. There are many right wing military governments in the world whose ideology, if any, might simply be defined as anti-Communist or anti-anarchist. They may not be overthrown but simply revert to a condition indistinguishable from neighbouring states, lacking apparently an alternative philosophy.

The same may be said of left wing governments. Arab socialism, the boast of President Nasser has been quietly buried in its homeland. The experiment lasted not more than twenty years before Egypt reverted into something remarkably like the pre-revolutionary style. It will be interesting to see whether Peronism in the Argentine survives long after President Peron's death in 1974.

From the viewpoint of the international enterprise, what matters is the practical, as opposed to the theoretical, attitude to private ownership. Enterprises may have to learn new rules when they find themselves in the 'Neither Capitalism nor Communism' situation. In the last analysis, it is their ability to cope with the alien culture and ideology that determines success or failure.

10. International Business—the National and International Viewpoint

We have been looking at the problems of international business from the viewpoint of the enterprise rather than the national government, whether parent or host. Now the process will be reversed and some of the issues previously discussed will be re-examined from the viewpoint of the nation states and the international community in general.

If the subject is to be treated in a logical manner, the argument has to be structured. This of course is true of any argument, including those advanced in the previous chapters. The main danger of structuring in this instance, however, is that it is only too easy to give the impression that issues are clearcut and government policies towards international business are logical and farsighted. Sometimes the reality is far short of this ideal, and national policies are not easily justified on a rational basis. Ignorance and prejudice play their part; or policy has been determined by factors which no longer have much relevance to current conditions.

So far as host governments are concerned, two facile assumptions have to be questioned. These are:

a) that the host government has a single interest, and coherent objective in dealing with the international enterprise.
b) that it can readily quantify the pros and cons of encouraging direct investment by the international enterprise.

So far as the parent government is concerned the issues are less confused. Briefly, however, it can be said that foreign investment in productive capacity by one of its domestic enterprises is, prima facie, against its national interests; unless, that is, it secures vital raw materials.

THE HOST GOVERNMENT

An earlier chapter listed three reasons why a host country might choose to give tax concessions to an incoming enterprise. These were:

    a) to encourage the introduction of new technology

    b) to create more employment

    c) To earn or save foreign exchange

It was acknowledged at the time that theses aims were not necessarily compatible: the most desirable type of industry might vary according to which of these was regarded as the most important at any one time. Even then, the choice is not likely to be decisively for one to the exclusion of the other two, but which of the three objectives should have the highest priority.

It is here that the first of the assumptions discussed above may be challenged because of the manner in which any government bureaucratic machine works. Quite simply, different government departments are likely to be concerned with technology, employment and foreign exchange, with only partial overlapping and common interests. Technology falls to a department concerned with industry, employment to a department of labour, foreign exchange to the Treasury and Central or Federal Reserve Banks. These departments or groups of departments may have different interests and relative importance, and this means a tendency to perceive the pros and cons of the investment differently and react accordingly.

The second assumption mentioned above was that it was possible to quantify the pros and cons of international investment. There are at least two areas where this assumption may be challenged. A national government may refuse to permit direct investment in the form of wholly-owned subsidiaries and insist instead on licensing or, at most, joint ventures with local industry. Whether or not it would achieve the desired industrial development on these terms is not all that certain, and would depend on the existing level of technical knowhow already available, as well as less definable social and cultural trends in the community. The point is, however, that it could be an error to assume that the community would be unable to get the benefits of foreign technology, or most of them, on its own terms. The Japanese, with a sufficient level of technical knowhow and an appropriate culture proved that point decisively.

In more general terms the question might be posed thus. How can a government balance the advantage of more industrial development, jobs, the prospect of foreign exchange earnings, against the disadvantages of having a very large proportion of its industry foreign owned? Most of the advantages can be expressed in economic terms, most of the disadvantages in political or perhaps cultural terms. They cannot therefore readily be compared.

RE-EXAMINING THE ARGUMENTS FOR INWARD INVESTMENT

A. THE INTRODUCTION OF NEW TECHNOLOGY

The basic issue has already been developed in earlier chapters, from the enterprise viewpoint, namely whether to introduce the most up to date technology even in a relatively backward market, and accept the expense and need to train personnel and possibly ancillary services up to the required standard; or whether to use relatively dated but still appropriate production methods and economize by using obsolescent equipment, plant, etc., replaced elsewhere.

The additional factor affecting the host government, is value for money, i.e. if any sort of subsidy is being paid to the enterprise it is important to know the real cost to the enterprise. It is not entirely unknown for a host government actually to pay out in subventions a sum greater than the total cost of the investment, because the valuation of obsolescent equipment has been incautiously accepted. Even paying up a sum greater than the immediate investment should still be an acceptable move if the long-term benefits appeared to warrant this. It is however political dynamite in the host country, if the government can be accused of being duped into paying well over the odds.

B. THE CREATION OF EMPLOYMENT

As was suggested earlier there is little or no distinction between a host government's regional policy, if it has one, and its policy of encouraging inward investment for employment purposes. In other words the enterprise will attract subsidies or tax concessions, not because it is foreign, but because it is moving into a region which is being given favourable fiscal treatment. The international enterprise attracts the same favourable treatment as would a domestic enterprise moving into the same region. The fact that the beneficiaries of such regional policies are often subsidiaries of an international enterprise, rather than branch plants of domestic enterprises, arises from two causes. Firstly, the foreign enterprise has no previous commitment to another area; secondly it may even be refused permission to build in an area of high employment.

Is there any obvious policy on the nature of employment? When a national government faces high unemployment in particular regions, it is not always very selective about the type of employment it brings in. It will try to ensure that the employment opportunities to be offered more or less correspond with the local needs, e.g. skilled male employment, light female labour, etc. But even when employment opportunities match up with the available skills, it does not follow that the incoming plant will mop up the unemployed. What may well happen is that the new plant recruits labour from existing industry and causes difficulties for existing employers. It is not difficult to see why this should be so. A man or woman who is already holding down a job may look a better prospect for the recruiter than someone who has been unemployed. Even if the person concerned has the wrong skill he is still a better prospect than the unskilled unemployed because his skill suggests he has an ability to be trained if necessary. Equally, since incoming companies, especially foreign companies, are likely to be paying at rather more than the prevailing rates, they are able to attract the more ambitious or more motivated worker. The local companies then find their industry being disrupted and have in turn to recruit and train from the unemployed, probably ending up with a less satisfactory labour force than before. The less efficient local enterprises may simply not be able to adjust and go out of business and the overall effects may be adverse.

The side effects may go further. Generally, an international enterprise going into a host country will use more capital intensive methods than local companies. After all, this is one of the implications of new technology. The total wage bill will then be a smaller proportion of total costs than for other firms and the newcomer will be less concerned about keeping labour costs down. This will certainly increase the difficulties of other companies; indeed to keep local goodwill the incomer may have to pay lower wages than he was willing to meet. But it may also embarrass a government facing inflationary pressures if the newcomer is prepared to offer little resistance to wage demands.

These problems are essentially economic. But other political or cultural problems may be created if the incomer's style of worker management relations, or ideas on labour rights form an unwelcome contrast with local practice. The 'demonstration' effect of vastly better conditions in a new plant can trigger off dormant discontents elsewhere.

C. THE FOREIGN EXCHANGE ISSUE

Foreign subsidiaries are almost always an immediate asset from the foreign exchange point of view, firstly in bringing in capital investment, and subsequently in replacing the foreign exchange drain of imports for smaller profit remittances. Even where there are no formal conditions applied to exporting, e.g. that the value of imported goods will be balanced by exports, the prospects are that the subsidiary will do rather better in exporting than local enterprises which have to develop their own export channels, instead of having them ready made.

Import Savings vs. Export Earnings

So far *import saving* and *export earning* have been taken as different sides of the same coin, i.e. it has been assumed that there is no real difference in the benefits to be derived. In practice, however, this is not so: there are far more advantages in the latter situation. Local production, merely for import saving in a relatively small market (i.e. most underdeveloped countries) will almost certainly result for purely technological reasons in very high cost production. The locally produced car may, for example, cost twice as much as the imported version, and be of a distinctly lower quality. Foreign exchange savings therefore are almost certainly being achieved at the expense of the local consumer who may have no choice but to tolerate rocketing prices and plummeting quality. Export earning plant, on the other hand, is likely to use more technically advanced production standards, with higher quality, to compete in the international market. The domestic consumer too has everything to gain from this type of product rather than merely an import substitute. The example was quoted earlier of the attempts of the Iranian government to persuade Toyota to produce vehicles locally on a scale which would require that the majority be exported. If the Iranians did succeed, the quality of the locally produced vehicles would immediately have to rise to international standards— to the benefit of the local buyer. In the same way Volkswagen have been acceding to local pressures by setting up assembly lines in several South East Asian countries. The local buyer in any of these countries is not likely to be happy at having to buy his next vehicle from the local, instead of the German, plant, unless the products are good enough for the German parent to be willing to sell them in markets which could be supplied from Germany.

THE PROBLEMS OF SUCCESS

The other major problem is possible conflict arising from success where the local plant, whether import saving or export earning, has profits to dispose of. The subsidiary may be required by the parent company to remit profits home to enable investment to take place in another part of the world. This is the other side of the coin to inward investment a few years before. The host government, however, would probably prefer more investment locally. If this is done, more and more of the nation's industry becomes foreign owned: and what may worsen the situation is that the foreign enterprise may choose to buy over locally owned production facilities instead of creating new investment—a practice increasingly frowned upon.

Either way, however, more and more of the nation's industry ends up foreign owned. The same end result follows if the host government attempts to limit the outflow because of the effects on the foreign exchange situation. In Brazil, for example, profit repatriation may not exceed twelve per cent of the capital of the subsidiary: elsewhere, in the Andean Pact countries the limit is fourteen per cent: and so on. The enterprise may attempt to evade the local ruling, or to obey it. In the first situation it may try to use transfer pricing or to reclassify profits as royalty payments, and if successful, defeat the legislation. If, however, it obeys the letter of the law, then any profits over and above the permitted level will inevitably, in a period of depreciating currency, be used to gain control of more and more local industry. The scope for conflict between national policy and the enterprise grows with success.

TAKEOVERS BY THE HOST GOVERNMENT

In the last analysis the host government can suppress, nationalize or simply expropriate the subsidiary established within its territory. That is why, however weak and poor, the nation state has greater power within its own boundaries than even the most powerful enterprise.

In underdeveloped nations professing Socialism and therefore public ownership of the means of production, the subsidiary must eventually cease to be part of the whole enterprise. In the great majority of cases, however, this is a highly theoretical and distant prospect for international enterprises in general, although the prospect of nationalization has to be considered as a serious risk. Increasingly too nation states are making it a condition of direct investment that sooner or later ownership passes to local hands, probably the public sector. Certainly this is now the practice for extractive industries where after a certain length of time, mines, oil wells or the like become the property of the host state, generally without compensation. The major problem is often that for one reason or another the host government may wish to accelerate the process, even after having solemnly agreed the timetable. Governments break agreements with impunity while enterprises cannot. The reasons are generally discreditable. A rising opposition politician may find it profitable to be more overtly anti-foreign than the government. Or the products covered by the agreement may assume a vital role in world affairs: the transformation in oil prices in the mid 1970's meant that many international oil companies found their assets being taken over long before the prevailing agreement made this legal. In part too host governments become increasingly captious as the handover date appears, because they fear that the assets will be run down in the last few years of the enterprise's lease, the enterprise having every interest in making immediate profits and little interest in long-term prospects.

The importance of this problem is seen whenever a host nation takes over foreign owned companies by a unilateral decision and only afterwards discusses compensation. The standard gambits of both disputants have been discussed earlier. The enterprise will place a very high value on the nationalized subsidiary, while the very low value on it by the expropriating government is justified on the grounds of failure to provide for future development by running down assets, pollution of neighbourhoods requiring to be compensated for, etc. International enterprises may be excused for feeling they are in a 'Heads I win, Tails you lose' situation. Low profits before nationalization show that the subsidiary was not worth much; high profits indicate that excess exploitation has taken place.

Realistically, one must assume that over large areas of Latin America, Africa, and Asia more and more assets of international enterprises may be at risk in the event of political quarrels, a vital role emerging for a commodity, or simply the growth of technical competence. The days of the extractive subsidiary therefore are numbered.

What precautions can be taken against the day of nationalization, whether the subsidiary is an extractive or a manufacturing one? It is as well to remember that although the nationalization of a subsidiary is likely to be a traumatic experience for the parent enterprise, both parties to the situation have an interest in remaining on speaking terms, even during the rape, so to speak. Outright denunciations and threats from the parent government of the enterprise are not likely to endear the latter to the national government from which it is trying to collect compensation. Equally the national government, unless it is in a transport of fury or delirium over getting rid of the foreigner, has to reckon its standing in the world finance markets and its ability to obtain financial credits or aid depend on it remaining relatively moderate in its attitudes about compensation. A record of expropriation or defaults wins no friends in international financial circles.

Emotional and non-rational attitudes are only too common in underdeveloped countries particularly when anti-foreign feeling can be whipped up to cover up an economic or political crisis. It used to be said that the way to unite a country in crisis was to go to war with another country. Today for many underdeveloped countries the way to a temporary unity is to expropriate foreign property, regardless of the relevance of that action to the real situation. The oil producing states led the way but others have followed

Where a political crisis is not acute, but capital can still be made out of causing difficulties to the foreigner, the tactics may not be direct expropriation but harassment and an officially inspired boycott to ruin the foreign enterprise.

At least such moves are less costly in human life than the old anti-foreign tactic. But it is just as irrational and stores up problems for the future. If nationalization is genuinely in the interest of the host society, then it is better for both parties that it be done coolly — not in passion or for short-term political expediency.

A major remedy would be some form of international arbitration on compensation, acceptable to both parties. Such an organization has been in existence since the middle 1960's, created under the auspices of the International Bank of Reconstruction and Development. This is the International Center for Settlement of Investment Disputes (ICSID) situated in Washington. ICSID provides an arbitration service, the use of which may now be written into agreements on investment; or it can be used on investment arrangements which predate the ICSID creation but which are only now giving rise to debate.

Both parties have to agree to its use and the judgments are binding. The practical limitation of this may be reduced by qualifications on what is to be discussed by one party or the other. The convention which set up the organization has now been ratified by between sixty and seventy nation states. Not surprisingly however, the states which have not signed the convention are in many instances those states where expropriation dangers are highest. And the difficulty is to know in advance whether a revolutionary movement which overthrew the existing government which had ratified the convention, would feel bound by the commitment undertaken by the overthrown regime if the new government decided on expropriation of foreign assets.

OTHER PRESSURES FROM HOST COUNTRIES

There are two major sources of these pressures, directly from the host government itself, and indirectly, but often with government encouragement, from local customers. The latter, almost certainly incorrectly, hope for lower costs and better service.

It is an error to assume that if a crisis arises from these pressures, then the parties originating the crisis always have a clear idea of what they want. It is possible for the host government, as has been suggested, to be uncertain what it does want most in the long run, i.e. jobs, technology or foreign exchange. Equally, local customers, in demanding local production, have not thought through the possible implications of higher prices and poorer quality.

A political crisis, only partly related to the issue, may precipitate a new demand on the enterprise quite unexpectedly. There is therefore no point in having an over rigid response worked out well in advance. But at least the enterprise should be clear in its own mind what it is prepared to concede and what *quid pro quo* it might wish to seek. If a host government is very anxious for local production to be expanded or extended in range, would it suit the enterprise to bargain for subsidies, tax concessions freer profit remission? If then the crisis does occur before the company is ready to move of its own accord, at least it will go into the dispute knowing what it wants out of the situation, rather than merely reacting defensively, with no initiatives of its own.

So far as pressure from the customer is concerned, it may be helpful to have worked out in advance detailed estimates of the cost in increased prices and reduced costs which the customer will have to meet.

THE PARENT GOVERNMENT

Foreign investment in productive capacity which could equally well be sited at home is prima facie against the interests of the parent government. It has precisely the opposite effect on technology, employment and foreign exchange earnings as it has for the host government.

This is of course a generalization and like all generalizations has to be qualified. Two examples illustrate these qualifications. Foreign investment may inhibit key research and development by local enterprises and so enable a national dominance of technology to be retained. As an illustration, however concerned the U.S. government may be about IBM dominance of computer and data processing technology in the U.S.A., its satisfaction with IBM dominance of this technology in most other Western nations is discreet, but wholehearted.

Secondly it may be politically expedient to permit such investment and aid in the industrialization of friendly countries in the underdeveloped world. The diversion of assembly operations by U.S. enterprises to low labour cost areas in South East Asia angers U.S. trade unions and would probably bring inhibiting legislation by the U.S. government, but for the fact that the countries involved, South Korea and Taiwan, and to a lesser extent Hong Kong and Singapore are deemed to be well worth supporting in U.S. national interests.

The major problem from the parent government's angle is that there is no organization available to screen the activities of the international enterprise as a matter of routine. Political embargoes can be directed at one or two hostile countries only. Currency controls may exist but they are intended to conserve foreign exchange, not to initiate or supervise a definite national policy in respect of the international enterprise. If non-controlled financial sources are used (e.g. the Eurodollar Market) then the national interest may not be involved so far as the parent government is concerned. In the parent country opposition to foreign investment by an enterprise comes from interested parties, e.g. trade unions, not from a more objective assessment of the national interest.

AREAS OF CONFLICT

We have discussed the possible conflict between the enterprise and one or other of the governments involved, i.e. host or parent. Another situation is possible, namely conflict between governments with the enterprise being the unhappy party in the middle. The cause is likely to be a directive from one government or the other to the enterprise whose implementation is likely to offend the other government; or even worse, contradictory directives from both governments. Generally speaking in both the above instances, the enterprise is more likely to pay attention to the parent government, even when directives are simply recommendations without legal sanctions.

Most of the reported clashes involve the U.S. authorities, executive or judicial. Why American authorities are more commonly involved than most other countries is complex. In part it arises simply because there are more American multinationals; in part too it may be that American public actions are more open than most. Two other factors are probably more important: the doctrine of the separation of power; and attitudes towards anti-trust legislation.

The fact that the U.S. Executives, Legislature and Judiciary are deliberately kept separate from each other by the Constitution, illustrates a point made earlier. It is dangerous to assume that a nation state has a single interest in dealing with international business. It is quite possible in the American situation for the Executive, through such departments as that of Commerce or the Attorney General, to have a distinct interest from that of Congress, and on top of this to find the Courts handing out legal judgements which cause embarrassment to the Executive and annoyance abroad.

Allied to the separation of powers issue, there is an historical tradition of anti-trust legislation which can be contrary to practice in other parts of the world where American enterprises operate.

In many other countries where the separation of powers is not practised (and in most democracies it would be unusual for the chief executive to represent a different political party from the legislative majority, as so often happens in the U.S.A.), then clashes do not arise so easily because of conflicts of interests. Moreover, the judiciary in other countries tends to pay rather more attention to what is politic in respect of other legal systems and will not in general issue judgements which require to be enforced outside their own jurisdiction.

The effect of this is that it is often U.S. legal decisions which hit the headlines because they appear to other governments or the foreign press as attempts to make the U.S. writ run within non-U.S. territory. When American Courts issue judgements affecting the operation of international enterprises, U.S. or foreign, within U.S. borders, this is regarded elsewhere as reasonable. When U.S. courts make decisions on how U.S. corporations shall operate in Europe, European governments are less happy. But when a U.S. court makes a ruling on how a non-American enterprise may act outside the U.S.A., in a third country, two national governments are likely to be very unhappy, the parent and the host government. All these situations have occurred from time to time.

The illustrations given so far have been in terms of court decisions. Executive directives have much the same consequences. The prohibition by Ford headquarters in Detroit of exports of vehicles from Ford of Canada to China attracted considerable publicity in Canada and elsewhere in the 1960's and, in the event, probably did the U.S.A. far more harm than the Chinese. The examination by the U.S. government of an agreement that Ford (Argentina) was to supply Cuba in the middle 1970's attracted less attention, but certainly did little to sweeten U.S. relations with either the Argentine or Cuba.[31]

It is perhaps inevitable that open government should cause this issue to be aired publicly, and attract to the U.S.A. the sort of criticism of interference in other nations' affairs, that open moves encourage. Other Western governments contrive to put their policies into effect much more discreetly, even though many, particularly the Japanese or the French, can and do use government pressure to advance the interests of their own multinationals.

Even allowing, however, for the unfortunate penchant of the U.S. government to achieve with the maximum of noise, what others may achieve more discreetly, the fact remains that there are few signs of consistent policies towards international enterprises by the parent country. It is often left to interested or injured parties within the society to urge more positive control on the foreign investment policy of the international enterprise. The trade unions are the most prominent. But intervention is sporadic and tends to be relatively ineffectual for that very reason.

CONTROLLING THE INTERNATIONAL ENTERPRISE

Any nation state wants to be able to regulate and, if necessary, limit the activities of private enterprise within its frontiers. And if the private enterprise company is also a foreign controlled one operating internationally, the desire and need for control is seen as that much greater. This is a truism whether the state is the most underdeveloped, or the most industrialized.

The Underdeveloped Countries

One of the most underdeveloped countries in the world is probably Papua, until recently an Australian protectorate and little more than a generation ago still in the stone age. A Papuan opposition party summed up in a political slogan in pidgin English the sentiments of many underdeveloped nations to foreign investment, and the international enterprise. The slogan was 'BISNIS BILONG AUTSIDE MAN'.[33] That simple statement, whether accurate or not, sums up more graphically than any official report the fears of underdeveloped societies that their industrial and commercial future may be controlled by outside interests. This section of the book deals with some of the methods open to such societies to attempt to control these developments.

Control of an enterprise does not necessarily require ownership. The U.S. Federal authorities and Western European governments effectively can exercise a degree of control on enterprises whether national or foreign, within their frontiers. Admittedly, their control in international enterprises is substantially less than those of national ones, and they constantly seek to remedy this. The remedies, however, follow the pattern of more effective regulation and public accountability rather than changing ownership patterns. In underdeveloped countries this rather sophisticated concept of control without ownership is not always practical. The administrative machinery to detect, for example, blatant transfer pricing or tax avoidance, is just not sufficiently advanced to deal with the sophisticated operation of the enterprise. To supervise and regulate the activities of the enterprise therefore it is often necessary to have inside knowledge—to insist at least on partial local ownership—whether by the state or by private citizens. Local ownership may be almost an atavistic drive.

Methods of control. There are several methods which may be used to bring a measure of regulation:

a) Licensing of investment, the import of capital equipment, and possibly of personnel. The first two tend to encourage the introduction at an early stage of local capital and therefore a measure of local control: the desirability of building up local managerial ability is obvious.

b) A sliding scale of taxation depending on the profits being made; this particular tax applying to foreign but not locally owned business. Such tax discrimination is politically a popular move. It is intended again to accelerate local ownership but is less easy to enforce than is sometimes thought, because of the possibility of transfer pricing.

Before going on to consider the other methods of control it may be useful to consider some aspects of the first two. In a sense they are old friends—but standing on their heads, being in fact the reverse of two policies already described to encourage investment. Some governments may actively be encouraging investment by concessions in these areas, others discouraging foreign investment by an exact reversal. Brazil might be taken as one extreme, India as the other, the former encouraging investments, and the import of capital equipment by permitting profit repatriation to take account of such imports, offering tax holidays and the like; while India, ideologically poles apart, follows the policies described in a) and b) above. Obviously, political ideology plays a part in deciding the policy; so too presumably does the stage of economic development. The same government might, as time passes, logically find it expedient to switch from one policy to the other, from discouragement of international business to encouragement, or vice versa. Sometimes because of the inertia in policy making, or simple irrational prejudice the appropriate policy for one decade may be carried on too long, and accelerate a process which ought expediently to be slowed down.

To revert, however, to listing the methods of control:

c) The encouragement of disinvestment. Here the international enterprise may be encouraged to sell off its holdings, and repatriate its capital, or simply allow the original investment to be run down and replaced by local enterprise. Logically, if disinvestment is the aim, then two consequences follow: 1) that the enterprise will not be allowed to sell assets to other foreign interests but only to local nationals; 2) having sold them the enterprise will not be allowed to invest the proceeds elsewhere in that society. If this policy is being carried to extremes the enterprise is in effect being distrained and forced to sell at any price regardless of real value since the number of local buyers may be small. There is then a tendency for local buyers to be front men either for the enterprise or for government officials administering the policy, with corruption becoming a major by-product. Finally, of course, such a policy of disinvestment by invitation so to speak requires ready repatriation of capital. Countries with substantial foreign reserves like the Arabs with oil, Zambia with copper, Malaysia with tin and rubber, may contemplate this. But if the foreign currency reserves are not available to enable capital repatriation to take place, disinvestment becomes indistinguishable from expropriation. Either the proceeds are blocked in a depreciating currency or repatriation is at a punitively low rate of exchange.

d) A requirement that ancillary or support industries should be in local hands. It was pointed out earlier that when local suppliers were unable to meet the quality requirements of an enterprise operating in a new territory, it might be necessary for the enterprise to undertake a range of support activity which it would not contemplate in its home market where adequate support industries were available. If, on the other hand, the enterprise is prevented from expanding into these areas and is required to 'buy local', then it is under some pressure to assist local industrialists to improve their standards. Such a policy will not give direct control over the enterprise, but will at least ensure that technological benefits are passed on. A variant on this already discussed is the tendency for assembly operations located in areas of cheap labour to be replaced by local companies performing the operation under contract.

Any or all of these methods of control may be tried. There is no doubt, however, that the most effective methods, as well as the most acceptable, are those which involve a measure of local ownership. In spite of the disadvantages of this from the point of view of overall strategy, that is a fact of life which the international enterprise operating in underdeveloped countries, may have to accept.

Variations on Local Ownership

There are three possible variants: a) the first of these is the sharing of ownership with a public sector company. The popularity of such organizations in the underdeveloped world has already been discussed along with their disadvantages, namely a tendency to be less efficient than privately owned companies. How successful such a joint venture will be depends on whether the enterprise can influence its partner to an essentially profit centred outlook: b) the second possibility is the straight joint venture with a local company, the pros and cons of which have been discussed; c) the third, and the one which has most variants, is the participation of local capital by individuals in the form of equity shares. The pros and cons of such an approach were discussed in passing in the section on finance. The basic problem is the extent to which equity share holding can be made a normal feature of society.

INCREASING LOCAL PARTICIPATION—THREE EXAMPLES

There are as many methods of encouraging local participation in subsidiaries of international enterprises as there are countries. The three examples given below are not therefore necessarily illustrative of broad principles. They have been chosen merely to demonstrate how one country in each of the three underdeveloped continents of South America, Africa and Asia have tackled the problem, and some of the potential difficulties which have followed.

A. South American Example—Peru

In 1968 a left wing military coup d'etat overthrew the existing government. The new government started to introduce a highly nationalistic and left wing policy on foreign investment. The pattern, however, was not overtly Marxist but claimed to derive from the cultural roots of the country, from the Inca concept of a Communidad, the local Community of which any foreign owned subsidiary was a part. The legislation was frankly confused, as most radical legislation is; but the basic principle was that laid down in the Andean Pact of which Peru became a founder member, i.e. that majority holdings in Peruvian located plant was to be reduced to a minority interest by the gradual transfer of 50 per cent of shares to the Community (or to any Peruvian national). The procedure was to be financed by a proportion of company profits being handed over to the Community which could then use this finance to increase its shareholding in the enterprise or any other foreign company. Subsidiaries that were more than 75 per cent foreign owned were to have the foreign holding reduced to 30 per cent; plants 50 to 75 per cent foreign owned were to reduce foreign ownership to 49 per cent.

It was clearly in the interest of the first group to reduce their holding below 75 per cent before the new legislation took effect. This tended to put shares on the market which were eagerly bought up by Peruvian nationals who felt that a share in a partially owned foreign venture had rather more security than a purely local holding. Because the share prices went to a premium the Communities had to pay higher prices than they might have expected—a point which tended to slow down the process and possibly give the Peruvian government time to consider whether running down foreign holdings was necessarily in the best interests of the economy.

The lack of a Peruvian stock exchange meant that the shares were sold through the banking system so that private buyers were probably well to do and buying in larger quantities than would have been the case if stock exchange facilities had been available. Even if the Peruvian government wished more shares to be held by the public sector (in this case the Communities) it would probably have suited its purposes better to have had the small private sector shares fairly widespread. Large shareholders would not necessarily be pro-government.

The other factor was the insistence that such nationalization was essentially in the historic pattern, not an imported variety of Marxism.

B.   An African Example — Kenya

In the early 1970's Kenya was a one party state with a moderate but ageing President, Jomo Kenyatta: its political and ideological commitment was not so left wing as (officially at least) were most newly independent African states.

The Kenya government was anxious to increase local ownership and share participation in foreign controlled subsidiaries, but by encouraging private shareholding in these companies, rather than the state having a share. To increase local participation, therefore, it experimented with controls in the Banking system. The effect of this was that the amount of overdraft facilities a foreign subsidiary might raise depended on the proportion of its shares held by Kenyan citizens. The higher the local share, the higher the credit facilities which would be made available.

How successful such a solution will be in the African context it is difficult to say. Basically of course the exercise depended on persuading Kenyans to buy shares instead of land or property which was the traditional way to deal with wealth in an under-developed country.

There was possibly less room for conflict if well-to-do Africans bought shares, because in general they preferred the Kenyatta government to any possible alternative which was likely to be more left wing. Potentially however if racialism ever broke out in Kenya, there could be problems. A substantial proportion of the middle class in Kenya were of Asian descent, having settled in Kenya during the British colonial regime. Those who had not claimed Kenyan nationality were gradually leaving, mainly for the United Kingdom. It was not inconceivable that in the future a black President might pursue an overtly racialist policy and dispossess or expel non-Blacks as President Amin had done in neighbouring Uganda. Possibly excessive holdings by Asians in foreign owned enterprises would increase the chance of such a racialist backlash.

The success therefore of the policy of Kenyanization by persuasion depended on two factors: the continuation of a moderate but strong government, and the conversion of a substantial proportion of the new African middle class to the concept of share buying as an alternative to land property or cattle.

C.   An Asian Example—Malaysia

Malaysia was a pro-Western society with potential racial problems. Malaysia had two major racial groups: the indigenous Malays who were largely Muslim, and the descendants of Chinese settlers. The Chinese minority were hardworking and, as in many other parts of South East Asia, dominated local trade and commerce, while foreign investors dominated key industrial companies. It was estimated by the Malaysian government that well over 60 per cent of the shares in Malaysian enterprises were foreign owned: 20 per cent or more were owned by non-Malay citizens (mainly Chinese). In part this reflected the country's colonial past, and overseas investment in Malayan raw materials, principally tin and rubber. Malays did not readily buy shares when they could buy property, a habit which in part reflected a conviction among the more conservative Muslim community that shareholding was a form of usury, with all the religious overtones that word carries.

Left to itself, the post-colonial pattern suggested that more and more foreign interests would be bought out by the prospering non-Malay groups; and in view of incipient distrust between Malay and Chinese such a situation would be at least as dangerous as having overwhelming foreign control.

The Malaysian government therefore planned to encourage more Malay ownership via share buying. The ideal was that by the end of two decades, share ownership would be about 30 per cent foreign, 40 per cent Chinese, and 30 per cent Malay. This would be accomplished, it was hoped, without transfer of existing equity because it was anticipated rapid growth in industry would take place. Provided some 50 per cent of all new shares were acquired by Malays in the 1970's, the redistribution would be achieved peacefully.

It was frankly a very ambitious aim, and again like the Kenyan system envisaged a change in cultural habits among the indigenous middle class of the economy. If it did not succeed there were some very ominous prospects of conflict, not so much between the foreign investors and the locals, but between Malay and non-Malays within the community.

CONTROL AT THE INTERNATIONAL LEVEL

This book started from the proposition that the international enterprise was outside the day to day control of any national government. It follows therefore that any effective control may have to be at an international level. This chapter examines the rudimentary international controls which now exist or are under consideration.

Such control may be exercised at two levels: regionally where groups of nation states have set up some international structure, e.g. a customs union or free trade zone; or globally, i.e. through the UN or its subsidiary organizations.

There are now a fair number of regional groupings with wide variations both of formalization and effectiveness. It would be tedious and unprofitable to examine all theses groupings in terms of their attitude towards the international enterprise, largely because few have any coherent policy and even those which tend to be evolving or changing that policy fairly quickly. Two groupings only will be considered: the EEC because its policy represents a response from Western developed nations, which are both the source and site of most international enterprises; and the Andean Pact Group of South America which represents a fairly rigid reaction in a less developed region and which, if successful, might well set the pattern followed by less developed countries elsewhere.

A.   THE EUROPEAN ECONOMIC COMMUNITY

The Treaty of Rome which set up the Community made no specific provision for regulating the international enterprise, although clearly international business is a key factor in what is intended to become in time a fully integrated economic and political union. Subsequent legislation evolved by the European Commission makes no distinction between international enterprises having origin within the Community and those originating outside, principally in the U.S.A., Sweden and Japan. There have at times been signs of hostility at the political level to the American corporations which were so swift to take advantage of the new conditions created by the Community. This has, however, tended to take the form of discussions on how to maximize the flow of information about financial and working conditions between members to enable national governments to detect tax avoidance or strategies by multinationals or to enable trade unions to compare practices and conditions from country to country, and so to co-ordinate their response. Such activities however have not moved beyond the discussion stage.

Of more direct consequence to the international enterprise has been the Community's attempts to develop competition policy based on the provisions of Clauses 85 and 86 of the Rome Treaty. These clauses attempt to limit restrictive practices or monopoly conditions and have tended, partly by deliberate action by the Commission and partly by case law precedent, to extend the somewhat vague powers incorporated in the clauses.[33]

One example of this has been the 1974 legislation on mergers which, while not as severe as U.S. Anti-trust Legislation, is likely to limit mergers and incidentally close one means of approach by a multinational seeking a foothold in the European market. Briefly, the Commission envisages a system of prior notification of mergers which would produce groupings of a turnover exceeding about $1,000 millions annually. The most effective part of the policy is not the undoubted right to prohibit mergers, but simply to delay them to the point that they are frustrated by mounting opposition. The criterion on which the proposed merger would be judged would be the probability of the merger weakening competition. Prenotification of the proposed merger generally means a three month moratorium on action, and this may be followed by up to nine months further consideration. American and British enterprises which are generally larger than continental enterprises are likely to be most affected.

Clauses 85 and 86 have given rise to legal action against international enterprises and it is perhaps significant that two of the seminal cases which have helped to establish case law involve American enterprises operating in or from the Community.

Another potential area of intervention is in respect of regional policy. It has been shown that international enterprises have been quick to take advantage of the very generous grants made for investment in regions of heavy unemployment. There are not too apocryphal stories of business rivals encountering each other in airports, going in opposite directions, each being tempted to set up plant in his rival's country, on the basis of central government grants. More blatantly, there have been instances of outside enterprises, American or Japanese, encouraging competitive bidding in investment incentives from the governments of various community members. An overall regional policy would probably put paid to the more ludicrous competitive stances now being adopted by member states.

Finally and somewhat speculatively, the steady if unspectacular progress towards standardization of legal commercial forms and accountancy standards will presumably lessen the room for manoeuvre of the international enterprise as between member states. And if and when the European Company form, the Societas Europea (SE) does emerge the machinery will exist for more detailed scrutiny of the actions of these international enterprises.

B. THE ANDEAN PACT GROUP

The Andean Pact Group emerged in the late 1960's when the Latin American Free Trade Association lost its momentum. The reasons for the relative failure of LAFTA are complex but can be summed up as the unwillingness of national governments to sacrifice their domestic industries by permitting the free import of goods from other member nations—precisely the factor which lies behind the failure of most such regional groupings.

The Andean Group consists of the signatories of the Cartagena Agreement of 1969, namely Bolivia, Chile, Colombia, Ecuador, Peru and Venezuela. Its intentions go further than the regulation of international business, requiring as it does the co-ordination of development plans of all the signatories and the harmonization of economic and social policies on a far more formal basis than was ever achieved by LAFTA. In the long term, its effects on economic and political development in Latin America could be as radical as the most visionary developments of the European Economic Community.

Not all aspects of the plan relate to international investment or the international enterprise: those which do are summarized very briefly below. What does stand out about these plans, as compared with EEC measures, is a greater degree of suspicion if not downright hostility to international business.

The two key limiting factors so far as international businesses are concerned are the requirements that the head office of any new enterprise must be located within the Andean Group area, and that the majority control shall be held by interests or nationals within the member country. The exact method of achieving this result is left to the individual nation. The Peruvian example of transfer of equity holdings to the local community which has been quoted is one example.

Foreign investment is therefore practical provided that the investor does not regard the conditions as too onerous. The positive side of the conditions are that guarantees are given that the value of the original investment may be repatriated, and profits may be remitted annually to a value of up to 14 per cent of the capital value. What therefore the system implies for the foreign investor is a reasonable degree of security against expropriation or currency blocking but without any real possibility of the investment forming part of a truly world wide set up. The limitations in fact are a very strict variation on those normally applying to a joint venture. Whether or not the proposition will be sufficiently attractive to bring in many international enterprises is a matter which only time will resolve.

The Andean Pact Group has developed to an extreme form the idea of sectorial programmes of industrial development, i.e. on the assumption that the domestic market of any one member state would be inadequate to permit the development of modern industry by large scale production techniques, industries have been allocated exclusively to one country or another. Colombia, for example, has what amounts to a monopoly in the development of light aircraft, Ecuador clocks and watches, Peru motor vehicles and so on. The Peruvian deal with Toyota illustrates how a franchise in motor vehicles for the whole area can be reinforced by eliminating competition from other vehicle manufacturers in the country.

Experience in LAFTA and elsewhere has shown that such sectorial arrangements are probably a sine qua non of a trading bloc in a developing area. Otherwise the tendency is for each nation to seek to use the export opportunities while at the same time attempting to protect its own industries from imports from other members.

Sectorial arrangements like these need not involve foreign enterprises: it is presumably up to the member nation concerned to decide whether to permit such investment. Indeed before the Allende government was overthrown Chile was in the process of nationalizing all foreign subsidiaries. And in more general terms tariff concessions within the area did not apply to exports from foreign owned factories. A major intention was to ensure that there would be no competitive bidding for foreign investment by laying down limits on the concessions or incentives open to such investment.

The Andean Group experiment has attracted wide interest in other parts of the underdeveloped world. If it proves a long-term success it will seriously inhibit the development of the international enterprise in these regions. The dangers however are precisely those of other trade blocs in the underdeveloped world, including LAFTA. Firstly, sectorial development is likely to have mixed successes and failures, and there is always a danger that those nations whose allocated industry sectors do not succeed will demand a reallocation of the more successful sectors. Secondly, political instability will have to be met with a remarkable tolerance in the event of internal disorders in any member state. Chile turned overnight from a revolutionary Marxist state to a right wing military establishment. Peru, by contrast, is a left wing self-styled revolutionary government and so on. The Cartagena agreement implied simultaneously a move towards economic union—by implication involving political union also—combined with the ability to accept overnight a political volte-face by any member state. The problems this creates are not likely to be felt only by international enterprises seeking a modus vivendi with such a grouping.

UN POLICIES ON INTERNATIONAL BUSINESS

There is a tendency to treat international business in general and the multinational corporation in particular as the villains of the piece so far as underdeveloped economies are concerned. Two approaches are illustrated below, one originating from a group representing the Third World, the other a more balanced view drawn up by a committee with representatives of the West, the Communist World and the Third World.

A.   UNCTAD, UNIDO, AND THE THIRD WORLD

Various agencies set up under UN auspices have their own policies towards international business, particularly the multinational corporations. The most important, UNCTAD, the UN Conference on Trade and Development and UNIDO, the UN Industrial Development Organization, tend to be dominated by underdeveloped countries, the so called Third World. These organizations tend to be more critical of the activities of the multinationals, although after ritual denunciations their proposals are not very extreme.

The proposals were summarized in the Algiers Conference of Non Aligned States in 1973 and included the following recommendations:

1) Central government control of foreign investment
2) Investment by foreign enterprises should introduce appropriate technology, save foreign exchange, ensure employment opportunities
3) Investment should create new industry, rather than buying over existing companies
4) Appropriate controls on profit remittances
5) Key industries should be prohibited to foreign investment: this might, where appropriate, include extractive industries.

All of these might be regarded as fairly conventional measures: in some cases more ideal than realistic guidelines.

In theory, any resolutions by an international organization ought to be far more effective in dealing with the international enterprise than action by individual nations. At the present moment, however, there is every sign that the nations, even of the Third World, are just as divided in their approach to the multinational corporation, as in anything else. Resolutions are likely to remain just resolutions for a long period of time. And if any action stops the spread of the multinational corporation it will have to be rather more convincingly backed up by international solidarity, than seems possible at present.

B.   THE GROUP OF EMINENT PERSONS REPORT

Following a resolution in the UN Economic and Social Council, a study was commissioned on the effects of the multinational corporations. The preliminary studies were carried out by staff members of ECOSOC basically assembling statistical information and posing the major issues. These were summed up as 'whether a set of institutions and devices can be worked out which will guide the multinational's exercise of power and introduce some form of accountability to the international community into their activities.'

The main report, however, was the responsibility of the so-called 'Group of Eminent Persons' drawn from politics, the academic world and business, with representatives from the Western developed countries, where the corporation originated, the underdeveloped world and the Communist world.

The recommendations made can be briefly summarized.

There should be a permanent UN Commission on Multinational Corporations, based on agreement among member nations.

The Report commented on the problems faced by developing countries in deciding what were reasonable terms for foreign investors. Thus a host government which had agreed terms with a multinational might conclude later on, in the light of experience, that the concessions given were too generous, and decide to change the terms unilaterally. Methods suggested to deal with this situation included the organizing of centralized negotiating services available to host governments; more co-ordination of policy among host nations; provision from the outset for the future review of terms; a clear indication from a prospective host government of those areas where foreign investment would be permissible, as well as a statement of long term national policies on the gradual reduction of foreign investment holdings.

The Report also considered specific fields where conflict between a host government and a multinational was most likely. Most of these have already been discussed earlier. The areas included ownership and control; finance, the evaluation of technology brought into the country, employment conditions for locally recruited staff; consumer protection, competition, taxation, transfer pricing, and standardized accounting procedures. None of the recommendations were particularly revolutionary although they were clearly written to protect the interests of the host country rather than the multinational. Indeed, to some extent the role of the parent government was seen as the defence of the host country's interest rather than the multinational's.

The conclusions were both balanced and moderate and reflected the fact that the Committee was not dominated by one political group. Nevertheless it would be unrealistic to assume that even such eminently practical suggestions will be implemented readily. The UN itself could not impose such measures on individual governments.

THE FUTURE OF THE INTERNATIONAL ENTERPRISE

The situation of international business and the international enterprise is changing so rapidly that it would be a rash man who attempted very definitive prophesies about future developments. One or two predictions however can be made.

The first is that certain types of enterprise have a limited future, namely those in the extractive industries, i.e. *Category I* industries. The future of manufacturing industries of *Category II* appears reasonably secure particularly in the developed world. *Category III*, i.e. the enterprise supplying markets in the developed world, with products manufactured in the underdeveloped world is however potentially the most significant in political terms if not in size. This type of enterprise may give the underdeveloped world more hope for prosperity than can be achieved by financial aid or self-help among the 'Have not' nations fuelled by hositility towards the 'Haves'.

So far as international control of the process is concerned, it is probable that regional efforts will remain more effective than global efforts, simply because regional groupings have more identity of interests than the world grouping. Guidelines can be laid down by UN bodies, but in the last analysis it is the individual nation state which will decide its own policy. In a paradoxical sort of way, the degree of freedom from international control enjoyed by the enterprises discussed in this book, exists because the nation states themselves are unwilling to limit their own freedom of action, in order to bring them under control.

Notes and References

1. J. J. Servan Schrieber, *The American Challenge*: Atheneum NY, 1969.
2. The reader may feel that the treatment of the subject rides roughshod over some painstaking efforts at systematic classification by writers on the subject. At present, however, businessmen do not make any very precise distinction between international, multinational, transnational or supranational. Until they do, it is premature to worry too much about definitions which are changing rapidly in any case. A further complication may be added by the growing importance of ideology and culture. The transideological enterprise is an increasingly important concept. So too may become the transcultural enterprise. Pushing classification to its logical conclusion one might apply the other three prefixes to either concept, and end up with twelve categories. Distinctions of this type, however, move further and further away from the realities of business.

   For the reader who is interested in the evolution of the terminology the best references are Y. Aharoni 'On the Definition of a Multinational Corporation' published in *The Multinational Enterprise in Transition*, Eds. A. Kapoor and P. D. Grub: Princeton, Darwin Press, 1972, and in the UN Publication *Multinational Corporations in World Development*, United Nations 1973, particularly Appendix II. The UN publication uses the Vernon definition, i.e. an annual turnover of $100 millions. The UN now favours 'Transnational' instead of 'Multinational'.
3. S. E. Rolfe defines an international corporation as one with a foreign content of 25 per cent or more, foreign content being the proportion of sales, investment production or employment abroad. See his paper 'The International Corporation in Perspective' in *The Multinational Corporation in the World Economy*, Eds. S. E. Rolfe and W. Damm: Praeger, NY, 1970.
4. H. V. Perlmutter 'The Tortuous Evolution of the Multinational Corporation' *Columbia Journal of World Business*, Vol 4, 1969.
5. J. H. Dunning 'The Multinational Enterprise—the Background', Chapter 1 of *The Multinational Enterprise*, Ed. J. H. Dunning: Allen and Unwin, London 1971.
6. R. Vernon *Sovereignty at Bay—the Multinational Spread of U.S. Enterprises*, Basic Books, 1971.
7. Another aspect of the tendency of the less developed nations to take over extractive industries as, and when they are technologically able to do so has been the creation of producer organizations which hope to limit output and raise prices. The most spectacularly successful has been OPEC (the Organization of Petroleum Exporting Countries) and less so CIPEC (the

Conseil Intergouvernemental des Pays Exporteurs de Cuivre). The latter has had less success than OPEC because there are more obvious substitutes for copper.

Some tentative attempts have been made to form a similar consortium among Bauxite producers, Bauxite being the most convenient source of aluminium. It is reported however that the major aluminium producers in the developed world are urgently seeking methods of extracting the metal from alumina-bearing clays and shales, which are a good deal more widely available than Bauxite and not therefore susceptible to output limitation by producer nations.

In general, however, international commodity agreements, administered solely by the producers, have been relatively unsuccessful because the countries have lacked financial resources to back up policies of limiting output.

8. At the 1968 Conference of UNCTAD (q.v.) demands were pressed for a Generalized System of Preference by which developed nations would reduce tariff duties on the import of manufactured goods from the underdeveloped nations. The U.S.A. refused to agree unless the European Economic Community were prepared to abolish discriminatory preferences to EEC Associate Members (largely ex-colonies of member states). The EEC and Japan have made some concessions.

9. The UN Industrial Development Organization has produced a 'Manual on the Establishment of Industrial Joint Ventures Agreement in Developing Countries' outlining acceptable terms. It is worth study by enterprises contemplating Joint Ventures anywhere, not merely in the underdeveloped world.

10. General Motors (U.S.A.) and the Nissan Motor Coy (Japan) were reported in 1974 to have concluded assembly plant agreements with Saudi Arabia. It is difficult to foresee that local manufacture could ever become profitable in a country, simultaneously immensely wealthy and sparsely populated.

11. UNCTAD (UN Conference on Trade and Development) was created in 1964 and in part complements, in part competes with, the General Agreement on Tariffs and Trade. UNCTAD has 142 member states and overwhelmingly represents the interests of the Third World. It seeks to establish closer economic co-operation among underdeveloped countries and to obtain unilateral tariff concessions for industrial exports from them to the developed world. Its four-yearly meetings tend to generate a good deal of hostility towards the developed world (including, on occasion, the Communist developed economies). The hostility is exacerbated when the underdeveloped countries—sometimes known as the 'Club of Seventy Seven'—use their numerical majority to pass resolutions imposing trade policies on the developed countries; resolutions which the latter refuse to regard as binding.

12. Comecon, otherwise the Council for Mutual Economic Assistance (CMEA) was founded in 1949, and comprises the U.S.S.R., Czechoslovakia, Poland, Hungary, Rumania, Bulgaria, East Germany and Mongolia. Other Communist states including Cuba have varieties of Associate Status.

13. GATT (The General Agreement on Tariffs and Trade) has now 80 member states. The principle on which GATT operates is that every four years or thereabouts individual members bargain with each other on tariff reductions on a *quid pro quo* basis: these tariff reductions then apply to all members, and in general tariff discrimination cannot be applied by any member against the others, except in a clearly defined emergency situation. GATT membership also prevents certain types of activities which amount to unfair competition, e.g. export subsidies.

In recent years GATT negotiations have tended to be dominated by the bargaining between the U.S.A. on the one hand and the EEC on the other. This situation has tended to drag out negotiations because of the necessity of EEC members to agree on a common policy beforehand.

Although, strictly speaking, the developed countries are in a numerical minority, economically they dominate the organization, and GATT has sometimes been referred to as the 'Rich Man's Club', as opposed to UNCTAD which is dominated by the underdeveloped nations

14. Arbitration procedures most widely used in foreign trade are those of the UN Economic Commission for Europe, and the International Chamber of Commerce. The latter operates a Court of Arbitration, and since its rules were formalized in 1955, has been of growing importance both for conciliation and arbitration. In direct investment disputes involving disagreements between international enterprises and host countries the main arbitration source is the International Center for the Settlement of Investment Disputes, discussed in Chapter 10.

15. Examples of this process are increasingly being found in the simplified vehicles manufactured or partially manufactured in the underdeveloped world. The General Motors Basic Transportation Vehicle, particularly in South East Asia, appears under local names and uses components from GM subsidiaries together with local suppliers. The Ford Fiera assembled in the same area, is also essentially a very simple and cheap vehicle which can be assembled anywhere with a minimum technological base.

16. Sometimes the nomenclature of regional divisions is unfortunate. The practice in American and European enterprises of labelling Asian operations as 'Far East' may on occasion arouse irritation among Japanese or other nationalities who do not regard their countries as being in a remote corner of the world. On a more trivial scale the use of the main title plus the name of the host country for a subsidiary requires tact. The British subsidiary of the Fiat SpA of Italy is Fiat (England) but also includes in its territory Scots, Northern Irish and Welsh, who might not object to being called British, but would object to being called English.

17. The term 'Joint Venture' is also used to describe an ad hoc arrangement between two or more enterprises of the same national origin to enter into a partnership to conduct negotiations for a large and complex foreign order, e.g. to build a factory, dam, power station, etc.: or even a partnership between two enterprises of different national origins to run such a capital project in a third country. In this book, however, Joint Venture implies that one partner is resident in the host country of the operation.

18. L. G. Franko *Joint Venture Survival in the Multinational Corporation:* Praeger 1971, describes research carried out into the permanence of these arrangements which suggests that about one-third of these eventually result in a takeover by one partner or the other, or a winding up of the operation.

19. The 1973 Algiers Conference of Non-Aligned States passed a resolution that such takeovers should normally be prohibited. See Chapter 10.

20. Subsequently British Leyland bought over Innocenti.

21. See R. Vernon, 'Sovereignty at Bay', *op. cit.,* and L. T. Wells, 'A Product Life Cycle for International Trade' *Journal of Marketing,* May 1966.

22. An example of contrasting viewpoints of trade unions and management can be found in two complementary articles in the *Columbia Journal of World Business,* volumes 1 and 3 for 1973. The first, entitled 'The Case for Hartke Burke' by N. Goldfinger, Director of Research for the AFL/CIO argues that the activities of American multinationals destroy the U.S. advantage in

technology, etc., and by implication weaken Labour in dealing with Management. The second, by D. M. Kendall, Chairman of the Board of PepsiCo entitled 'The Need for Multinationals' argues on the contrary that they benefit the U.S. economy. A soft drink manufacturer has virtually no prospect of reaching a foreign market by exporting and represents, par excellence, the type of enterprise which has to produce locally in the market.

23. The tendency of U.S. multinationals to appoint Americans only to key executive posts was illustrated in an article by K. Simmonds 'Multinational? Well not Quite' in the *Columbia Journal of World Business*, Vol 4, 1966. The study was repeated on British companies with similar conclusions—see K. Simmonds and R. Connell 'Breaking the Boardroom Barrier' *Journal of Management Studies,* May 1974.

24. The Berne Union (Union d'Assureurs des Credits Internationaux) was created in 1934 and includes the principal credit insurance organizations of the major trading nations. It recommends maximum credit terms for standard export products but has no power to enforce these. The tendency under increasing competition has been for credit terms to be extended, and each member tends to reserve the right to provide matching credits, comparable with those offered by anyone else.

25. The Eurocurrency market emerged in the 1950's, primarily in terms of dollar deposits which were attracted to Europe, partly by the higher interest rates obtainable there than were legal in the U.S.A., but also fuelled by dollar holdings from other sources which preferred to remain outside the control of the U.S. Financial Authorities. The main operators in Eurodollar deals were European and particularly English banks. With the relative weakening of the U.S. dollar, other hard currencies have come into the market, e.g. German Marks and Swiss Francs. The term Eurocurrency is therefore tending to replace Eurodollar. Generally speaking, Eurocurrency is used to describe short-term borrowing and Eurobonds longer term borrowing.

26. See R. B. Stobaugh and S. M. Robbins *Money in the International Enterprise*: Basic Books 1973.

27. The Hartke-Burke proposals would inter alia extend taxation liabilities of U.S. Corporations on overseas earnings.

28. The problems of financial and accounting practices in some parts of the Third World were commented upon frankly and rather engagingly by the Governor of the Indonesian Central Bank. Discussing proposals that foreign enterprises including joint ventures would soon have shares quoted on the Indonesian stock exchange, he added,

> 'We would like to be careful as we have no tradition of public companies which issue properly inspected profit and loss accounts . . . We cannot afford to rush because we have not got a sufficient number of public accountants who will do the job. So I expect that the first shares quoted will be those of joint venture companies. They have a better book-keeping tradition and, let's put it frankly, they have a reputation to uphold in publishing a profit and loss account.'

Quoted from the *Financial Times,* London 18 July, 1974.

29. It is always dangerous to quote the Yugoslav situation as an illustration of East European practice. Nevertheless a useful article by M. Sukijasovic on 'Foreign Investment in Yugoslavia' illustrates the problem of permitting direct foreign investment while not conceding property rights. See *Foreign Investment—the Experience of Host Countries*, Eds. I. A. Litvak and C. J. Maule: Praeger, NY, 1970.

30. H. V. Perlmutter, 'The Transideological Enterprise', *Columbia Journal of World Business*, Vol 5, 1969.
31. Examples of the impact of U.S. jurisdiction on foreign enterprises operating outside U.S. territory are to be found in Rolfe and Damm (*op. cit.*), Chapter 3 by J. J. Ellis; J. N. Behrman *National Interests and the Multinational Enterprise*: Prentice Hall 1969, which quotes sixteen instances, largely of executive action by the U.S. government where subsidiaries of American corporations were required to act in a manner which conflicted with policies followed by the host governments.
32. *Financial Times*, London.
33. Recent decisions by the European Court suggest that EEC Legislation is being regarded as binding even outside the Community and that for example U.S. enterprises may be liable for penalties for actions committed outside the Community which affect Community interests.

Further Reading

There are now hundreds of books and several times that number of articles on aspects of International Business. The list which follows is at best a selection. Articles have not been listed separately except in the *Notes and References* preceding this section.

Y. Aharoni, *The Foreign Investment Decision Process*, Harvard University Press (1966).

T. Aitken, *Multinational Man,* Allen and Unwin (London, 1974).

J. S. Arpan, *International Intercorporate Pricing,* Praeger (New York, 1972).

J. N. Behrman, *National Interests and the Multinational Enterprise,* Prentice Hall (New Jersey, 1970).

U.S. International Business and Governments, McGraw Hill (New York, 1971).

J. Boddewyn, *Comparative Management and Marketing,* Scott Foresman and Co. (Glenwood, Illinois, 1969).

International Business Management, McGraw Hill (New York, 1969).

W. C. Broehl, *The International Basic Economy Corporation*, National Planning Association (Washington, 1968).

C. C. Brown (Ed.), *World Business,* Macmillan Co. (New York, 1970).

M. Z. Brooke and H. L. Remmers, *The Strategy of the Multinational Enterprise,* Longman (London, 1970), Elsevier Publishing Co. (New York, 1970).

The Multinational Company in Europe, Longman (London, 1972). Business International, *Managing the Multinationals,* Allen and Unwin (London, 1972).

J. Dunning, *The Role of American Investment,* PEP (London, 1969).

The Multinational Enterprise, Allen and Unwin (London, 1971).

W. A. Dymza, *Multinational Business Strategy,* McGraw Hill (New York, 1972).

Economist Intelligence Unit, *The Growth and Spread of International Companies,* EIU (London, 1969).

EEC Commission, *Multinational Undertakings and Community Regulations* (Brussels, 1973).

R. N. Farmer and B. M. Richman, *International Business: an Operational Theory,* R. D. Irwin (Homewood, Illinois, 1966).

J. Fayerweather, *Management of International Operations,* McGraw Hill (New York, 1960).

International Business Management, McGraw Hill (New York, 1969).

L. E. Franko, *Joint Venture Survival in the Multinational Company,* Praeger (New York, 1971).

Government of Canada Task Force, *Foreign Ownership and the Structure of Canadian Industry,* Queens Printer (Ottawa, 1968).

J. Greene and M. G. Duerr, *Intercompany Transactions in the Multinational Corporation,* Conference Board (New York, 1970).

H. J. Heck, *The International Business Environment,* American Management Association (1969).

A. O. Hirschmann, *How to Divest in Latin America and Why,* Princeton Essays in International Finance (1969).

M. Hodges, *Multinational Companies and National Government,* Saxon House (London, 1974).

International Labour Office, *Multinational Enterprises and Social Policy,* ILO (1974).

International Chamber of Commerce, *Guidelines for International Investment,* ICC (Paris).

E. Jacobs, *European Trade Unionism,* Croom Helm (London, 1973).

C. P. Kindleberger, *American Business Abroad,* Yale University Press (New Haven and London, 1969).

E. J. Kolde, *International Business Enterprise,* Prentice Hall (New Jersey, 1968).

C. Levinson, *Capital, Inflation and the Multinationals,* Allen and Unwin (London, 1971).

I. A. Litvak and C. J. Maule, *Foreign Investment; the Experience of Host Countries,* Praeger (New York, 1970).

D. C. McLelland, *The Achieving Society,* Van Nostrand (New York, 1969).

W. A. P. Manser, *Financial Role of the Multinational Enterprise,* Associated Business Programmes (London, 1973).

R. H. Mason, R. Miller and D. Weigel, *Economics of International Business,* John Wiley (New York, 1974).

R. Mazzolini, *European Transnational Concentrations,* McGraw Hill (U.K.) Limited (1974).

L. C. Nehrt, *The Political Climate for Foreign Private Investment,* Praeger (New York, 1970).

S. Pisar, *Coexistence and Commerce,* McGraw Hill (New York, 1970), Allen Lane/Penguin (Harmondsworth, 1971).

W. B. Reddaway *et al., The Effects of U.K. Direct Investment Overseas,* Cambridge University Press (1968).

B. M. Richman and M. G. Copen, *International Management and Economic Development,* McGraw Hill (New York, 1972).

S. H. Robock and K. Simmonds, *International Business and Multinational Enterprises,* R. D. Irwin (Homewood, Illinois, 1973).

R. D. Robinson, *International Business Policy,* Holt Rinehart and Winston (New York, 1964).
International Business Management, Holt Rinehart and Winston (New York, 1973).

S. E. Rolfe, *The International Corporation,* ICC (Paris, 1969).

S. E. Rolfe and W. Damm, *The Multinational Corporation in the World Economy,* Praeger (New York, 1970).

J. J. Servan Schrieber, *Le Defi Americain,* Denoel (Paris, 1961). Translated as *The American Challenge,* Atheneum (New York, 1969), Penguin Books (Harmondsworth).

H. Stieglitz, *Organizational Structure of International Companies,* Conference Board (New York, 1965).

R. B. Stobaugh and S. M. Robbins, *Money in the International Enterprise,* Basic Books (New York, 1973), Longman (London, 1974).

J. M. Stopford and L. T. Wells, *Managing the Multinational Enterprise,* Basic Books (New York, 1972), Longman (London, 1972).

M. J. Thomas, *International Marketing Management,* Houghton Mifflin (Boston, Massachusetts, 1968).

J. W. C. Tomlinson, *The Joint Venture Process in International Business,* MIT Press (Cambridge, Massachusetts, 1970).

C. Tugendhat, *The Multinationals,* Penguin (Harmondsworth, 1973), Random House (New York, 1972).

L. Turner, *The Multinational Company and the Third World,* Allen Lane (London, 1974).

United Nations, *Manual on the Establishment of Joint Venture Agreements in Developing Countries,* UN (New York, 1971).
The Impact of Multinational Corporations on Development and on International Relations, UN (1974).

Bureau of International Commerce, *The Multinational Corporation,* Bureau of International Commerce (Washington, 1972).

R. Vernon, *Sovereignty at Bay,* Basic Books (New York, 1971), Penguin (Harmondsworth, 1974).
The Manager in the International Economy, Prentice Hall (New Jersey, 1972).

J. J. Ward, *The European Approach to U.S. Markets,* Praeger (New York, 1973).

D. B. Zenoff and J. Zwick, *International Financial Management,* Prentice Hall (New Jersey, 1969).

Index